D0499364

"Grof is one of the great explorers of this century. In this book, he has given us a collection of stories that, like those of Marco Polo, are so outside most of our experience that at first one tends to doubt their reality. However, if you are able to stay open, you see how profound, valid, and important these stories are and how much they extend our understanding of our own and humanity's possibilities. Freud illuminated a few rooms of consciousness, as did Jung; Grof tours the entire house. Thank goodness psychology will never be able to ignore these areas again."

—JAMES FADIMAN, PH.D.
Institute for Transpersonal Psychology

"Stan Grof's life is full of dramatic adventures and wild stories, as he leads the expedition of Western psychology deeper into the inner world, where we find grand peak experiences and the wild jungles of consciousness. Dr. Grof is one of the great explorers of the human condition, and in this book you take the journey with him."

—WES NISKER
Buddhist meditation teacher and author of *The Essential Crazy Wisdom*

"Dr. Stanislav Grof's extraordinary life stories are indeed adventures of the Heroic Journey. I have had the privilege of participating in a number of these seemingly impossible happenings; they have all been life transforming. With great admiration and respect for Dr. Grof's lifelong, dedicated work in transpersonal research, reading this book is such a pleasurable 'wu wei' joyride along the 'Watercourse Way' of the Great Tao."

—CHUNGLIANG AL HUANG
Founder-president, Living Tao Foundation

"When the Impossible Happens *offers benefit for oneself and for everyone around one, for if it spreads among us, the 'holotropic consciousness' that makes the impossible happen—which is also the consciousness that can create a world inhabited by mature human beings, children of the Earth and of the cosmos, able to live with each other and with nature in peace and with solidarity, and the love that is born of the knowledge that we are truly one with the universe."*

—ERVIN LASZLO
Philosopher and author of *Science and the Akashic Field*

"*Stan Grof is one of the world's foremost researchers of the further reaches of the human mind. His understandings, which have helped so many, now become even more accessible and fascinating as he shares a multitude of powerful personal experiences, his adventures in non-ordinary reality.*"

—CHARLES T. TART, PH.D.
Author of *Altered States of Consciousness*

"*Stan Grof's mastery is to braid the wisdom found in the world's spiritual traditions with scientific research. His own accounts of non-ordinary realities are validating, insightful reminders of how prevalent and important these realities are to our own spiritual development and creative contributions in the world.*"

—ANGELES ARRIEN, PH.D.
Cultural anthropologist and author of *The Four-Fold Way* and *The Second Half of Life*

"Stanislav Grof is a pioneering psychiatrist, world-renowned for his immense contributions to the field of psychotherapy (through methods involving LSD, as well as Holotropic Breathwork™) and also to an expanded scientific paradigm that takes the spiritual or transpersonal dimensions of existence seriously. In this utterly fascinating book we encounter Grof the storyteller sharing numerous anecdotes from his personal and professional experience that involve non-ordinary states of consciousness and contact with mysterious phenomena, inexplicable from the conventional materialist worldview. These are factual observations, confirmed in many cases by multiple witnesses, that can only be understood (if at all) by acknowledging the existence of a cosmos far more awesome and more meaningful than we have ever imagined. I believe this book will be recognized as a watershed work in the transition to a new cosmology for our time."

—RALPH METZNER, PH.D.
Professor of psychology, author of *The Unfolding Self* and *The Well of Remembrance*

"Stanislav Grof challenges mainstream science and current views of reality with marvelous and exciting personal stories from a life of exploration at the frontiers of consciousness. A must-read for anyone interested in his pioneering work and the nature of reality."

—MICHAEL HARNER
Author of *The Way of the Shaman*

WHEN THE
IMPOSSIBLE
HAPPENS

WHEN THE
IMPOSSIBLE
HAPPENS

ADVENTURES IN NON-ORDINARY REALITIES

STANISLAV GROF
M.D., PH.D.

Sounds True, Inc.
Boulder CO 80306

© 2006 by Stanislav Grof. All rights reserved.

Published 2006
Printed in Canada

ISBN: 1-59179-420-X

Library of Congress Control Number 2006922552

✪ This book is printed on 100% postconsumer-waste recycled paper.

TO CHRISTINA—my wife, lover, best friend, co-worker, and fellow seeker—who shared with me many of the adventures in non-ordinary realities described in this book and saw the impossible happen.

Contents

PREFACE

Almost half a century ago, a powerful experience lasting only several hours of clock-time profoundly changed my personal and professional life. As a young psychiatric resident, only a few months after my graduation from medical school, I volunteered for an experiment with LSD, a substance with remarkable psychoactive properties that had been discovered by the Swiss chemist Albert Hofmann in the Sandoz Pharmaceutical Laboratories in Basel.

This session, particularly its culmination period during which I had an overwhelming and indescribable experience of cosmic consciousness, awakened in me an intense, lifelong interest in non-ordinary states of consciousness. Since that time, most of my clinical and research activities have consisted of systematic exploration of the therapeutic, transformative, and evolutionary potential of these states. The five decades that I have dedicated to consciousness research have been for me an extraordinary adventure of discovery and self-discovery.

I spent approximately half of this time conducting therapy with psychedelic substances, first in Czechoslovakia at the Psychiatric Research Institute in Prague and then in the United States at the Maryland Psychiatric Research Center in Baltimore, where I participated in the last surviving American psychedelic research program. Since 1975, my wife, Christina, and I have worked with Holotropic Breathwork, a powerful method of therapy and self-exploration that we jointly developed at the Esalen Institute in Big Sur, California. Over the years, we have also supported many people undergoing spontaneous episodes of non-ordinary states of consciousness—psychospiritual crises, or "spiritual emergencies," as Christina and I call them.

The common denominator of these past experiences with psychedelics is that they involve non-ordinary states of consciousness or, more specifically, an important subcategory of them that I call "holotropic." This composite word literally means "oriented toward wholeness" or "moving in the direction of wholeness" (from the Greek *holos*, whole, and *trepein*, moving toward or in the direction of something). This term suggests that in our everyday state of consciousness we identify with only a small fraction of who we really are. The best way of explaining what holotropic means is to refer to the Hindu distinction between *namarupa* (the name and shape that we have in our everyday existence) and *Atman-Brahman* (our deepest identity, which is commensurate with the cosmic creative principle). In holotropic states of consciousness, we can transcend the narrow boundaries of the body ego and reclaim our full identity. We can experientially identify with anything that is part of creation and even with the creative principle itself.

Holotropic experiences play an important role in shamanic initiatory crises, healing ceremonies of native cultures, Aboriginal rites of passage, and systematic spiritual practice, such as various forms of yoga, Buddhist or Taoist meditation, Sufi dhikrs, Kabbalistic exercises, or the Christian Jesus Prayer (hesychasm). They have also been described in the literature on the ancient mysteries of death and rebirth conducted in the Mediterranean area and other parts of the world in the names of Inanna and Tammuz, Isis and Osiris, Dionysus, Attis, Adonis, Mithra, Wotan, and many other deities. In everyday life, holotropic experiences can occur in near-death situations or spontaneously, without any obvious trigger. They can also be induced by powerful forms of experiential therapy developed in the second half of the twentieth century.

In psychedelic therapy, holotropic states are brought about by administration of mind-altering substances, such as LSD, psilocybin, mescaline, and tryptamine or amphetamine derivatives. In Holotropic Breathwork, consciousness is changed by a combination of faster breathing, evocative music, and energy-releasing bodywork. In spiritual emergencies, holotropic states occur spontaneously, in the middle of everyday life, and their cause is usually un-known. If they are correctly understood and supported, holotropic states have an extraordinary healing, transformative, and even evolutionary potential.

In addition, I have been peripherally involved in many disciplines that are, more or less directly, related to holotropic states of consciousness. I have spent much time exchanging information with anthropologists and have participat-ed in sacred ceremonies of native cultures in different parts of the world with and without the ingestion of psychedelic plants, such as peyote, ayahuasca, and magic mushrooms. This involved contact with various North American, Mexican, South American, and African shamans and healers. I have also had extensive contact with representatives of various spiritual disciplines, includ-ing Vipassana, Zen, and Vajrayana Buddhism, Siddha Yoga, Tantra, and the Christian Benedictine Order.

Another area that has received much of my attention has been thanatology, the young discipline studying near-death experiences and the psychological and spiritual aspects of death and dying. In the late 1960s and early 1970s, I participated in a large research project studying the effects of psychedelic therapy in individuals dying of cancer. I should also add that I have had the privilege of personal acquaintance and experience with some of the great psy-chics and parapsychologists of our era, pioneers of laboratory consciousness research, and therapists who developed and practiced powerful forms of expe-riential therapy that induce holotropic states of consciousness.

My initial encounter with holotropic states was very difficult and intellec-tually, as well as emotionally, challenging. In the early years of my laboratory and clinical research with psychedelics, I was bombarded daily with experi-ences and observations for which my medical and psychiatric training had not prepared me. As a matter of fact, I was experiencing and seeing things that, in the context of the scientific worldview I was brought up with, were considered impossible and were not supposed to happen. And yet, those obviously im-possible things were happening all the time.

After I had overcome my initial conceptual shock, incredulity concerning my observations, and doubts about my own sanity, I began to realize that the problem might not be in my capacity to observe or in my critical judgment, but in the limitations of current psychological and psychiatric theories and of the monistic, materialistic paradigm of Western science. Naturally, it was not easy for me to come to this realization, because I had to struggle with the awe and respect a medical student or a beginning psychiatrist feels toward the academic establishment, scientific authorities, and impressive credentials and titles.

My initial suspicion about the inadequacy of academic theories concerning consciousness and the human psyche gradually turned into certainty, nourished and reinforced by thousands of clinical observations. Eventually, I reached a point where I had no more doubts that the data from the research of holotropic states represent a critical conceptual challenge for the scientific paradigm that currently dominates psychology, psychiatry, and psychotherapy, and I expressed this opinion in a series of professional books. I came to the conclusion that thinking in these disciplines requires a radical revision that in its nature and scope would resemble the conceptual cataclysm that Newtonian physicists had to face in the first three decades of the twentieth century.

The observations challenging the worldview, which I imbibed from the culture I grew up in and inherited from my academic teachers, came from many different areas and sources. Most of this information was drawn from extraordinary experiences reported by my clients undergoing psychedelic therapy, participants in our Holotropic Breathwork workshops and training, and people undergoing spiritual emergency. A critical factor in the transformation of my worldview were the holotropic experiences of various kinds that I experienced myself and those that my wife, Christina, shared with me.

However, not all of the evidence involved in the profound change of my worldview was directly related to special states of consciousness. Over the years, many extraordinary things happened in our everyday life that have significantly contributed to this transformation. These included remarkable encounters and experiences with shamans of different cultures, renowned spiritual teachers and psychics, as well as many astonishing coincidences and synchronicities. The common denominator of all these events was the fact that they should not have happened if the universe were the way traditional science portrays it—a strictly deterministic material system governed by chains of causes and effects. This is what inspired the title of this book.

When the Impossible Happens: Adventures in Non-Ordinary Realities is a collection of stories describing various events in my professional and personal life that forced me to abandon my skeptical and materialistic scientific perspective on life and embrace the Eastern spiritual philosophies and mystical teachings of the world. They also generated in me great respect for the ritual and spiritual life and for the healing traditions of native cultures that Western science dismisses as products of primitive superstition. I am aware of the fact that reading these stories will not convey the full power of the actual real-life experiences that they describe. However, I hope that in their totality they will give the reader a taste of the reenchantment of the universe that they brought into my own life.

The first part of the book consists of stories that involve what C. G. Jung described as *synchronicity*—highly implausible coincidences that cannot be explained by the principle of linear causality, the principle that is the cornerstone of Western scientific thinking. By showing that the world of matter can enter into playful interaction with the human psyche, the existence of synchronicities undermines the very foundations of the Cartesian-Newtonian paradigm and of the monistic materialistic worldview. It abolishes the basic metaphysical assumptions held by the Western academic community that consciousness and matter are two separate entities, that matter is primary and consciousness its epiphenomenon, and that the events in the world are governed exclusively by chains of causes and effects.

Parts 2, 3, and 4 of the book feature stories that challenge the current scientific understanding of the nature of memory and its limits. Mainstream psychiatrists and neurophysiologists assume that the brain of the newborn is not mature enough to record the memory of hours of stressful and painful experiences during biological birth. The work with holotropic states of consciousness clearly demonstrates that each of us carries in the unconscious psyche not only the memory of our delivery and the trauma associated with it, but also memories of our prenatal life and early embryonal existence, our conception, and of the lives of our human and animal ancestors.

It is not very plausible that our entire biological history could be stored in the DNA and that, under special circumstances, this record could be translated into a vivid experience. However, the above memories—embryonal, ancestral, racial, and phylogenetic—at least come from situations for which it is possible to imagine material substrate capable of carrying information. Many experiences in holotropic states present an even more formidable conceptual problem because they suggest the existence of memory without any material substrate whatsoever.

Here belong, for example, experiential sequences portraying events from human history stored in the archives of the collective unconscious as envisioned by C. G. Jung, past-life memories, and experiential identification with the members of other species. All these experiences clearly transcend ancestral, racial, and biological lines of any kind, and it is impossible to imagine any physical medium in which they could be recorded. They seem to be stored in fields that are currently unknown to science or embedded in the field of consciousness itself.

The fifth part of the book consists of stories illustrating phenomena traditionally studied by parapsychologists—telepathy and clairvoyance, psychometry, experiences of astral realms, communication with discarnate entities and spirit guides, encounters with archetypal beings, channeling, mind-over-matter phenomena (*siddhis*), and out-of-body experiences during which disembodied consciousness accurately perceives immediate or remote environments. Unbiased study of these extraordinary experiences and events suggests that materialistic science has been premature in ridiculing this entire realm and the researchers who study it. These observations reveal the existence of "anomalous phenomena" that might in the future lead to a radical revision of the scientific worldview and its basic metaphysical assumptions.

A special section in the book (Part 6) is dedicated to stories describing observations that challenge the most fundamental assumptions of mainstream psychiatrists concerning the nature of psychotic episodes, currently considered manifestations of serious mental diseases. It also includes accounts of surprising positive results of highly unorthodox and controversial approaches to treatment. An example of such psychiatric "heresy" is seeing episodes of non-ordinary states of consciousness as crises of spiritual opening ("spiritual emergencies"), rather than as psychotic episodes. Another example is approaching symptoms as expressing a self-healing attempt of the psyche and working with them. The most radical and unusual situations described in this section of the book involve the use of psychedelics to activate, rather than suppress, psychotic symptoms, dramatic improvements achieved by a method resembling exorcism, and therapeutic breakthroughs featuring psychodynamic mechanisms that would not make any sense to traditional psychiatrists.

The appendix of the book focuses on the attitude of traditional scientists toward the paradigm-breaking observations generated by consciousness research and transpersonal psychology, the extension of traditional psychological study into the realm of spirituality, body-mind connections, and transformation. The first story is an extreme but typical example of resistance to the new data found in many members of the academic community. It involves a brilliant, world-renowned scientist who defends his intellectual convictions with such stubbornness and determination that it matches the position of a religious fundamentalist. The second story illustrates what happens when traditionally trained professionals with a materialistic orientation have the opportunity to experience holotropic states of consciousness. The third one describes how my own determined resistance to astrology, a discipline mocked and ridiculed by "serious" scientists, had to succumb to the influx of convincing observations.

This book is a very personal statement, revealing many intimate details of my private and professional life. Most clinicians and researchers would hesitate to disclose so much subjective information because of their concern that this would damage their scientific reputation. The reason that I share with so much honesty the trials and tribulations of my personal quest is that I want this information to ease the struggle and quandary of people involved in serious self-exploration and help them avoid the mistakes and pitfalls that are integral parts of any venture into new, unexplored territories.

I hope that open-minded readers will see the personal stories that I share in these memoirs of my unconventional quest as a testimony to the passion with which I have pursued the search for knowledge and wisdom hidden in the deep recesses of the human psyche. If this book provides useful information and assistance for even a small fraction of the thousands of people experiencing holotropic states of consciousness and exploring non-ordinary realities, my sacrifice of personal privacy has not been in vain.

Stanislav Grof, M.D., Ph.D.
Mill Valley, California
August 2005

Acknowledgments

This book is a rich tapestry of extraordinary adventures in my inner world and everyday reality that I have experienced in the course of five decades of research into non-ordinary states of consciousness induced by psychedelic substances, by various nondrug methods, and those occurring spontaneously in the middle of everyday life. This quest has taken me to realms and dimensions of reality my culture and my professional colleagues were telling me did not exist, except in the minds of severely disturbed psychiatric patients. It took years of intellectual struggle before I reached certainty that the normally invisible beings I was encountering and the domains I was visiting in my inner journeys had objective existence in the collective unconscious and lent themselves to consensual validation. In most cases, such validation required individuals who had the opportunity to experience personally these realities in non-ordinary states of consciousness.

This challenging journey of discovery and self-discovery would have been incomparably more difficult had I undertaken it alone. It has been extremely helpful and validating to meet open-minded individuals who shared the new understanding of consciousness, reality, and the human psyche that was emerging from the study of non-ordinary states or who were open to it. I am extremely grateful for the encouragement and support I have received from like-minded colleagues, who have independently confirmed, on the basis of their own research and personal experiences, various aspects of the new understanding of reality emerging from my work. Over the years, the number of such individuals kept increasing, and at present there are too many to acknowledge all of them individually by name. I will mention only a few, whose support was particularly important and meaningful.

Immediately after my arrival in the United States, it was Joel Elkes, head of the psychiatric department at Johns Hopkins University, who had invited me to this country as Experimental and Research Fellow and later offered me the position of assistant professor of psychiatry. A brilliant scientist with impeccable academic credentials, Joel was very open-minded and showed keen interest in the new vision of the human psyche and of reality emerging from psychedelic research. His intellectual and administrative support was invaluable for our team at the Maryland Psychiatric Research Center in Catonsville, Maryland, conducting in the late 1960s and early 1970s the last surviving psychedelic research in the United States. It is difficult to find appropriate words for the gratitude I feel to Albert Kurland, director of the Maryland Psychiatric Research Center, and the members of our research team, particularly Sandy Unger, the late Walter Pahnke, Charles Savage, Bill Richards and his late wife, Ilse, Bob and Karen Leihy, Sidney Wolf, Rich Yensen, the late Franco di Leo, and Nancy Jewel, who received me with open hearts into their professional and personal lives; their families became for me my second home.

I am extremely grateful to Michael Murphy, who invited me as Scholar-in-Residence to the Esalen Institute in Big Sur, California, a unique center for exploration of the human potential that he had founded jointly with Dick Price. My stay at Esalen between 1973 and 1987 was for me an exceptionally validating and affirming experience. Thanks to the extraordinarily rich program of workshops offered by the institute, I had the opportunity to meet personally most of the pioneers of new paradigm science, founders of various schools of experiential psychotherapy, and prominent spiritual figures, who came to Esalen as visiting teachers. My wife, Christina, and I conducted thirty monthlong workshops at Esalen, which gave us the opportunity to invite these remarkable people as guest faculty, get acquainted with their teachings, and establish friendships with them. Esalen also provided for us an ideal setting for developing Holotropic Breathwork, a powerful experiential method of self-exploration and therapy.

The bonds we formed at Esalen with visiting teachers made it possible for Christina and me to launch a series of large transpersonal conferences held in different parts of the world—North and South America, Europe, Australia, and Asia. The stellar cast of these meetings and their rich interdisciplinary program provided further validation for the new emerging vision of reality and understanding of the psyche, consciousness, and human nature. It was particularly encouraging that many presenters at these conferences sharing this new perspective had solid educational backgrounds, extraordinary intelligence, and impressive academic credentials.

My special thanks go to a circle of our close friends and fellow seekers in the Bay Area that has been meeting regularly since we moved from Big Sur to Mill Valley—Angeles Arrien, Michael and Sandra Harner, Jack and Liana Kornfield, Bokara Legendre, Ram Dass, Frances Vaughan, and Roger Walsh. Our joint dinners, meditation groups, and exchange of information about various subjects have been for me a treasure trove of new ideas, inspiration, useful suggestions, and critical comments but, above all, provided powerful support and validation based on our general consensus about the basic tenets of the transpersonal vision and the spiritual worldview. Rick Tarnas, another close friend, brilliant astrologer, and archetypal psychologist, has helped me enormously in our countless discussions and courses and workshops we have co-led over the years to appreciate and embrace astrology, a discipline that— more than any other—stretched my conceptual boundaries and expanded my intellectual horizons. Independently, I have also received much inspiration, validation, and support from Ervin Laszlo and Ralph Metzner.

I am deeply grateful to Michael Marcus, Janet Zand, John Buchanan, Bokara Legendre, and Betsy Gordon for their friendship and generous support they have granted our work over the years. My brother, Paul, psychiatrist specializing in research of affective disorders, represents a unique combination of excellent probing intellect, scientific passion, and extraordinary generosity. He has been my intimate friend, confidant, enthusiastic fan, and honest and sincere critic. Special thanks go to Tav and Cary Sparks, our dear friends and co-workers for more than two decades. They both have played a pivotal role in our lives as codirectors of Grof Transpersonal Training (GTT) and as cocoordinators of workshops and international transpersonal conferences we have organized in many different parts of the world. Tav has been for years my travel companion and coleader, and Cary has been the soul of all our joint projects.

The normally invisible non-ordinary dimensions of reality would have remained hidden for me without the epoch-making discovery and life's work of Albert Hofmann, who gave the world extraordinary tools for exploring the human psyche—LSD, psilocybine, psilocine, and monoethylamid of lysergic acid. I would like to use this opportunity to express my profound gratitude to him for everything that his discoveries brought into my personal and professional life and the lives of countless others who used his gift responsibly and with the respect that this extraordinary tool deserves.

I have had the privilege to know Albert personally and meet him on various occasions. Over the years, I have developed great affection and deep admiration for him, not only as an outstanding scientist, but also as an extraordinary human being. After more than a century of a full, blessed, and productive life, he radiates amazing vitality, curiosity, and love for all creation. A few months ago, when he spent a day with the group of our trainees in Gruyères, Switzerland, we all felt that we were not listening to a scientific lecture, but had a darshan with a spiritual teacher. We had no doubt that Albert had joined the group of great scientists—like Albert Einstein and Isaac Newton—whose rigorous pursuit of their discipline brought recognition of the miraculous divine order underlying the world of matter and the natural phenomena. He will remain a model and shining example for me for the rest of my life.

My list of acknowledgements would not be complete without expressing my profound gratitude to Christina, my wife, lover, best friend, co-worker, and fellow seeker, for all the inspiration I have received from her over the years and for everything she has contributed to my life and to our joint projects. Among others, she founded the Spiritual Emergence Network (SEN), has made unique contributions to the understanding of the relationship between addiction, attachment, and the spiritual quest, and has codeveloped with me Holotropic Breathwork, a powerful form of therapy and self-exploration. The breathwork workshops and training we have jointly conducted all over the world have been the source of extraordinary observations that provided the material for many of the stories in this book. Christina played an important role in many of these stories and was present "when the impossible happened." I am aware that writing this book and many others before often encroached on our private life. I would like to use this opportunity to thank Christina for her patience and understanding and extend to her my apologies.

My special thanks go to two people who have played an important role in the publication of this book. Tami Simon, whom I admire and appreciate very much, has created single-handedly Sounds True, an audio, video, book, and music publishing company, which has grown from one person working in a single room to an organization that has its own state-of-the-art facilities and employs over fifty people. Sounds True recordings have made it possible for hundreds of thousands of listeners to get acquainted with the ideas of spiritual teachers and pioneers of new paradigm science, alternative healing, consciousness research, and transpersonal psychology. I appreciate very much that Tami decided to include the present work in her new publishing project. I am also grateful to Alice Feinstein for the expertise and enthusiasm with which she edited the manuscript and for her advice and suggestions that I have found very helpful in finding the most appropriate format for sharing my stories with the readers.

Discovering Cosmic Consciousness
My First LSD Session

The experience I am about to relate was without any doubt the single most important and influential experience of my entire life. Although it lasted only a few hours—and its most significant part only about ten minutes—it sent me professionally on a radically different course than the one for which I had been trained and prepared. It set for me a trajectory that I have been following with great passion and determination until this very day. It also instigated in me a process of profound personal transformation and spiritual awakening. Today, almost fifty years later, I look at this experience as an initiation similar to that offered to the participants in ancient mysteries.

This story will take us back to the end of my medical studies and beginnings of my professional career as a psychiatrist. In the mid-1950s, the psychiatric department of the School of Medicine of Charles University in Prague, where I had worked as a student volunteer since the fourth year of my medical studies, conducted research with Melleril. This was one of the early tranquilizers, produced by the Sandoz Pharmaceutical Laboratories in Basel, Switzerland. My preceptor had a good working relationship with Sandoz and received from time to time complimentary samples of their products. As part of this cooperation, he received for testing a supply of diethylamide of lysergic acid, or LSD-25, a then-new experimental substance with extraordinary psychoactive properties.

The astonishing effects of this compound on the human psyche had been discovered in April 1943 by the leading chemist at Sandoz, Dr. Albert Hofmann, who accidentally intoxicated himself when he was synthesizing it in his lab. When it happened, he was forced to interrupt his work in the laboratory in the middle of the afternoon, because he felt remarkable restlessness and dizziness. This developed into a dreamlike state with a stream of fantastic images and a kaleidoscopic play of colors that lasted approximately two hours.

Three days later, Dr. Hofmann decided to take a measured dose of LSD to confirm his suspicion that his abnormal mental state was due to intoxication by LSD-25. Although this was a reasonable assumption, he could not imagine how the drug would have gotten into his system. In this planned self-experiment, he ingested 250 micrograms or gammas (millionths of a gram) of LSD which, "being a conservative man," he considered to be a "miniscule dose." This assessment was based on the fact that ergot alkaloids are usually taken in milligram dosages. He had no way of knowing that he ingested a substance of unprecedented efficacy, the most powerful psychoactive drug ever discovered. In clinical work conducted in the 1950s and 1960s, the dose Albert Hofmann had taken was considered a high dose, requiring hours of preparation, supervision by two guides, overnight stay in the treatment center, and subsequent follow-up interviews.

Because many of the stories in this book describe events associated with LSD, I will give here a brief description of this historical experiment. Within an hour after ingesting 250 micrograms of LSD-25, Albert Hofmann was unable to work and asked his assistant to accompany him home. Because of war restrictions imposed on the use of automobiles, a car was not available, and they had to use bicycles. Hofmann's account of what it was like to cycle through the streets of Basel under the influence of a high dose of LSD has since become legendary. After arriving home, he felt possessed by demonic forces that had taken control of his mind and body and was afraid that he was going insane. His friendly neighbor, who brought him some milk, had the appearance of a dangerous witch and seemed to be hexing him. His physical distress was so extreme that he was sure he was dying, and he asked his assistant to call a doctor.

By the time the doctor arrived on the scene, the peak of the crisis had already passed, and Hofmann's condition had radically changed. He was not dying any longer. He had experienced his own birth and felt reborn, revitalized, and rejuvenated. On the day after the LSD experiment, he was in excellent physical and mental condition. He wrote a report about his extraordinary experience to his boss, Dr. Arthur Stoll. It just happened that Dr. Stoll's son Werner A. Stoll was a psychiatrist practicing in Zurich and was very interested in exploring the effects of LSD in a clinical trial. His pioneering report about the effects of LSD-25 in a group of "normal volunteers" and psychiatric patients was published in 1947 and became overnight a sensation in the scientific world.

Werner Stoll's early LSD study showed that minuscule dosages of this extraordinary substance—in the order of millionths of a gram—were able to profoundly change the consciousness of his experimental subjects for a period of six to ten hours. Sandoz representatives now made samples of LSD available to researchers and therapists all over the world and requested feedback about its effects and its potential. They wanted to know if there was legitimate use for this substance in psychology and psychiatry. Dr. Stoll's pilot study suggested some interesting similarities between the LSD experience and the symptomatology of naturally occurring psychoses. It seemed, therefore, that the study of such "experimental psychoses" could provide interesting insights into the causes of naturally occurring psychotic states, particularly schizophrenia, the most enigmatic of psychiatric disorders.

The insert from Sandoz accompanying the sample of LSD also contained a little note that profoundly changed my personal and professional life. It suggested that this substance could be used as a revolutionary, unconventional teaching tool for mental health professionals working with psychotic patients. The possibility of experiencing a reversible "experimental psychosis" seemed to provide a unique opportunity for psychiatrists, psychologists, psychiatric nurses, social workers, and students of psychiatry to gain intimate personal knowledge of the inner world of their clients and make it possible to understand them better, to be able to communicate with them more effectively, and as a result, to treat them more successfully.

I was extremely excited about such an extraordinary training opportunity and asked my preceptor, Dr. George Roubíček, for an LSD session. Unfortunately, the staff of the psychiatric clinic decided that, for a variety of reasons, students would not be accepted as volunteers. However, Dr. Roubíček was too busy to spend hours at a time in the LSD sessions of his experimental subjects and needed help. There were no objections to my supervising psychedelic sessions of others and keeping the records of their experiences. I thus had sat in on the LSD sessions of many Czech psychiatrists and psychologists, prominent artists, and other interested people before I myself was qualified as an experimental subject. By the time I graduated from the medical school and qualified for a session, my appetite had been repeatedly whetted by fantastic accounts of the experiences of others that I had witnessed.

In the fall of 1956, after my graduation from medical school, I was finally able to have my own session. Dr. Roubíček's area of special interest was research of the electric activity of the brain. One of the conditions for participating in the LSD study was to agree to have an EEG recording taken before, during, and after the session. In addition, at the time of my session, he was particularly fascinated by what was called "driving" or "entraining" the brain waves. This involved exposure to various frequencies of flashing stroboscopic light and finding out to what extent the brain waves in the suboccipital area of the brain could be "entrained," that is, forced to pick up the incoming frequency. Eager to have the LSD experience, I readily agreed to have my EEG taken and my brain waves "driven." My brother, Paul, who was a medical student at that time and was deeply interested in psychiatry, agreed to supervise my session.

I started feeling the effects of LSD about forty-five minutes after ingestion. At first, it was the feeling of slight malaise, lightheadedness, and nausea. Then these symptoms disappeared and were replaced by a fantastic display of incredibly colorful abstract and geometrical visions unfolding in rapid kaleidoscopic sequences. Some of them resembled exquisite stained glass windows in medieval Gothic cathedrals, others arabesques from Moslem mosques. To describe the exquisite nature of these visions, I made references to Sheherezade and *A Thousand and One Nights* and to the stunning beauty of Alhambra and Xanadu. At the time, these were the only associations I was able to make. Today, I believe that my psyche somehow managed to produce a wild array of fractal images, similar to graphic representations of nonlinear equations that can be produced by modern computers.

As the session continued, my experience moved through and beyond this realm of exquisite aesthetic rapture and changed into an encounter and confrontation with my unconscious psyche. It is difficult to find words for the intoxicating fugue of emotions, visions, and illuminating insights into my life and existence in general that became available to me on this level of my psyche. It was so profound and shattering that it instantly overshadowed my previous interest in Freudian psychoanalysis. I could not believe how much I learned in those few hours. The breathtaking aesthetic feast and the rich plethora of psychological insights would have been sufficient, in and of themselves, to make my first encounter with LSD a truly memorable experience.

However, there was another aspect of my session that surpassed everything else that happened. Between the third and fourth hours of my session, Dr. Roubiček's research assistant appeared and announced that it was time for the EEG experiment. She took me to a small cabin, carefully pasted electrodes all over my scalp, and asked me to lie down and close my eyes. Then she placed a giant stroboscopic light above my head and turned it on. At this time, the effects of the drug were culminating, and that immensely enhanced the impact of the strobe.

I was hit by a vision of light of incredible radiance and supernatural beauty. It made me think of the accounts of mystical experiences I had read about in spiritual literatures, in which the visions of divine light were compared with the incandescence of "millions of suns." It crossed my mind that this was what it must have been like at the epicenter of the atomic explosions in Hiroshima or Nagasaki. Today, I think it was more like Dharmakaya, or the Primary Clear Light, the luminosity of indescribable brilliance that, according to *The Tibetan Book of the Dead* (*Bardo Thödol*), appears to us at the moment of our death.

I felt that a divine thunderbolt had catapulted my conscious self out of my body. I lost my awareness of the research assistant, the laboratory, the psychiatric clinic, Prague, and then the planet. My consciousness expanded at an inconceivable speed and reached cosmic dimensions. There were no more boundaries or difference between me and the universe. The research assistant carefully followed the protocol. She gradually shifted the frequency of the strobe from two to sixty hertz per second and back again, and then put it for a short time in the middle of the alpha band, theta band, and finally the delta band. While this was happening, I found myself at the center of a cosmic drama of unimaginable dimensions.

In the astronomy literature that I later discovered and read over the years, I found names for some of the fantastic experiences that I underwent during those extraordinary ten minutes of clock time—Big Bang, passage through black and white holes, identification with exploding supernova and collapsing stars, and other strange phenomena. Although I had no adequate words for what had happened to me, there was no doubt in my mind that my experience was very close to those I knew from the great mystical scriptures of the world. Even though my psyche was deeply affected by the effects of LSD, I was able to see the irony and paradox of the situation. The Divine manifested and took over in the middle of a serious scientific experiment, involving a substance produced in the test tube of a twentieth-century chemist, and conducted in a psychiatric clinic of a country that was dominated by the Soviet Union and had a Marxist regime.

This day marked the beginning of my radical departure from traditional thinking in psychiatry and from the monistic materialism of Western science. I emerged from this experience touched to the core and immensely impressed by its power. Not believing at that time, as I do today, that the potential for a mystical experience is the natural birthright of all human beings, I attributed everything to the effect of LSD. I felt strongly that the study of non-ordinary states of consciousness, in general, and those induced by psychedelics, in particular, was by far the most interesting area of psychiatry I could imagine. I realized that, under the proper circumstances, psychedelic experiences—to a much greater degree than dreams, which play such a crucial role in psychoanalysis—are truly, using Freud's words, a "royal road into the unconscious."

And right there and then, I decided to dedicate my life to the study of non-ordinary states of consciousness.

PART 1

THE MYSTERY
OF SYNCHRONICITY

Twilight of the Clockwork Universe

Many of us have experienced instances in our lives when the seemingly logical and predictable fabric of everyday reality, woven from complex chains of causes and effects, seems to tear apart, and we experience stunning and highly implausible coincidences. During episodes of holotropic states of consciousness—holotropic meaning "moving toward wholeness"—these violations of linear causality can occur so frequently that they raise serious questions about the worldview with which we have all grown up. Since this extraordinary phenomenon plays an important role in many stories described in this book, I will briefly discuss its relevance for the understanding of the nature of reality, consciousness, and the human psyche.

The scientist who brought the problem of meaningful coincidences defying rational explanation to the attention of academic circles was the Swiss psychiatrist C. G. Jung. Aware of the fact that unswerving belief in rigid determinism represented the cornerstone of the Western scientific worldview, he hesitated for more than twenty years before making his discovery public. Expecting strong disbelief and harsh criticism from his colleagues, he wanted to be sure that he could back his heretic claims with hundreds of examples. He finally described his groundbreaking observations in his famous essay entitled "Synchronicity: An Acausal Connecting Principle" (Jung 1960).

Jung began his essay with examples of extraordinary coincidences occurring sometimes in everyday life. He acknowledged the Austrian Lamarckian biologist

Paul Kammerer, whose tragic life was popularized in Arthur Koestler's book *The Case of the Midwife Toad* (Koestler, 1971), as one of the first people to be interested in this phenomenon and its scientific implications. One of the remarkable coincidences Kammerer had reported involved a situation wherein one day his streetcar ticket bore the same number as the theater ticket he bought immediately afterward. In addition, later that evening, the same sequence of digits was given to him as a telephone number for which he had asked.

In the same work, Jung also related the amusing story told by the famous French astronomer Flammarion about a certain Monsieur Deschamps and a special kind of plum pudding. As a boy, Deschamps was given a piece of this rare pudding by a Monsieur de Fontgibu. For the ten years that followed, he had no opportunity to taste this delicacy until he saw the same pudding on the menu of a Paris restaurant. He asked the waiter for a serving, but it turned out that the last piece of the pudding had already been ordered and eaten by Monsieur de Fontgibu, who just happened to be in the same restaurant at that time.

Many years later, Monsieur Deschamps was invited to a party where this pudding was served as a special treat. While he was eating it, he remarked that the only thing lacking was Monsieur de Fontgibu, who had introduced him to this delicacy and had also been present during his second encounter with it in the Paris restaurant. At that moment, the doorbell rang and an old man walked in looking very confused. It was Monsieur de Fontgibu, who burst in on the party by mistake because he had been given the wrong address for the place to which he was supposed to go.

The existence of such extraordinary coincidences is difficult to reconcile with the understanding of the universe developed by materialistic science, which describes the world in terms of chains of causes and effects. And the probability that something like this would happen by chance is clearly so infinitesimal that it cannot be seriously considered as an explanation. It is certainly easier to imagine that these occurrences have some deeper meaning and that they are playful creations of cosmic intelligence. This explanation is particularly plausible when they contain an element of humor, which is often the case. Although coincidences of this kind are extremely interesting in and of themselves, the work of C. G. Jung added another fascinating dimension to this challenging, anomalous phenomenon.

The situations described by Kammerer and Flammarion involved highly implausible coincidences, and the story about the plum pudding certainly did not lack an element of humor. However, both stories described happenings in the world of matter. Jung's observations added another astonishing dimension to this already baffling phenomenon. He described numerous instances of what he called "synchronicity"—remarkable coincidences, in which various events in consensus reality were meaningfully linked to internal experiences, such as dreams or visions. He defined synchronicity as "a simultaneous occurrence of a psychological state with one or more external events which appear as meaningful parallels to the momentary subjective state." Situations of this kind show that our psyche can enter into playful interaction with what appears to be the world of matter. The fact that something like this is possible effectively blurs the boundaries between subjective and objective reality.

Struggling with this phenomenon, Jung became very interested in the developments in quantum-relativistic physics and in the radically new worldview to which they were pointing. He had many intellectual exchanges with Wolfgang Pauli, one of the founders of quantum physics, who was his client and personal friend. Under Pauli's guidance, Jung became familiar with the revolutionary concepts in modern physics, including the challenges to deterministic thinking and linear causality it had introduced into science. Jung was aware of the fact that his own observations appeared much more plausible and acceptable in the context of the new emerging image of reality. Additional support for Jung's ideas came from no less than Albert Einstein who, during a personal visit, encouraged Jung to pursue his idea of synchronicity because it was fully compatible with the new discoveries in physics (Jung 1973). Toward the end of his life, Jung became so convinced about the important role that synchronicity played in the natural order of things that he used it as a guiding principle in his everyday life.

The most famous of many synchronicities in Jung's own life is one that occurred during a therapy session with one of his clients. This patient was very resistant to psychotherapy, to Jung's interpretations, and to the notion of transpersonal realities. During the analysis of one of her dreams featuring a golden scarab, when therapy had reached an impasse, Jung heard a sound of something hitting the windowpane. He went to check what had happened and found on the windowsill a shiny rose chafer beetle trying to get inside. It was a very rare specimen, the nearest analogy to a golden scarab that can be found in that latitude. Nothing like that had ever happened to Jung before. He opened the window, brought the beetle inside, and showed it to his client. This extraordinary synchronicity became an important turning point in the therapy of this woman.

The observations of synchronicities had a profound impact on Jung's thinking and his work, particularly on his understanding of archetypes, primordial governing, and organizing principles of the collective unconscious. The discovery of archetypes and their role in the human psyche represented Jung's most important contribution to psychology. For much of his professional career, Jung was very strongly influenced by the Cartesian-Kantian perspective dominating Western science, with its strict division between subjective and objective, inner and outer. Under its spell, he initially saw the archetypes as transindividual, but essentially intrapsychic, principles, comparable to biological instincts. He presumed that the basic matrix for them was hardwired into the brain and was inherited from generation to generation.

The existence of synchronistic events made Jung realize that archetypes transcended both the psyche and the material world and that they were autonomous patterns of meaning, which informed both the psyche and matter. He saw that they provided a bridge between inner and outer and suggested the existence of a twilight zone between matter and consciousness. For this reason, Jung started referring to archetypes as having a "psychoid" (psychelike) quality. Stephan Holler described Jung's fully advanced understanding of the archetypes in a succinct way and using poetic language: "The archetype, when manifesting in a synchronistic phenomenon, is truly awesome if not outright miraculous—an uncanny dweller on the threshold. At once psychical and physical, it might be likened to the two-faced god Janus. The two faces of the archetype are joined in a common head of meaning" (Holler 1994). Following the publication of Jung's essay on synchronicity, this concept has become increasingly important in science and has been the subject of many articles and books (von Franz 1980, Aziz 1990, Mansfeld 1995) .

During the fifty years I have been involved in consciousness research, I have observed numerous extraordinary synchronicities in my clients, heard many stories about them from my fellow researchers and therapists, and personally experienced hundreds of them myself. I have selected for this chapter a small representative sample of the most interesting stories from my collection. The first of them bears some similarity to Jung's encounter with the golden beetle in that it involves the appearance of an insect in a place and at a time that was highly unlikely.

THE WAY OF THE ANIMAL POWERS

Praying Mantis in Manhattan

During one of his many workshops at the Esalen Institute in Big Sur, California, our friend and teacher Joseph Campbell gave a long talk on his favorite subject—the work of C. G. Jung and his revolutionary contributions to the understanding of mythology and psychology. During this lecture, he made a fleeting reference to the phenomenon of synchronicity. One of the participants, who was not familiar with this term, interrupted Joe and asked him to explain what synchronicity was. After giving a brief, general definition and description of this concept, Joe decided to illustrate his explanation with a practical example. Instead of telling Jung's story of the scarab, which one usually hears on such an occasion, Joe decided to share with the audience an example of remarkable synchronicity from his own life.

Before moving to Hawaii in their advanced age, Joe and his wife, Jean Erdman, had lived in New York City's Greenwich Village. Their apartment was on the fourteenth floor of a high-rise building on Waverly Place and Sixth Avenue. Joe's study had two pairs of windows, one of them facing the Hudson River, the other up Sixth Avenue. The first set of windows offered a beautiful view of the river, and during nice weather both of them were open all the time. The view from the other two windows was uninteresting, and the Campbells very seldom opened them. According to Joe, they might have not opened them more than two or three times during the forty-odd years they had lived there.

One day in the early 1980s, Joe was in his study working on his magnum opus, *The Way of the Animal Powers*, a comprehensive encyclopedia of shamanic mythologies of the world. At that time, he was writing the chapter on the mythology of the African Bushmen, a tribe living in the Kalahari Desert. One of the most important deities in the Bushman pantheon is Mantis, who combines the characteristics of a Trickster figure and Creator God. Joe was deeply immersed in this work, surrounded by articles and books on the subject. He was particularly impressed by the story Laurens van der Post wrote about his half-Bushman nanny, Klara, who had taken care of him since the moment of his birth. Van der Post vividly remembered instances from his childhood when Klara was able to communicate with a praying mantis (*Mantis religiosa*). When she talked to the member of this species, asking specific questions, the insect seemed to be responding appropriately with movements of its legs and body.

In the middle of this work, Joe suddenly felt an irresistible and completely irrational impulse to get up and open one of the windows facing Sixth Avenue. These were the windows with a boring view that normally remained closed all the time. After he opened it, he immediately automatically looked to the right without understanding why he was doing it. The last thing you would expect to encounter in Manhattan is a praying mantis. And yet, there it was, a large specimen of its kind, on the fourteenth floor of a high-rise building in downtown Manhattan, climbing slowly upward. According to Joe, it turned its head toward him and gave him a meaningful look. Although this encounter lasted only a few seconds, it had an uncanny quality and left a powerful impression on Joe. He said that he could confirm what he had read just minutes earlier in Laurens van der Post's story: there was something curiously human about the face of the mantis; its "heart-shape pointed chin, high cheek bones, and yellow skin made it look just like a Bushman's."

The appearance of a praying mantis on the fourteenth floor of a high-rise building in the middle of Manhattan is a very unusual occurrence, in and of itself, to say the least. But if one considers the timing of its appearance, coinciding with Joe's intense immersion in the mythology of Kalahari

Bushmen, and his unexplainable impulse to open the window and actively seek the meeting, the statistical improbability of this concatenation of events is truly astronomical. Only a hardcore materialist committed to his or her worldview with a quasi-religious fervor could believe that something like this might have happened by pure chance.

Traditional psychiatry does not distinguish between true synchronicities and psychotic misinterpretations of the world. Since the materialistic worldview is strictly deterministic and does not accept the possibility of "meaningful coincidences," any intimation of extraordinary synchronicities in the client's narrative will automatically be interpreted as "delusion of reference," a symptom of serious mental disease. However, there cannot be any doubt about the existence of genuine synchronicities, where any person who has access to the facts has to admit that the coincidences involved are beyond reasonable statistical probability. This certainly is the case with Joe's extraordinary encounter with the praying mantis.

THE DYING QUEEN

When Dreams Foretell What Comes by Day

I n 1964, I was invited by Joshua Bierer, a British psychiatrist, to participate in the Congress of Social Psychiatry in London; Joshua was the organizer and program coordinator of this conference. My lecture was part of a symposium on LSD psychotherapy, which gave me the opportunity to meet several prominent psychedelic pioneers, whose work I had previously known only from their writings. There I connected with two remarkable women, British therapists Joyce Martin and Pauline McCririck. Both of them had traditional training in Freudian psychoanalysis, but were now practicing LSD psychotherapy in Joyce's palatial house on London's famous Welbeck Street. They had jointly developed what they called "fusion therapy," a form of psychedelic treatment that was too revolutionary even for many therapists who were open-minded and courageous enough to administer LSD to their patients.

This method, particularly suited for patients with a history of abandonment, rejection, and emotional deprivation in infancy, involved close physical contact between therapists and clients during LSD sessions. During their sessions, these clients spent several hours in a deep age regression, lying on a couch covered with a blanket, while Joyce or Pauline lay by their side, holding them in close embrace, as a good mother would do to comfort her child. Their revolutionary method effectively polarized the community of LSD therapists. Some of the practitioners realized that this was a very powerful and logical way to heal "traumas by omission," emotional problems caused by maternal deprivation and bad mothering. Others were horrified by this radical "anaclitic* therapy"; they warned that close physical contact between therapist and client in a non-ordinary state of consciousness would cause irreversible damage to the relationship.

I was among those who were fascinated by Joyce and Pauline's "fusion therapy" because it was clear to me that "trauma by omission" could not be healed by talking therapy. I asked many questions about their unorthodox approach, and when they saw my genuine interest, they invited me to spend some time at the Welbeck clinic, meet their patients, and have a personal experience with their approach. I was impressed when I found out how much their clients benefited from the nourishing physical contact they had received in their psychedelic sessions. It also became clear to me that Joyce and Pauline encountered considerably less transference problems than an average Freudian analyst with his or her detached "deadpan" approach to therapy.

At the International Conference on LSD Psychotherapy held in May 1965 in Amityville, Long Island, Joyce and Pauline showed their fascinating film on the use of the fusion technique in psychedelic therapy. In a heated discussion that followed, most of the questions revolved around the transference/countertransference issues. Pauline provided a very interesting and convincing explanation why this approach presented less problems in this regard than the orthodox Freudian approach. She pointed out that most patients who come to therapy experienced in their infancy and childhood lack of affection from their parents. The cold attitude of the Freudian analyst tends to reactivate the resulting emotional wounds and triggers desperate attempts on the part of the patients to get the attention and satisfaction that had been denied to them.

By contrast, according to Pauline, fusion therapy provided a corrective experience by satisfying the old anaclitic cravings. Having their emotional

---

*An infant and a toddler have strong primitive needs for instinctual satisfaction and security that pediatricians and child psychiatrists call *anaclitic* (from the Greek *anaklinein*, meaning to cling or lean upon). These involve the need to be held, caressed, comforted, played with, and be the center of the caregivers' attention. If these needs are not met, it has serious consequences for the future of the individual.

wounds healed, the patients recognized that the therapist was not an appropriate sexual object and were able to find suitable partners outside of the therapeutic relationship. Pauline explained that this paralleled the situation in the early development of object relationships. Individuals who receive adequate mothering in infancy and childhood are able to emotionally detach from their mothers and find mature relationships. By contrast, those who experienced emotional deprivation remain pathologically attached and go through life craving and seeking satisfaction of primitive infantile needs.

Having heard enthusiastic stories from Joyce and Pauline's LSD patients at their Welbeck Street clinic, I became deeply interested in having a firsthand experience of the "fusion technique." My own session with Pauline was truly extraordinary. Although both of us were fully dressed and separated by a blanket, I experienced a profound age regression into early infancy and identified with an infant nursing on the breast of a good mother and feeling the contact with her naked body. Then the experience deepened, and I became a fetus in a good womb blissfully floating in the amniotic fluid. For more than three hours of clock time, a period that subjectively felt like eternity, I kept experiencing both of those situations—"good breast" and "good womb"—simultaneously or in an alternating fashion. I felt connected with my mother by the flow of two nourishing liquids—milk and blood—both of which felt at that point sacred. The episode culminated in an experience of sacred union with the Great Mother Goddess, rather than human mother. Needless to say, I found the session profoundly healing.

In 1966, during a conference on LSD psychotherapy in Amsterdam, I had the opportunity to have another equally remarkable session with Pauline and experience the "fusion therapy" the second time. We became good friends and saw each other occasionally at professional meetings or during my visits to London. In the late 1960s, after Joyce Martin's death, Pauline did not have anybody to sit for her in her own psychedelic sessions, and she asked me to step into Joyce's shoes and become her guide. At this time, I was not in Europe anymore; having received a scholarship to Johns Hopkins University, I now lived and worked in Baltimore. It reflected Pauline's deep conviction about the value of psychedelic sessions that she was willing to travel repeatedly over the Atlantic with all the expenditure of money, time, and energy involved. In connection with one of these sessions, I experienced a remarkable synchronicity.

Between four and five o'clock in the morning before Pauline's session, I woke up from a very disturbing dream. It took place in a gloomy castle, or rather burg, sometime in the Middle Ages. There was a general atmosphere of alarm and chaos, with many people running through dark corridors with torches in their hands. I heard distressing and agitated voices crying aloud: "The Queen … the Queen … the Queen is dying!" I was one of the people running in panic through the castle. After a breathless dash through the labyrinth of poorly lit corridors, I finally arrived at a chamber, where an old woman—clearly the Queen—was lying in a large bed with four carved wooden pillars and an ornate canopy. She was gasping for air, and her face was contorted in agony, as she was facing the final moments of her life. I stared at her in despair, overwhelmed with powerful emotions, knowing that the dying woman was my mother.

I woke up from this dream early in the morning in a state of great uneasiness and apprehension. I had a strong feeling that this dream had something to do with Pauline's session that I was about to run, and I experienced great reluctance to go ahead with it. This was something very unusual for me; I had never experienced anything like it before. The uneasiness I was sensing sharply contrasted with the enthusiasm I had usually felt about forthcoming psychedelic sessions. I lay in bed, reflecting on the dream, and trying to understand the uncanny feelings I was experiencing. As the morning broke and sunshine entered the bedroom, this strange state of mind gradually dissipated. I became more grounded and regained my usual confidence vis-à-vis the psychedelic session I was about to run.

During the first few hours of Pauline's session nothing extraordinary happened. By this I mean nothing that I had not seen before and that would make this session stand out in any particular way. Naturally, having taken a high dose of LSD, Pauline had very powerful experiences. Some of them were memories of emotionally charged episodes from her childhood and infancy, others involved reliving of her difficult birth, and a few were transpersonal elements from the collective unconscious. We were about five hours into the session when Pauline encountered a memory from her childhood involving a royal parade. At one point, she started singing the British anthem: "God save our gracious Queen, long live our noble Queen, god save the Queen. ... "

As she was singing, she suddenly became very alarmed. "My God, Stan, I am singing 'God save the Queen.' When I was a child, we had a king, not a queen; why am I singing 'God save the Queen'?" Then all her facial muscles suddenly contracted, giving her an expression of great agony, one that bore uncanny similarity to the face of the dying queen that I distinctly remembered from my dream. "Stan, this is not about my childhood anymore," she continued obviously distressed, in great panic, and heavily gasping for air. "I am the Queen, and I am dying." By that time, I had seen enough people in psychedelic sessions experience their death, and I was not particularly alarmed and concerned about Pauline's physical condition. However, I was astounded to see her enacting my dream from the preceding night and embodying with great accuracy the dying Queen who so prominently featured in it.

Pauline's session had a happy ending; her experience of death in identification with the old Queen was followed by an experience of rebirth and a "psychedelic afterglow" lasting several days. She felt that her experience was drawn from the collective unconscious or possibly from her own karmic record. She connected it with her lifelong fascination with royalty and her tendency to wear expensive and extravagant dresses and jewelry. I have not been able to find an explanation for why I had this astonishing precognitive dream. From time to time, I recall this extraordinary synchronicity, trying to understand its origin and meaning. I wonder if this strange bond between us was related to the psychedelic sessions I had with Pauline, during which I experienced symbiotic fusion with her as a fetus in a good womb and an infant on a good breast.

THE RAINBOW BRIDGE
OF THE GODS

In the Realm of the Nordic Sagas

Profound and auspicious synchronicities can initiate and accompany a powerful spiritual awakening; however, they are not without pitfalls. They can convey a convincing sense that we not only are embedded in a larger ground of cosmic meaning and purpose but also in some sense a focus or center of it. However, the overwhelming feeling of numinousness that is often associated with these synchronicities can be deceptive and should not be naively trusted and acted upon. As we will see in the following story, even the most glorious synchronicities do not guarantee a positive outcome of the situation of which they are part.

The events I will describe here happened about four years after my arrival in the United States, a time when I was looking for a life partner, with unsolicited assistance of my well-meaning, concerned friends. At the end of 1971, I received a call from Leni and Bob Schwartz, who belonged to the closest circle of my friends. Their house in lower Manhattan, testimony to Leni's impeccable taste, was a favorite hangout of many cultural figures of the time, from Joseph Campbell to Betty Friedan. Leni and Bob were both on the phone at the same time and, with great excitement, they alternated in describing their recent discovery: "We've just met somebody really special. She lives in Miami, and her name is Joan Halifax. She is an anthropologist, and she's beautiful and brilliant. She has done fieldwork with the Dogon in Sub-Saharan Africa, and she studies Santeria and other Caribbean religions. You'll have so much in common! You'll love her."

I wrote down Joan's name and telephone number and thanked Bob and Leni for their effort. But after one tumultuous relationship (see page 140), I was not ready to throw myself headfirst into another relationship. Occasionally, I let my fantasy wander to Joan, trying to imagine what our meeting would look like and toying with the idea of calling her. Finally, after several months, I decided to give it a try. I was about to attend the Annual Conference of the American Psychiatric Association in Dallas, Texas, to present the results of our research of LSD psychotherapy with terminal cancer patients. The conference ended on Friday, and it would have been easy for me to make a side trip and spend the weekend in Miami on the way back to Baltimore.

I dialed Joan's number, and when she picked up the phone, I introduced myself and said: "I'm Stan Grof from Baltimore. Our joint friends, Bob and Leni Schwartz, keep telling me that the two of us should meet. Is that something you would be interested in? I could come to Miami next weekend. Any chance we could get together?"

"I'm sorry," was Joan's response. "I won't be here. I'll be in Dallas. Next week I am going to the APA meeting to give a paper on my work with Santeria."

"That's very interesting," I said, marveling at the coincidence. "I will be in Dallas, too, going to the same meeting. I wanted to stop in Miami on the way back. Which hotel are you staying in?"

Things were rapidly getting denser. "In the Baker Hotel," was Joan's answer.

Of all the hotels in Dallas, this was the one for which I had made my reservation. It turned out that I had actually booked the room, that was directly under Joan's, one floor lower. Because we were staying in the same hotel, we decided that after our arrival we would connect with each other by telephone. When I arrived in the hotel, the meetings had already started. Joan was not in her room, and she had not left me a message. I decided to go to the meetings and find her. The program had many parallel tracks, eight if I remember correctly, and the meetings were held in several hotels. I looked at the program, trying to guess to which lecture Joan would go. I was using as a clue the fact that she was an anthropologist and also Leni and Bob's assurance that Joan and I had similar interests. After some deliberation, I chose a movie that was shown in a large auditorium of one of the conference hotels.

When I entered the hall, the lights were already out and they were showing the movie. I looked around and sat down in a nearby seat that was free. As I was watching the movie, my attention was repeatedly drawn to a woman who was sitting in the row in front of me, about three seats to my left. I actually started seeing something like a light aura around her head. After a while, she started turning her head in my direction, which was very unusual because she had to do it at a fairly large angle for our eyes to meet. This went on for quite a while and, by the time the movie ended, both of us felt so much certainty, that we simply went over to each other and confirmed our suspicions by introducing ourselves. Another extraordinary coincidence was thus added to those that preceded our arrival in Dallas.

Our Chinese dinner, an assortment of northern Chinese dishes, probably of average quality, seemed very special. We talked nonstop about our various interests, discovering that Leni and Bob were right; we really had much in common. At the end of the dinner, the waiter brought us the obligatory fortune cookies, something that we usually would not have taken very seriously. But in the context of all the unusual synchronicities that had happened already, the messages seemed absolutely right on and they sounded like an ancient I Ching reading. My cookie said: "Your heart was hers from the moment you met," and hers revealed: "After long waiting, your dream is finally coming true!" Needless to say, we decided not to go back to our respective homes but to spend the weekend together in Dallas.

After this auspicious beginning, our relationship moved very fast. The weekend following our encounter in Dallas, I flew to Miami to spend several days with Joan. The following weekend, Joan came to see me in Baltimore, and we had a wonderful time together. The two visits further deepened our relationship. By the end of the weekend, we felt so close that we wanted to continue seeing each other as much as possible, and the idea of separation was quite painful. However, my forthcoming schedule presented a serious problem in this regard. I was to go for about ten days to Iceland to attend the First International Transpersonal Conference.

To my great surprise and delight, Joan made a sudden decision to take a leave of absence and join me on my trip. We met at Kennedy Airport in New York and boarded Loftleidir, the Icelandic airline, for a flight to Reykjavik. In those days, I conducted many workshops at the Esalen Institute in Big Sur, California, and in various other parts of the United States. On many occasions, this involved taking the "red eye express," as I called the overnight flights back to Baltimore. A friend of mine gave me for these occasions a special kind of candy that he personally prepared. It seemed to be a perfect solution for the lack of comfort and sleep that these flights entailed. I was later able to obtain from him the recipe for this culinary panacea for jetlag and other forms of discomfort associated with long travel.

My friend's candy looked and tasted like a Middle Eastern dessert from *A Thousand and One Nights*. It was a mixture of cut-up nuts, dates, dried figs, and raisins rolled into little balls about the size of a large walnut. The most important ingredient in the mixture was "bhang ghee," melted butter containing an extract of sinsemilla, dried leaves, and blossoms of hemp native in Big Sur. Embarking on long night flights, I would swallow this before boarding the airplane. By the time it started taking effect, I had a greatly enhanced sense of taste and voracious appetite, which turned the airplane dinner into a gourmet feast. Following the dinner, I put on my eyeshades and listened to music until I fell asleep. I woke up relaxed and refreshed after a good night's sleep, usually just at the time when they were serving breakfast.

Joan and I each took two of these magic balls to ease our night flight to Reykjavik. When we landed, we were in a euphoric state of consciousness, one that was known among therapists as "the psychedelic afterglow," and we seemed to have remained in this special state of mind for many of the following days of our stay in Iceland. We rented a Land Rover for the three days before the conference started and decided to explore the island. The Icelandic scenery is incredible—majestic snow-capped mountains, volcanic craters, sparkling glaciers, luscious meadows and pastures, pristine rivers, and giant waterfalls. Everything seemed ancient—beginning and end of the world coming together.

We found an idyllic place, a lodge in the mountains with several A-frame cottages scattered in a fairy-tale-like landscape, quite far apart from each other and from the lodge, each with a private little geyser and pool. We were several hours' drive north of Reykjavik, in a region that lies far beyond the polar circle. It was the end of May, and the magic of the white nights, enhanced by the "psychedelic afterglow," was an unforgettable experience. We now felt even closer than we had before, and we started toying with the idea of taking advantage of the beautiful Icelandic natural setting and getting married here before our return home.

The romantic time in our little eyrie came to an end, and we drove to Bifrost, the site of the First International Transpersonal Conference, to join the other seventy participants. The Bifrost conference center, located in a stunningly beautiful volcanic landscape, had a central lodge, residential units, and a large sauna, built of natural wood. The conference brought together a group of very special people, including Joseph Campbell with his wife, Jean Erdman, philosopher and religious scholar Huston Smith, professor of religion Walter Houston Clark, and the Icelandic mythologist Einar Palsson. Among the participants were my brother, Paul, with his wife, Eva, and our joint friend Leni Schwartz, who had brought Joan and me together.

It is well-known that the population of the areas that lie beyond the polar circle has a strikingly large incidence of psychic phenomena. We could certainly confirm that during our stay in Iceland. We met many people who were precognitive, telepathic, and clairvoyant, and others who had reputations as healers, were successful dowsers, or saw elves and fairies. Various ESP phenomena were also rampant among the participants of our Bifrost group. This Icelandic experience helped me understand a book I had always loved, the *Gösta Berling Saga* by Selma Lagerlöf, the first woman awarded the Nobel Prize for literature. I had always been deeply moved by the intriguing way this author was able to merge everyday life and the mythic realm into an inextricable amalgam.

After our arrival in the Bifrost lodge, we sat down with Leni Schwartz to have a cup of tea. We decided to tell her that we were toying with the idea of getting married in Iceland. But we barely had a chance to tell her that we had some interesting news for her. "I know what you want to tell me; you would like to get married here," she said, and her face lit up. She was so convinced about the correctness of her guess that she got up and walked away without waiting for our confirmation. We found out later that she immediately broke the news to the rest of the group. Everybody got excited about the prospect of a nuptial ritual, and collective preparations for the ceremony started almost immediately.

Einar Pâlsson, an Icelandic mythologist who for the previous twenty years had studied Nordic mythology, came to the conference specifically to meet his hero, Joseph Campbell. The two became engaged in an ongoing series of profound discussions. Joseph, who had incredible encyclopedic knowledge of world mythology, was teaching Einar new things about the symbolic significance of some geographical locations in Iceland and the magic meaning of numbers involved. When the two of them heard about the planned wedding, they decided to provide a solid mythological foundation for our joining.

They reconstructed an ancient Viking wedding ritual that had not been performed in Iceland since the Christians had arrived. The joining of the bridegroom and the bride reflected *hierosgamos*, the sacred union of Father Sky and Mother Earth, and the symbol of this union was the rainbow. The conference was organized by an Icelandic couple, Geir and Ingrid Vilhjamsson. Ingrid's father was the mayor of Reykjavik, and her mother had an old Icelandic costume. They brought it from Reykjavik as a wedding dress for Joan, and it fit as if it had been custom-made for her. The wedding outfit we had chosen for me was a beautiful hand-knitted Icelandic sweater.

In the free time between the sessions of the conference, all the participants were involved in making costumes and masks for the wedding ritual, and some of them worked on the menu for the banquet. Joe Campbell's wife, Jean, an accomplished dancer and Broadway choreographer, choreographed the wedding ceremony and began rehearsing it with the group. Although neither Joan nor I had explicitly told anybody—except each other—that we wanted to get married, the preparations were in full gear.

The wedding began in the afternoon with a purification ceremony in the sauna, performed separately according to the Icelandic tradition for the bride and the bridegroom. Then the women in the group combed Joan's hair and dressed her up, singing songs and preparing her for the experience of the wedding night. Led by Ingrid, they tried to detach from their modern minds and emulate the discussion that might have occurred on this occasion in the old times. I met with the male part of the group to celebrate the end of my bachelorhood. We drank mead, sang appropriate songs, and told many jokes. Trying to tune in to the Viking mentality, my friends offered me their support and encouragement for what was lying ahead of me.

Following our sauna experience, we all gathered in the dining hall for a festive dinner. The exquisite menu featured many gifts of the Earth and a selection of freshwater fish and assorted seafood. The colors, tastes, and textures of the food, good wine, and the eerie light of the white night conspired in creating a magical atmosphere. After dinner, as we were dancing, somebody looked out the window and noticed that it had started to drizzle and that a giant, unbelievably rich full double rainbow was gracing the sky. Everybody walked out into the rain and continued to dance on the wet lawn.

While the dancing inside was jubilant and Dionysian, the rhythm of the movements now became leisurely and flowing, as if slowed by the command of an invisible conductor. People were moving in a tai chi manner, some individually, others in pairs or small groups. Somebody intuitively changed the music inside the dining hall; it was now meditative and timeless, perfectly matching the rhythm of the dance. Illuminated by the magic light of the white night and against the backdrop of the double rainbow, the scene looked otherworldly, surreal, like a Fellini movie.

To our astonishment, the double rainbow appeared and disappeared three times. In the mood we were in, it was difficult not to interpret this magnificent display as a very auspicious sign. This incredible celestial spectacle would have been enough, in and of itself, to impart to the wedding an air of numinosity. But it also involved some extraordinary synchronicities. We found out that the name of the place, Bifrost, meant in the old Icelandic language the "Rainbow Bridge of the Gods" and, in the ancient Viking wedding ritual we were performing, the rainbow was the symbol for the joining of Father Sky and Mother Earth. It was easy to infer that this event had some deeper cosmic significance.

In addition, for me the rainbow had a profound personal significance and was connected with another interesting synchronicity. During my first year in the United States, I invited my parents to join me, and we spent two months traveling around the country, combining visits to prominent representatives of psychedelic and consciousness research with sightseeing and camping in national parks and other places of natural beauty. Eager to see everything there was to see, we covered more than 17,000 miles in eight weeks.

Needless to say, our ambitious itinerary included the spectacular American Southwest. One day, late in the afternoon of a very hot day, as we were crossing the New Mexico desert on our way to Santa Fe, it started to rain. It was a very welcome change after many hours of scorching heat. The sun was setting, gracing the sky behind us with a rich panoply of beautiful colors. All of a sudden, a magnificent full rainbow appeared in the sky in front of us. The highway was absolutely straight, like an arrow shot from our car toward the horizon, crossing it precisely at the rainbow's right radix. I instinctively stepped on the gas pedal, eager to come as close as possible before the rainbow would disappear.

The rainbow remained in the sky, and it grew bigger and brighter as we approached. It stayed in place until our car drove directly into its radix. At that moment, it was as if we had passed through a gateway into another reality. We were suddenly in a realm of indescribable beauty, with gossamer veils of rainbow colors dancing and swirling around us, exploding into myriad shining little diamonds. I stopped the car, and the three of us sat there astonished, admiring this incredible spectacle. For me this event triggered the most powerful ecstatic experience I have ever had in my life without the help of any mind-altering substances or devices. It lasted the rest of the evening, and even next morning I could feel its afterglow.

After a good night's sleep, we decided to visit the Museum of Navajo Art in Santa Fe. Its main hall was a large round structure resembling a kiva, ceremonial chamber of American Pueblo Indians. The most conspicuous piece of decoration in it was a large and very thin stylized female figure, whose body consisted of parallel longitudinal stripes. It stretched in a U shape all around the entire hall, with the exception of the entrance, which was flanked by her head on one side and a short skirt and legs on the other. The native guide explained to us that this was the Rainbow Maiden, a very popular Navajo deity. She played a crucial role in Navajo mythology, which reflected the importance of rain in this arid region. The guide shared with us the Navajo belief that if the Rainbow Maiden liked some people, she would envelop, embrace, and kiss them. This would result in an experience of ecstatic rapture that these individuals remember their entire lives. He essentially described what had happened to me on our way to Santa Fe; this auspicious experience has remained vivid in my memory until this very day.

The set and setting for the Bifrost wedding ceremony could not have been more magnificent. We got married at three o'clock in the morning in an old volcanic crater at the time when the rising sun reappeared in the sky after disappearing for only an hour behind the horizon. Joseph Campbell was the surrogate father who brought Joan to the improvised altar, and the joiner and officiator was Huston Smith. Walter Houston Clark offered as benediction Sarah's pledge from the Old Testament: "I will go where you go and your people will be my people." After exchanging rings of a Viking design and sealing the union with a kiss, we ran through a gauntlet of our friends, who were holding branches with green foliage and looked like Macduff's army from *Macbeth,* carrying Birnam woods to Dunsinane castle.

We got only about an hour's sleep because the group had to leave early for a long hike to one of Iceland's spectacular glaciers. I woke up after an hour of dozing off, ready to embark on the trip. As soon as I opened my eyes, I sensed that something was terribly wrong. All the thrill and ecstatic feelings of the preceding day were gone; I felt sober and somber. The wave of excitement we had experienced the last few days suddenly felt illusory and deceptive. And what was worse, marrying Joan suddenly seemed like a serious error.

Our final destination was a primitive lodge on one of Iceland's largest glaciers that had a communal dormitory and one single room. The group unanimously decided that this precious commodity would serve as the bridal chamber, where Joan and I would spend the next night. I managed to keep my concerns to myself, and things continued to look wonderful on the outside. The group was still feeling the emotional echoes of the Viking nuptial ritual, and the spellbinding Icelandic scenery was truly extraordinary. After a glorious day in the mountains and a night stay in the lodge, we returned to Bifrost for the closing ceremony of the conference.

The Icelandic meeting, the first of a series of international transpersonal conferences, was an unforgettable event for all of us who shared in it, and our wedding was without any doubt its highlight. However, once we returned to the United States, my dismal premonitions began to materialize. Various problems Joan and I encountered shortly after our return started to take a toll on our relationship.

On the way back from Iceland, we stopped in Miami, where Joan introduced me to her parents, John and Eunice. They had no idea that Joan had plans to be married until she broke the news about our Icelandic wedding in a telephone call. I clearly did not meet the standards of the nouveau riche world of their Miami island house. However, they reluctantly accepted me, probably because, knowing Joan's rebellious spirit, they expected worse. The first three sentences Joan's father, John, asked after she told him she was married were: "Is he black? Is he a Communist? Does he have a beard?" And he felt somewhat reassured when the answers to all three of those questions were negative.

Joan left her job with the anthropological department of the University of Miami and moved to my apartment in Baltimore. She made several unsuccessful attempts to get a teaching or research position at the Johns Hopkins University and at the University of Maryland. The loss of her academic identity seemed to take a big toll on her emotional condition. I offered her to join me in our project of psychedelic therapy with terminal cancer patients. She enjoyed being a cotherapist in LSD and DPT (dipropyltryptamine) sessions, but had to do it gratis, because there was no salaried position available at the Maryland Psychiatric Research Center. A trip to Japan intended as a honeymoon further increased the tension between us.

Fortunately, I was offered an advance royalty from Viking Press to write two books on LSD. At a party in Leni and Bob Schwartz's house in New York City, we ran into an old friend of mine, Michael Murphy, the cofounder of the Esalen Institute. After a brief discussion, Michael invited us to move to Big Sur as Esalen's guests and offered me the position of Scholar-in-Residence. A vacation in Austria and Italy and the move to Esalen temporarily took some of the pressure from our relationship and brought a momentary relief. However, it did not last very long; the differences between us continued to grow, and our relationship rapidly deteriorated. For some time, we tried to stay together, mostly because we did not want to disappoint the group of our Bifrost friends, who had created and experienced our beautiful wedding ceremony, and particularly Joe Campbell. Joe criticized, in his lectures, modern marriage for lacking a solid mythological grounding and offered a glowing description of our wedding as a model of a mythologically informed marriage that would last forever. When our marriage finally fell apart, and it was clear that divorce was inevitable, dealing with Joe's disappointment was one of the most difficult parts of the process.

The Icelandic adventure was a fascinating experience of archetypal energies breaking into everyday life and creating astonishing synchronicities. However, it taught me an important lesson. I learned not to trust unconditionally the seductive power of such experiences and the enchantment and ego inflation that they engender. The ecstatic feelings associated with emergence of archetypal forces do not guarantee a positive outcome. It is essential to refrain from acting out while we are under their spell and not to make any important decisions until we have again both feet on the ground.

THE PLAY OF CONSCIOUSNESS

Swami Muktananda and Siddha Yoga

O ver the years, my wife, Christina, and I have observed in our work and personally experienced many remarkable synchronicities. Sometimes these were isolated occurrences; other times they came in entire chains and aggregates. However, there was a period of eight years in our lives when we had the opportunity to encounter and observe synchronicities on a mass scale. This was the time of our close relationship with Swami Muktananda, Indian spiritual teacher and head of the ancient Siddha Yoga lineage. In 1975, when Christina and I met in Big Sur, California, and started working and living together, Christina was Swami Muktananda's student and ardent follower. She had met him when he had stopped in Honolulu during his first world tour, accompanied by Ram Dass, famous Harvard psychology professor and psychedelic researcher turned spiritual seeker and teacher.

Christina was at that time experiencing a powerful awakening of Kundalini, which had started during the delivery of her first child, Nathaniel, and had been further intensified and deepened by the delivery of her daughter, Sarah, two years later. According to the yogic tradition, Kundalini, also called the Serpent Power, is the generative cosmic energy, feminine in nature, which is responsible for the creation of the universe. It has its representation in the subtle or energy body, a field that pervades and permeates, as well as surrounds, the human physical body. In its latent form, it resides in the sacral area, at the base of the spine. The name Kundalini means literally "the coiled one," and it is usually depicted as a snake twisted three and half times around the lingam, symbol of the male generative power. This dormant energy can become activated by meditation, specific exercises, the intervention of an experienced spiritual teacher (guru), or for unknown reasons.

The activated Kundalini, called *shakti*, rises through the *nadis*, channels or conduits in the subtle body. As it ascends, it clears old traumatic imprints and opens the centers of psychic and spiritual energy, called *chakras*. Awakening of Kundalini is thus conducive to healing, spiritual opening, and positive personality transformation. This process, although highly valued and considered beneficial in the yogic tradition, is not without dangers and requires expert guidance by a guru whose Kundalini is fully awakened and stabilized. The most dramatic signs of Kundalini awakening are physical and psychological manifestations called *kriyas*. The kriyas involve intense sensations of energy and heat streaming up the spine, which can be associated with violent shaking, spasms, and twisting movements.

Powerful waves of seemingly unmotivated emotions, such as anxiety, anger, sadness, or joy and ecstatic rapture, can surface and temporarily dominate the psyche. This can be accompanied by visions of brilliant light or various archetypal beings and a variety of internally perceived sounds. Many people involved in this process also often have powerful experiences of what seem to be memories from past lives. Involuntary and often uncontrollable behaviors complete the picture: speaking in tongues, chanting unknown songs or sacred invocations (*mantras*), assuming yogic postures (*asanas*) and gestures (*mudras*), and making a variety of animal sounds and movements.

Swami Muktananda had the reputation of being a perfected master, an accomplished Kundalini yogi, capable of awakening spiritual energy in his disciples. Christina heard about his visit to Hawaii from her friends and decided to attend an "intensive," as Muktananda called weekend retreats he was offering. During one of the meditations in this retreat, Christina received from him *shaktipat*, which is the Sanskrit name for transfer of spiritual energy from the guru, mediated by a touch, a look, or even a thought. For Christina, this powerful energy transfer occurred when Muktananda looked at her and their eyes met. At this point, she experienced a penetrating lightning bolt radiating from the guru's eyes and hitting her between her eyes in the area where the spiritual traditions place the "third eye." This triggered intense *kriyas,* waves of overwhelming emotions and shaking.

The experience with Muktananda greatly intensified Christina's process of Kundalini awakening, which had already been well underway before she met him. This was the beginning of her important relationship with this remarkable Siddha yogi, which lasted until 1982, when he died at the age of seventy-four. After the weekend retreat, Christina offered as a meeting place for Muktananda's devotees her small apartment in Honolulu, where she lived after her divorce with her children, Than and Sarah. Muktananda accepted her offer, visited her apartment, and blessed it as a Siddha Yoga meditation center. After leaving Hawaii, Christina tried to use any opportunity to reconnect with her teacher.

Shortly after Christina and I started living together at Esalen, Swami Muktananda came to the Bay Area to spend several months in his ashram in Oakland, near San Francisco. Oakland is only about a three-hours' drive from Big Sur, where we lived, and Christina used this occasion to arrange for the two of us a personal audience, or *darshan*, with her spiritual teacher. As I found out later, she was uncertain whether Swami Muktananda would approve of our relationship and wanted to find out. I could certainly understand her concerns. Being a "transcendental hedonist," as I often jokingly referred to myself, I did not exactly meet the conventional Indian criteria for an austere spiritual seeker. I was not a vegetarian, enjoyed sex, and was known for my work with LSD and other psychedelic substances.

I had heard about Swami Muktananda before I met Christina, and had the chance to leaf through a manuscript of his autobiography, entitled *Guru*, later to become *The Play of Consciousness.* I was not particularly eager to drive to Oakland to meet him because I had somewhat mixed feelings about him. Two of my friends had converted to Siddha Yoga and were showing what I saw as an uncritical passionate devotion to Muktananda. They were certainly not the best advertisements for Muktananda and the influence he had on his followers.

Their behavior drastically changed following their attendance of a Muktananda weekend intensive and created much commotion at Esalen. Instead of covering the topic they had promised in the Esalen catalog, they brought into their workshops little drums and cymbals and tried to engage the participants in chanting "Shree Guru Gita," "Om Namah Shivaya," and other Hindu devotional chants.

Devotional yoga had never been my favorite spiritual practice. According to the ancient Indian tradition, people with different personalities need and seek different types of yoga. While Christina's preference was without any doubt bhakti yoga, an approach emphasizing devotion to the guru, I felt great affinity to jñana yoga, a spiritual strategy that pushes the intellect to its utmost limits, where it has to surrender. I also resonated very much with raja yoga, a system that focuses on psychological experiment and a direct experience of the divine. I could easily accept karma yoga, the yoga of service accumulating karmic merits, but bhakti yoga was low on my scale of values.

But because I am very curious by nature, my reservations about devotional practice did not override my interest in meeting a Siddha Yoga guru with Muktananda's reputation. And I knew that this darshan was very important for Christina. As we were driving toward the Bay Area, Christina kept telling me some remarkable stories about her spiritual teacher, as a preparation for our meeting. We overestimated the time it would take us to drive from Big Sur to Oakland because this was not our usual route, and arrived at the ashram about twenty minutes before our scheduled meeting.

While we were sitting in the car waiting for the darshan, we continued our discussion about Swami Muktananda. At one point, Christina mentioned that he was a Shaivite, which means a follower of Shiva. This captured my attention and increased my interest in meeting him. I knew that among the methods the Shaivites were using to get into non-ordinary states of consciousness was ingestion of bhang and datura seeds. And I considered Shiva to be my most important personal archetype because the two most powerful and meaningful experiences I have ever had in my psychedelic sessions involved this Indian deity. As we were waiting, I described these two experiences at some length to Christina.

My first encounter with Shiva occurred in one of my early LSD sessions, when I was still in Prague. I spent the first four hours of this session in the birth canal, reliving the trauma of my birth. As I was emerging from the birth canal, all battered, covered with blood, and tasting vaginal secretions, I had a terrifying vision of the Hindu goddess Kali and experienced a complete unconditional surrender to the power of the feminine principle in the universe. At that moment, I saw a gigantic figure of Bhairava, Shiva in his Destroyer aspect, towering above me. I felt crushed by his foot and smeared like a piece of excrement on what seemed to be the deepest bottom of the universe. It was a complete annihilation of what I then considered to be my identity, a shattering death of my body and ego. But having become nothing, I became everything. I had a sense of dissolving in a source of light of indescribable intensity and exquisite beauty. I realized that I was experiencing what had been called in the ancient Indian scriptures the union of Atman and Brahman.

My second encounter with Shiva happened many years later, during my vision quest in the Ventana wilderness in Big Sur. In an overnight LSD session that took place near a waterfall in a redwood dell, I had the vision of a giant archetypal river, representing time and the impermanence of all creation. It flowed back into what appeared to be the source of all existence—an immense ball of radiating energy that was conscious, possessed infinite intelligence, and was simultaneously creative and destructive. I heard a compelling sound and knew instantly that it was dambaru, the drum of Shiva Bhairava, the Destroyer, commanding all creation to return where it came from.

The history of the universe and of the Earth was passing in front of my eyes. As if in an incredibly sped-up movie, I saw the birth, development, and death of galaxies and stars. I observed the beginning, evolution, and extinction of species and witnessed cultures and dynasties originating, flourishing, and facing destruction. The most memorable sequence of this session was a procession of dinosaurs of all shapes and sizes entering after millions of years of existence the River of Time and disappearing in it. Permeating this amazing scenery like a magnificent cosmic hologram was a giant figure of Shiva Nataraja, Lord of the Cosmic Dance, performing his dance of the universe. After sunrise, when my attention turned from my inner world to the incredible beauty of nature around me, I heard for many hours in my ears the enticing and irresistible chant "Om, hare Om, hare Om, Shri Om," which I had heard throughout this unforgettable experience as a leitmotif of the River of Time.

I finished telling Christina about these two experiences, which had transformed my life, just when it was time for our darshan. As we entered the room and saw Swami Muktananda, I was struck by his extraordinary appearance. He wore a thick red ski cap, large dark glasses, and the lunghi, an orange robe. In his right hand he held a wand of peacock feathers, which—as I found out later—was heavily scented with fragrant sandalwood essence. Hitting people with peacock feathers over the head was one of Swami Muktananda's principal tools for imparting the shaktipat.

Baba, as his followers fondly called him, invited me to sit down next to him and turned his head toward me. He then took off his dark glasses, something he very rarely did, and he started to inspect my face from a short distance. I saw in a close-up his widely dilated pupils, which seemed to be floating freely on his eyeballs; this was something I was used to seeing in my clients who had taken large doses of LSD. He focused his sight on my eyes and examined them with the thoroughness of an ophthalmologist. As if summarizing his professional observations, he suddenly uttered a phrase that sent chills up my spine: "I can tell you are a man who has seen Shiva."

I was astonished by this extraordinary synchronicity. Muktananda's statement came only a few minutes after I had finished telling Christina about my experiences of Shiva and their importance for my life. It was absolutely impossible for Muktananda to have any knowledge of this fact had he relied on ordinary information channels. It was also hard to imagine that this was only a meaningless coincidence. The probability of something as specific as this being a result of chance was so low that it could be practically excluded. I could see only two possible explanations for what had just happened. Swami Muktananda had to have paranormal access to information about facts in the surrounding world or be part of a field that fostered meaningful synchronicities in the Jungian sense.

My curiosity concerning Muktananda and interest in spending some time with him increased considerably after what had just happened. Our exchange following this dramatic opening seemed at first anticlimactic, although the topic of our discussion was quite interesting for me from a professional point of view. Muktananda knew that I had worked with LSD and initiated a discussion about the use of psychoactive substances in spiritual practice. He expressed his belief that the experiences induced by them were closely related to those sought in Siddha Yoga.

"I understand you have been working with LSD," he said through his interpreter, Malti, a young Indian woman whom he many years later appointed as his successor under the name Swami Chitvilasananda. "We do something very similar here. But the difference is that, in Siddha Yoga, we teach people not only to get high, but to stay high," he stated with confidence. "With LSD you can have great experiences, but then you come down. There are many serious spiritual seekers in India, Brahmans and yogis, who use sacred plants in their spiritual practice," Swami Muktananda continued, "but they know how to do it properly."

He then talked about the need for a respectful ritual approach to cultivation, preparation, and smoking or ingesting of Indian hemp (*Cannabis indica*) in the form of bhang, ganja, or charas and criticized the casual and irreverent use of marijuana and hashish by the young generation in the West. "The yogis grow and harvest the plant very consciously and with great devotion," he said. "They first soak it in water for fourteen days to get rid of all the toxic ingredients and then dry it. They put it in a *chilam* (a special pipe) and smoke it. And then they lie naked in the snow and ice of the Himalayas in ecstasy." Talking about smoking the chilam and the ecstatic rapture of the yogis, Baba acted out the appropriate facial expressions, movements, and postures as if remembering what it was like.

In the course of our discussion, I asked Baba about soma, the sacred potion of ancient India that is mentioned more than a thousand times in the *Rig Veda* and that clearly played a critical role in the Vedic religion. This sacrament was prepared from a plant of the same name, the identity of which got lost over the centuries. I found the reports about soma fascinating and hoped that Swami Muktananda might know something that would lead to its botanical identification and, ultimately, to the isolation of its active principle. Discovering the secret of soma was at the time the dream of many of us who were involved in psychedelic research.

Talking about soma, Muktananda dismissed the theory expounded by mycologist Gordon Wasson that this plant was *Amanita muscaria*, the fly agaric mushroom. He assured me that soma was not a mushroom, but a "creeper." This seemed to make sense and did not particularly surprise me because another important item in the psychedelic pharmacopoeia, the famous Mesoamerican sacrament ololiuqui, was a preparation containing the seeds of morning glory (*Ipomoea violacea*), which would qualify as a creeper plant because it grows with the help of tendrils.

But what followed came as a great surprise to me. Baba not only knew what soma was, but he assured me that it was still being used in India to this very day. As a mater of fact, he claimed that he was in regular contact with Vedic priests who were using it in their rituals. And, according to Baba, some of these priests actually came every year down from the mountains to Ganeshpuri, a little village south of Bombay that hosted his ashram, to celebrate his birthday. On this occasion, they regularly conducted soma ceremonies. At the end of our discussion, Baba extended his invitation to Christina and me to visit his ashram at the time of his birthday and promised to make arrangements for us to participate in this ancient ritual.

By and large, it seemed that the darshan would have the form of a quasi-professional exchange of information about "technologies of the sacred." But then the situation took a sudden, unexpected turn. Without any preparation or warning, Muktananda brusquely reached for a pink can of Almond Rocca that was displayed on a small table on his side. There were always many sweets around the ashram because Baba made it clear that Shakti, the divine feminine energy, had a great affinity for sweets. Amrit, the ashram's well-stocked cafeteria, abounded in the most incredible confections of all kinds. Muktananda now fished out of the can two pieces of this candy, skillfully unwrapped them, and stuffed them into my mouth while simultaneously slapping me quite strongly on both of my cheeks, hitting me on the forehead, and kicking me on my shins.

Then he stood up, making it clear that the darshan was coming to an end. At the door, as we were on the way out, he looked at Christina and me and said: "We'll have two weekend intensives on Kashmir Shaivism; I invite you both as my guests." Before I left the room, he gave me a meaningful look and said: "It will be very interesting for you." At that time, I did not know anything about Kashmir Shaivism; I could only infer from the name that it had something to do with Shiva and with Kashmir. We thanked Muktananda, said good-bye, and walked out of the darshan room into the spacious meditation hall of the ashram.

Outside the darshan room was a large crowd of people, waiting for us to come out. Most of them seemed to be people who had been brought to Siddha Yoga by their psychedelic experiences. They suspected that my discussion with Muktananda would include psychedelics and wanted to know if he had said anything about this subject. I had to walk through a gauntlet of these people showering me with questions, such as: "What did you talk about? Did Baba say anything about acid? Did Baba think psychedelics were okay?"

I did not feel the least inclination to socialize. I was aware of some strange sensations in my body and felt that something was churning inside my head. I apologized, disentangled myself from the crowd, and walked into the farthest area of the meditation hall. There I sat down in a cross-legged position, with my back pressed into the corner, and with my eyes closed. I felt this would be the best way to get a better insight into what was happening to me.

Siddha yogis have the reputation of being able to awaken the inner psychic energy by shaktipat, and I knew that what Muktananda had done with me belonged to this category. However, I did not expect any significant reaction because I did not consider myself particularly suggestible. I did not think, at that time, that anything short of a potent psychoactive drug would significantly change my consciousness. And I knew from literature and from my experience with Christina that a typical response to shaktipat involved kriyas—intense emotions, involuntary sounds, and dramatic motor responses. My own reaction took me by surprise.

Seconds after closing my eyes, I found myself in a state of complete nothingness and emptiness, in a void that had cosmic dimensions. One way of describing my condition would be to say that it felt like being suspended in interstellar space, somewhere midway between the Earth and Alpha Centauri. However, this would pertain only to a very superficial aspect of this experience and would not capture the sense of profound peace and tranquility of this condition and the extraordinary metaphysical insights associated with it. I felt that I was in a state that transcended all polarities and that I had a total understanding of existence. It seemed that this cosmic vacuum somehow held the secret of being and creation. When I opened my eyes again, I found out that more than an hour had elapsed since the darshan had ended.

We gladly accepted Baba's invitation for the weekend intensives on Kashmir Shaivism, Christina because of her devotion to the guru and myself because of the curiosity aroused by the peculiar synchronicity and my unusual experience. The first intensive turned out to be another surprising and very interesting experience. It started with an introductory lecture on Kashmir Shaivism, delivered by Swami Tejo, a member of the Muktananda staff. As the swami began talking, I found myself increasingly baffled and slightly paranoid. He seemed to be reading passages from an article that I had written and published several years earlier in one of the last issues of a short-lived, obscure periodical, *Journal for the Study of Consciousness*. The similarity was astonishing, down to specific images and metaphors.

In the late 1960s, when I was still working at the Maryland Psychiatric Research Center, I decided to write a paper describing the ontological and cosmological insights that become available in non-ordinary states of consciousness. It was based on observations from over five thousand psychedelic sessions that my colleagues and I had conducted in Prague and in Baltimore. I extracted those parts of our clients' reports where they tackled some fundamental problems of existence—the nature of reality, mystery of the cosmic creative principle, the process of creation of the universe, the relationship between humans and the divine, the role of evil in the universal fabric, reincarnation and karma, the enigma of time and space, and the like.

I found to my surprise that the individual metaphysical insights of my clients were strikingly similar from person to person and that they constituted various partial aspects of one overarching cosmic vision. This extraordinary perspective on the cosmos and human existence that emerged from this analysis was radically different from the one formulated by Newtonian-Cartesian materialistic science. However, it bore striking similarity to various spiritual systems to which Aldous Huxley referred to as perennial philosophy.

Many aspects of this vision also showed impressive convergence with the worldview of quantum-relativistic physics and other revolutionary advances in modern science, usually described as the "new" or "emerging" paradigm. The article discussing my findings, entitled "LSD and the Cosmic Game: Outline of Psychedelic Cosmology and Ontology," had been published in 1972, three years before the Oakland intensive took place. Twenty-six years later, this article became the basis for my book *The Cosmic Game: Explorations of the Frontiers of Human Consciousness*.

And, in his introductory talk in the Oakland intensive, Swami Tejo seemed to shamelessly plagiarize my ideas. It took me a while before I realized that what he was describing was actually Kashmir Shaivism and not passages from my paper. This was truly astonishing because more than a millennium and thousands of miles separated the origins of this spiritual philosophy and the insights of my clients. The beginnings of Kashmir Shaivism can be traced back to the eighth century A.D., when a Kashmiri sage had a vision that directed him to a specific location outside of Shrinagar, the country's capital. There he found sacred inscriptions carved in the rock that later became *Shiva Sutras*, the principal sacred text of Kashmir Shaivism. Nobody knows who their author was or how long they had been there before their discovery.

It was difficult to believe that the experiences of twentieth-century subjects, central Europeans of Slavic or Jewish origin, caucasian Americans, and African Americans, who had ingested LSD-25, could bear such a deep resemblance to passages from ancient Kashmiri texts. What was the relationship between the effects of a semisynthetic psychoactive substance, discovered by a strange serendipity by a Swiss chemist, and philosophical insights described in the scriptures of an ancient spiritual discipline? And what was the explanation for the fact that they were not erratic and delirious products of the individual psyches, but took the form of a shared, internally consistent, well-integrated, and comprehensive cosmic vision?

It took me some time to find the solution to this puzzle, but once I had it, the answer seemed quite obvious. LSD was not a pharmacological agent generating exotic experiences by its interaction with the neurophysiological processes in the brain. This remarkable substance was clearly an unspecific catalyst of the deep dynamics of the human psyche. The experiences induced by it were not neurochemical artifacts, symptoms of a toxic psychosis as mainstream psychiatrists called it, but genuine manifestations of the human psyche itself. These experiences could then naturally be triggered by many other approaches, including various "technologies of the sacred," developed by Eastern spiritual disciplines.

Our friendship with Swami Muktananda continued until his death seven years later and formed an important part of our life. Christina and I had many additional personal darshans with him and attended a number of Siddha Yoga meditations and weekend intensives in different parts of the world. During these years, I also had ample opportunity to compare spontaneous experiences of people who had received shaktipat with those that were induced by psychedelics, and could confirm their remarkable similarity.

Shortly after my first meeting with Baba, Christina and I developed Holotropic Breathwork, a powerful nonpharmacological method of self-exploration and therapy. With this approach, non-ordinary states of consciousness are induced by very simple and natural means—faster breathing, evocative music, and release of blocked energies by a certain form of bodywork. The experiences triggered by this approach can be very powerful, and they resemble both the states induced by psychedelics and those described in Kashmir Shaivism. They thus represent an additional proof that the phenomena induced by LSD and other similar substances are not chemical artifacts, but genuine expressions of the human psyche.

Our relationship with Swami Muktananda deepened and intensified in the last years of his life. During a darshan following the conference of the International Transpersonal Association (ITA) in Danvers, Massachusetts, he suggested that we hold one of the future ITA meetings in India, and he offered us his personal support, as well as the help of his staff and of the Ganeshpuri ashram. The conference was held in the Oberoi Hotel in Bombay in February 1982, several months before Baba's death. It was called Ancient Wisdom and Modern Science and provided a forum for exchange between new paradigm scientists and spiritual teachers.

The program had a stellar cast; it featured brain researcher Karl Pribram, physicist Fritjof Capra, biologist Rupert Sheldrake, family therapist Virginia Satir, neurophysiologists Elmer and Alyce Green, child development expert Joseph Chilton Pearce, and many other scientists. The spiritual world was represented by Swami Muktananda, Mother Teresa, Parsee high priest Dastoor Minocheer Homji, Turkish Sufi Sheik Muzafer Ozak Al-Jerrahi, Taoist Master Chungliang Al Huang, Aurobindo scholar Karan Singh, Benedictine monk Father Bede Griffith, and rabbis Zalman Schachter-Shalomi and Shlomo Carlebach. Among the highlights of the cultural program was an evening of Hassidic dances, sufi zikr of the Halveti Jerrahi dervishes, musician Paul Horn, and Alarmel Valli, the rising star of Indian classical dance. The meeting was a thundering success in spite of the absence of the Dalai Lama, who could not deliver his opening address because he fell ill on his way from Dharamsala to Bombay, and of the Karmapa, who had died a few months before the conference and was not able to close the conference with the promised Black Crown ceremony.

On the day following the conference, Baba invited all 700 participants to his ashram in Ganeshpuri for a *bandara*, a traditional Indian feast. As it turned out, Baba's presentation at the Bombay ITA conference was his last public appearance. When the meeting ended, he retreated into his quarters in the Ganeshpuri ashram, where he spent most of his time in silence, making gradual preparations for the transmission of the Siddha lineage and his own demise. Christina and I spent two weeks on a pilgrimage to various sacred sites in India and then returned to Ganeshpuri for our final two weeks with Baba. He appeared in the marble-covered courtyard twice a day and sat there in silence, while the ashram residents and visitors paid homage to him and offered various gifts.

Everything seemed to indicate that we would not have another chance to talk to him or see him privately. That unexpectedly changed two days before our departure. Noni, Baba's personal valet, delivered to us a message that Baba wanted to see us. He wanted us to come at five o'clock to the meditation hall, where he would "tune up our meditation." The meditation Hall was the spiritual heart of the ashram. It was built around the place where Muktananda's own guru and powerful Siddha yogi Nityananda lived in a cottage. This place was marked by a large hide of a tiger, the animal consecrated to Shiva. One of its doors opened into Baba's bedroom, another one to the staircase descending underground to the Tiger Cave, another favorite place for meditation.

Christina and I arrived in the dark meditation hall at the appointed hour and sat down on a large hide. We might have meditated for about five minutes, when the door of Baba's private quarters quietly opened up and he walked in. Without saying a word, he approached Christina and pressed on her eyeballs, maintaining the pressure for about fifteen or twenty seconds. Then he moved on to me and did the same. I felt his thumbs delving so deep into my eyes that they seemed to be touching my retinas. I experienced an indescribable pain and pressure in my head and had to control my impulse to interrupt this procedure. I felt that nobody, not even a Siddha guru, should be allowed to do with my eyes what Muktananda was doing. But my curiosity took over, and I said to myself: "This is very interesting; stay with it!" And I did.

The pressure grew to intolerable intensity and then my head exploded into a brilliant light that gradually turned into a vision of star-filled sky. I experienced an ecstatic rapture of truly cosmic proportions, which ended in a state of blissful emptiness, similar to the one I had experienced after I had first received shaktipat from Muktananda. This experience matched those in my high-dose psychedelic sessions in terms of its intensity, but it was of shorter duration. Christina's experiences were equally powerful, but they continued throughout the night. They brought a chain of memories of abuse that she had suffered from various male figures in her life. She felt that it was a major emotional clearing and healing of old traumas.

The next day, Noni brought us a message that Baba wanted to see us in the meditation hall at the same hour for "round two," as he called it. This time, he repeated the same procedure of compressing the eyeballs, but added another element. He pressed his forehead, decorated with several ashen horizontal stripes—the sign of Shiva—against ours and forcefully blew air into our nostrils. This time, the resulting experience was very positive for both of us. In the morning of our last day in the ashram, shortly before our departure, Baba unexpectedly invited us into his private quarters for a darshan. In retrospect, it became clear that this was meant to be the final good-bye.

At the beginning of this meeting, he gave us each a meditation shawl and a beautiful dark amethyst. Then he broke his silence and told us that we should have the amethysts set in gold and made into rings. He emphasized that it was very important that we wear these rings all the time. As we were parting, Baba surprised us with an enigmatic sentence: "Go back and continue to work with people! I will help you. You are doing my work!" And he motioned us to leave. This was the last time we saw Baba, and all that remained were memories of this remarkable human being and of the play of consciousness that he represented.

Devotees often try to explain scandalous events that happen around their gurus by saying that large light casts a big shadow and that such problems are caused by dark forces fighting enlightenment. Swami Muktananda's light must have been very bright because its shadow was large and dark. The final months of his life were tainted with ugly rumors about his sexual abuse of young girls. Some of his devotees were appalled by what they considered hypocrisy and an inexcusable flaw of their guru and left the movement. Others decided not to believe these rumors or tried to excuse this behavior by seeing it as some advanced Tantric practice, culturally acceptable in India but misunderstood in the West.

After Muktananda's death, the situation was further confounded by a profound dissent between Chitvilasananda and Nityananda, the two siblings to whom he passed the Siddha Yoga lineage. The ugly intrigues that were involved were widely publicized by Indian and American press and further deepened the already existing rift in the inner circles of Siddha Yoga, as well as in the larger group of followers all over the world that, according to some estimates, exceeded one hundred thousand.

Christina and I visited the Ganeshpuri ashram twice more, but the magic of the old days was gone. We have dissociated ourselves from the movement and its politics, but remain connected to the Siddha movement on another level. Baba continued to appear in our dreams and various non-ordinary states of consciousness. We also have repeatedly had experiences of participation in powerful Siddha rituals in which we felt a strong connection with what we call "Shiva energy."

THE GURU IN THE LIFE
OF HIS DEVOTEES
Is the Siddha Yogi a Cosmic Puppeteer?

One of the most extraordinary aspects of our experience with Swami Muktananda and Siddha Yoga was the astonishing incidence of synchronicities in the lives of Muktananda's followers. We heard about them on a regular basis from our friends and acquaintances who were associated with the Siddha Yoga movement. The weekend intensives offered by the various ashrams regularly featured speakers who told their remarkable stories about meeting Baba. These stories contained without any exception descriptions of fantastic coincidences similar to those that introduced me to the world of Siddha Yoga.

One example came from a man who spent some time in an Australian ghost town looking for leftover gems in abandoned mines. At the time, he lived alone in a ramshackle cabin. During the long evenings, he tried to read using the light of a candle. One of the previous dwellers had left on the wall of the cabin a picture of a strange dark-skinned man in a red ski cap holding a wand of peacock feathers. It happened to be a portrait of Swami Muktananda, although there was no inscription on the photograph identifying him as such.

In one of his lone evenings, the gem hunter lifted his eyes from the book he was reading and became captivated by the face of the man on the picture. As he was focusing on the eyes, he experienced a radiant thunderbolt that seem to emanate from the portrayed man's pupils and hit him between the eyes. It triggered powerful waves of emotions and a strong physical response. These experiences continued on the following days, and in the next two weeks a series of events led this man to Baba's Melbourne ashram. He decided to take a weekend intensive, where he learned about shaktipat and the many different forms it can take. He remained Baba's ardent follower in the years to come.

One of Muktananda's senior swamis, a friend of ours, shared with us the following story from her early devotee years. One of the things that Muktananda liked to do was to give Westerners Indian spiritual names—Yamuna, Sadashiva, Durghananda, Shivananda, Lakshmi, and so on. His students and followers usually received their new names in the darshan line, which involved brief contact with the guru, a few words, and an offering, or *prasad*. Our friend, at the time an eager student and aspiring novice, stood in the darshan line with a friend of hers, both of them waiting to receive a spiritual name from Swami Muktananda. She felt slightly nervous and channeled her anxious anticipation into jovial conversation. "I think I know what name Baba will give us," she said grinning. "He'll call us Creepa and Creepie." To her astonishment, the name she received just minutes later was Kripananda, or the bliss of grace, and has been known as such ever since.

Among the hundreds of stories told in weekend intensives, one deserves special notice. It involved a Malibu veterinarian who was summoned to take care of one of Baba's dogs. As Swami Muktananda journeyed all over the world, an envoy of people from his inner circle traveled ahead of him to find temporary quarters for his visit. They often chose for this purpose poorly maintained buildings in bad neighborhoods and renovated them, creating temporary ashrams; it was seen as karma yoga to leave the premises in much better shape than they had been initially.

Baba liked to go for regular walks wherever he was and did it fearlessly, without any regard to the reputation of the place. While he himself was not worried, this caused deep concern in his followers. One of them gave Baba two large dogs to protect him during his strolls. During Baba's stay in Malibu, one of the dogs became very sick. A woman from Baba's inner circle looked up the phone number of a local veterinarian.

The veterinarian arrived at the ashram and examined the dog, without meeting Baba or having any contact with him. On the way home, he started having kriyas—intense welling-up of emotions and body tremors. Within a few days, as a result of a few coincidences, he was sitting in the meditation hall chanting "Om Namah Shivaya." Eventually, he too became one of Baba's dedicated followers. Swami Muktananda often jokingly likened Shakti, the energy involved in the shaktipat and in kriyas, to the common cold, something that is eminently contagious, something that one can "catch."

Instead of describing more experiences of Baba's followers that we heard about, I would like to give some examples from our own life. The first story involves an entire series of synchronicities that occurred in the early 1980s. It began when Christina and I received in our house in Big Sur, California, a phone call from Gabriel, a medical doctor who was a member of Swami Muktananda's inner circle. He told us he was passing through Big Sur and asked if he could stop by to discuss something important.

The reason for his visit was that the media people from the ashram were not satisfied with an interview that Baba had given on the subject of death. The reporter had not been sufficiently familiar with the topic and did not ask very interesting questions. Gabriel knew that I had done psychedelic therapy with terminal cancer patients and that I was very interested in psychological, philosophical, and spiritual aspects of death and dying. He sat down with a notebook and asked me to tell him what might be the most interesting questions about death that a Western psychiatrist and consciousness researcher would like to ask a yogi.

After about three hours of our discussion, Gabriel realized that what we were doing did not make much sense. It became obvious that, instead of formulating the questions for somebody else, I should be the one actually asking the questions. He suggested that we visit the Miami ashram, where Baba was at the time, and that I conduct the interview with him. However, there was a problem: the ashram would not cover our expenses, and we did not have, at the time, a lot of money to spare. In addition, we were about to travel in the opposite direction, to conduct some workshops in

Australia and to continue to India to prepare ground for the 1982 International Transpersonal Conference.

After a long discussion, we decided to go to Miami after all. It was always interesting to see Baba, and the opportunity to hear his ideas about death was particularly tempting. Just before leaving for Miami, we had a workshop scheduled at Esalen. The Esalen program typically had four parallel events, and there was a limit for the number of participants in each of them. Shortly after our decision to go to Miami, the enrollments for our workshop started rushing in. One of the other workshops had to be canceled for lack of interest, and two others were not filling. As a result, Esalen extended the quota for our workshop. It filled to such an extent that we ran out of floor space for the breathwork; we had a long waiting list and had to turn people down.

The sudden interest in our workshop was unprecedented. As a legacy of Fritz Perls, Esalen offered complimentary Gestalt sessions for all residents and seminarians who needed it. The week before our workshop started, several people actually did emotional work on the Gestalt "hot seat," working on their disappointment and anger that they were not able to participate in our workshop. When we got the check for the workshop, we discovered that the difference between our fee and what we would have made had the other workshops filled amounted exactly to two roundtrip tickets from Monterey to Miami. It was difficult not to see it as "the grace of the guru," or guru kripa, as Muktananda followers used to call similar events.

When we arrived at the Miami ashram on Thursday, we found out that the interview with Baba scheduled for Friday was canceled. He was not feeling well and needed some rest before the weekend intensive. Instead of interviewing Baba, I did an interview with one of the ashram media people on transpersonal psychology. Because we already were in Miami, we wanted to participate in the weekend program, but our flight to Melbourne was leaving on Saturday late in the evening. We asked Baba for permission to take only half of the intensive, which was a highly unusual and irregular request. To our pleasant surprise, the permission was granted, but then the question arose whether we had to pay for the entire intensive or just half of it. Baba made another exception and allowed us to pay just half of the usual cost, one hundred and fifty dollars.

Another big surprise came when we were just about to enter the meditation hall. The young woman at the door gave us a big smile and handed us three pristine fifty dollar bills that looked as if they just had come from the printer's press. "Here's your money back," she said. "Baba does not want you to pay; you are coming as his guests." Everything seemed to indicate that the guru was giving us special treatment. However, this feeling rapidly dissipated at the end of the first day of the intensive, when we approached him in the darshan line with an offering and wanted to thank him. He kept talking with the man who was ahead of us in the line and brushed us off with a dismissive gesture of his hand without exchanging a single word with us.

This "Swedish shower" approach, combining outpouring of love and favors with complete disinterest, outwardly cold behavior, or even ego-deflating comments, seemed to be Baba's strategy of reducing his followers' sense of self-importance and exclusivity. We got into a taxi and drove to the airport, facing a long flight to Melbourne. The plane was full and the seats in the economy class seemed exceptionally narrow, particularly for people with long legs, like ourselves. Tired after a long day and jammed into our uncomfortable seats, we felt defeated and surrendered with a sense of resignation to our grim predicament.

"Staaan, Christiiina!" the loud voice of one of the stewards aroused us from our melancholic mood. "What a surprise! Had I known you were on this flight, I would have put you in the first class. But I have two seats for you in the business class." It turned out that a couple of years earlier this steward had been in one of our Esalen workshops and had very positive life-transforming experiences in Holotropic Breathwork sessions. Seated comfortably in the business class, we wondered if this was just an incredibly improbable coincidence or another crest in the sea of guru's grace.

When we finally reached Melbourne, we were met at the airport by our dear friends and hosts, Muriel and Al Foote. As we were driving to the city, they told us that they arranged for us to spend the first day and night in the house of their close friends, the famous Australian opera singer Greg Dempsey and his wife, Annie. When we arrived at the Dempsey residence, we discovered to our surprise that Greg and Annie were both dedicated followers of Swami Muktananda. The house was full of Baba's photographs, and there was one even in the bathroom.

As we were sitting down for breakfast, Muriel suddenly started looking very sheepish and told us that she had invited a young woman to join us for breakfast and spend some time with us. "I'm really sorry. I know you guys must be dead tired," she apologized. "Many people called me and wanted some private time with you while you're in Melbourne. I managed to turn down all of them, except this one. There was something special about her. She has done work with dying people, like yourselves, and she sounded so nice!"

When the woman arrived, it turned out that, unbeknownst to Muriel, she was from the Melbourne Siddha Yoga ashram. She told us that just as she was walking out of the door, the phone rang and she happened to pick up the phone. It was Baba notifying the ashram people that we were coming to Melbourne and that they should help us because we were "doing his work." During breakfast, we heard many Baba stories and learned about the growing Siddha Yoga movement in Australia, getting used to the Australian accent.

We spent the night at Greg and Annie's, and the next day the Footes drove us to nearby Blackwood, where they had their house and seminar center. In the evening that day, we started our Holotropic Breathwork workshop. The Siddha magic seemed to continue. Out of twenty-five people in the group, eight had experiences of Blue Light, Blue Pearl, and Blue Person, which in Siddha Yoga are considered very auspicious and important steps on the spiritual journey. One participant started spontaneously chanting "Om Namah Shivaya," without having any idea what that was. None of the participants knew about our connection with Swami Muktananda.

Another interesting event I would like to describe happened two years later. I have already mentioned earlier, describing our last meeting with Baba, that he had given us each a beautiful dark amethyst and suggested that we have them made into rings and wear them all the time. We later found out that the choice of the stones might have had a deeper meaning. Since antiquity, amethysts have had the reputation to protect the owner against intoxication, as indicated by their Greek name. "*Methystos*" means intoxicated and *a-* is *alpha privativum*, expressing negation. This seemed to make sense in view of my work with psychedelics and Christina's problems with alcohol.

Shortly after our return from India, a series of natural disasters devastated the Big Sur coast. A catastrophic fire that had destroyed 160,000 acres of the Ventana wilderness stripped the coastal mountain range of all vegetation for about twenty miles, from the Hermitage of the Immaculate Heart almost to Ventana Inn. The following onslaught of torrential rainstorms on the unprotected mountain slopes resulted in massive landslides. Highway 1, the stunning scenic road connecting the Esalen Institute with Monterey and its airport, was blocked for a number of weeks. All the Esalen workshops, including ours, had to be canceled.

This had serious financial repercussions for Esalen, but particularly for us. We lived at that time on a very limited budget, and loss of income from several workshops was very painful. It was not a very good time to follow Baba's suggestion and have our amethysts set in gold and made into rings. I, being the more rational member of our marital dyad, would have postponed the project, but Christina felt strongly that we should go ahead. During our next shopping trip to Carmel, which with the detour caused by the landslides now took seven hours instead of the usual two, we stopped at the jeweler's shop and ordered our rings.

Two weeks later, when we were leaving for France, our first stop on a European workshop tour, we picked up our rings on the way to the airport. Our first workshop in Paris was a Holotropic Breathwork weekend with about thirty participants. As we were going around the circle introducing ourselves, one of the group members, Simone, presented as her main complaint severe chronic pain in her belly, which seriously interfered with her everyday life. She described that repeated examinations had failed to detect any medical reason for this difficulty. Since the problem seemed to be psychosomatic, she hoped to use the breathwork to get some insight into its causes.

Eager to begin her explorations, she asked her breathing partner if she could go first. Her process was very intense, with much crying and physical struggle.

About an hour into the session, she started to make loud sounds and asked for me. She shared with me that her belly pain was greatly intensified and asked me if I could do something about it. Our usual approach to such situations was to intensify the pain by external pressure and encourage the person to find a way to express his or her feelings. I asked Simone to tense up her belly and applied pressure on the center of the painful area, using my right hand on which I had the amethyst ring. I then encouraged her to express fully with sounds and physical movements her emotional reaction to this intervention.

Simone pushed against me with her tensed-up belly, and her face was showing more and more strain. She was holding her breath, and her face was turning purple. Suddenly, there was a bloodcurdling scream like I had never heard before in my life. Simone started to breathe normally, went into a deep relaxation, and a blissful smile appeared on her face. A little later, she told me that she felt completely pain free for the first time in years. In the evening, when the group got together for sharing, she described what had happened during her session.

At the beginning of her experience, she relived several memories from her postnatal life that involved pain in the belly, including repeated sexual abuse by a relative. Then the experience deepened and took her to the memory of her biological birth. As she was reliving her difficult passage through the birth canal, she discovered that part of her abdominal pain was related to the agonizing discomfort she had experienced as a fetus struggling to be born. As her session continued, Simone started envisioning scenes from human history that involved violence and sexual abuse. This was the time when she decided to call me, because her pain kept increasing and was rapidly reaching the limit of her tolerance.

"It was incredible when you put pressure on my belly," she recounted later in the sharing group. "The pain was increasing every moment and became absolutely unbearable. But I wouldn't let go and was determined to stay with it. At one point, the pain was not just mine; it was all of humanity that was suffering! And then everything exploded into deep-blue light, which was indescribably beautiful. And in that light appeared the image of that Indian guru, whose posters are all over Paris. He had dark glasses and a red woolen cap and was holding a bunch of peacock feathers."

A couple of weeks before our arrival in Paris, Swami Muktananda's successor, the young Nityananda, had visited the city and held a weekend intensive. The posters, which one could still see on many walls and pillars all over the city, featured him with his teacher. Christina reached into her wallet, took out a picture of Swami Muktananda she happened to have, and showed it to Simone with a questioning look. "Yeah, that's the one; a funny guy!" she confirmed and then she added: "But my experience also had something to do with your amethyst ring. The blue light seemed to come right out of that ring!"

It was interesting that Simone associated her healing experience not only with the amethyst ring and with Swami Muktananda, from whom it came, but also with blue color. As I mentioned earlier, visions of Blue Light and Blue Person play an important role in Siddha Yoga and are considered to be very auspicious. Simone connected with me several years later in another French workshop and gave me a follow-up; she told me that since our Paris workshop her pain had not returned.

The number of synchronicities we have experienced ourselves and observed in Baba's followers was truly astonishing. He appeared in his followers' dreams, meditations, and psychedelic sessions, and these visionary visitations seemed to be closely linked to events in these people's everyday lives. Many of his followers concluded from these astonishing coincidences that Baba was aware of everything that was happening in their lives and was actually actively arranging all these situations for their spiritual benefit. This gave him a superhuman stature of a cosmic puppeteer, supervising the lives of tens of thousands of his followers and students and pulling the strings behind the scenes of material reality.

I was fascinated by this phenomenon and, at one point, I asked Swami Ama, who had been with Baba for more than twenty-five years, to find out from Baba how he himself saw this situation. She agreed and subsequently told me that Baba laughed at this grandiose fantasy of his followers. He explained to her that during the forty-some years of his pilgrimage in India and rigorous spiritual search, he had had many experiences in higher, normally hidden dimensions of existence. Because of that, he had become part of these domains and of the mechanisms through which they influence everyday reality.

He also told Ama that if he needed, he was able to focus his mind in meditation to different areas and get the necessary information, which is something that many good psychics can do. But, more than anything else, his arduous spiritual quest brought him to a sharper focus on the here and now and appreciation of simple things in everyday life. For example, he told Ama, he loved to cook. And while he was focusing with single-pointed consciousness on all the colors, textures, smells, and tastes of the food he was preparing, thousands of his followers were experiencing him as the conscious and active architect of their lives. He was very amused by the idea that he would monitor the lives of thousands of his devotees and orchestrate for them custom-made astonishing synchronicities and spiritually meaningful events. "That would be too much work; I like my life simple," he said with a mischievous smile.

DANCE OF THE WHITE SWAN
Underworld Journey in the Salish Spirit Canoe

I solated synchronicities are extremely frequent in the lives of people experiencing spontaneous or induced holotropic states of consciousness; however, it is not uncommon for them to appear in impressive series or clusters. Over the years, we have observed and personally experienced many aggregate synchronicities in connection with psychedelic therapy, Holotropic Breathwork sessions, and episodes of psychospiritual crises. The events described in this story happened during one of our monthlong seminars at Esalen, at a time when Christina was experiencing her spiritual emergency.

Christina's spontaneous experiences were very rich and combined elements from various levels of the personal and collective unconscious. In some of them, she regressed to various painful memories from her childhood and infancy; others involved reliving of the trauma of her biological birth. She also encountered powerful experiential sequences that appeared to be memories of her past lives in Russia, Germany, and seventeenth-century North America. On occasion, she also had visions of various archetypal figures and animals. Particularly significant among them were peacocks and white swans, the birds associated with Siddha Yoga and with Christina's spiritual teacher, Swami Muktananda. One day during the mentioned monthlong seminar, Christina had particularly intense and significant visions involving a white swan.

Our guest faculty for the following day was Michael Harner, a well-known anthropologist and dear friend. Michael belonged to a group often referred to as "visionary anthropologists." In contrast to traditional mainstream anthropologists, Michael and his colleagues, such as Barbara Meyerhoff, Peter Furst, Dick Katz, Christian Raetsch, and Carlos Castaneda, did not do their anthropological fieldwork as detached academic observers. They actively participated in the ceremonies of the cultures they studied, whether these involved mind-altering substances, such as peyote, magic mushrooms, ayahuasca, and datura, or all-night trance dance and other nonpharmacological "technologies of the sacred."

Michael's discovery of the way of the shamans and their incredible inner world work began in 1960, when the American Museum of Natural History invited him to make a yearlong expedition to the Peruvian Amazon to study the culture of the Conibo Indians of the Ucayali River region. His informants told him that if he really wished to learn, he had to take the shaman's sacred drink. Following their advice, he ingested ayahuasca, a brew containing a decoction of the jungle liana *Banisteriopsis caapi* and the cawa plant, which the Indians called "soul vine" or "little death." He had an indescribable visionary journey through ordinarily invisible dimensions of existence, during which he experienced his own death and obtained extraordinary insights and revelations about the nature of reality.

When he later found that a Conibo elder, a master shaman, was quite familiar with everything he himself had seen and that his ayahuasca experience also paralleled certain passages from the book of Revelation, Michael became convinced that there was indeed a hidden world to be explored. He decided to learn everything that he could about shamanism. Three years later, Michael returned to South America to do field work with the Jivaro, an Ecuadorian tribe that Michael had lived with and studied in 1956 and 1957. Here he experienced another important initiatory experience, which was basic to his discovery of the way of the shaman. Akachu, a famous Jivaro shaman, and his son-in-law took him to a sacred waterfall deep in the Amazonian jungle and gave him a drink of maikua, juice of a brugmansia species of datura, a plant with powerful psychoactive properties.

As a result of these and other experiences, Michael—an anthropologist with good academic credentials—became an accomplished practitioner and teacher of shamanism. He also started with his wife, Sandra, the Foundation for Shamanic Studies, an institution dedicated to teaching shamanic methods to interested students and to offering shamanic workshops for the public. Michael had written a book entitled *The Way of the Shaman*, in which he gathered together various methods of shamanic work from all over the world and adapted them for use in experiential workshops and in shamanic training of Westerners.

During our Esalen monthlong workshop, Michael led us in a healing journey, using the method of the spirit canoe practiced by the Salish Indian tribe in the American Northwest. He began the session by beating his drum and invited participants to move and dance until they felt identification with a specific animal. It did not take long, and people were crouching, crawling on all fours, and jumping around, simulating all kinds of climbing, digging, clawing, swimming, and flying movements. The main room in Esalen's Big House was filled with various recognizable and unrecognizable voices of animals and birds. When everybody made the connection with a specific animal, Michael asked the group members to sit down on the floor in a spindlelike formation, creating an imaginary "spirit canoe." He then asked if there was a person who needed healing, and Christina volunteered. Michael stepped into the "boat" holding his drum, beckoned Christina to join him, and instructed her to lie down.

With the scene for the healing voyage all set, Michael asked us to imagine that we were an animal crew undertaking a journey into the underworld to retrieve Christina's spirit animal. The specific target that Michael chose for this imaginary expedition was the system of interconnected underground caverns filled with hot water that is believed to stretch under much of California. The entry into it was easy to find because this system feeds the Esalen hot springs. As the captain of this spirit boat, Michael explained, he would indicate the pace of the paddling by the beat of his drum. During the journey, he would look for spirit animals. When a particular power animal appeared three times, this would be the sign that he found the one he was looking for. At that point, he would seize it and would signal to the crew of the boat by rapid beat of the drum that it was time for a hasty return.

We had done the Salish spirit canoe with Michael several times before. The first time we did it, we did not go into it with great expectations. The whole thing sounded like innocent fun—a great idea for children's play, but a somewhat silly activity for mature adults. But the very first thing that happened made us change our mind. In that group was a young woman who behaved in a way that had antagonized the entire group. She was very unhappy about it because the same thing had happened earlier in her life in just about every group she had ever been part of, and she decided to volunteer for a healing journey.

As the imaginary boat was traveling through the "underworld," she had a very violent reaction, just at the moment when Michael identified and seized her spirit animal. She suddenly sat up and, as Michael was giving the signal for return by rapid beats of his drum, she went through several spastic episodes of projectile vomiting. As she was throwing up, she lifted the front part of her skirt, trying to contain what was coming out, and completely filled it with her vomit. This episode, lasting not more than twenty-five minutes, had a profound effect on her personality. The change in her behavior was so dramatic that before the month ended, she became one of the most loved and popular people in the group. This episode and similar ones later on made us approach this process with respect.

Michael began drumming, and the journey into the underworld started. We all paddled and made sounds of the animals with which we had identified. Christina went into intense convulsions that were shaking her entire body. This, in and of itself, was not unusual because she was in the middle of Kundalini awakening, during which experiences of powerful energy tremors are very common. After about ten minutes, Michael greatly accelerated the rhythm of his drumming, letting us know that he had succeeded in finding Christina's spirit animal. Everybody began paddling in a fast rhythm, imagining rapid return to the Middle World.

Michael stopped drumming, indicating that the journey had ended. He put down the drum, pressed his mouth on Christina's sternum, and blew with all the force he could muster, making a loud sound. He then whispered into her ear: "Your spirit animal is a white swan." Following this, he asked her to perform in front of the group a dance, expressing her swan energy. It is important to mention that Michael had no prior knowledge of the content of Christina's inner process and of the fact that this bird had figured importantly in her life. He also had no idea that the swan had been for her a very important personal symbol.

The story continued the next morning, when Christina and I walked to our mailbox on Highway 1 to get our daily mail. Christina received a letter from a person who had attended a workshop we had given several months earlier. Inside was a photograph of Christina's spiritual teacher, Swami Muktananda, which this person thought she might like to have. It showed him sitting with a mischievous expression on a garden swing, near a large flowerpot shaped like a white swan. The index finger of his left hand was pointing at the swan; the tips of his right thumb and index finger were joined, forming the universal sign indicating bull's eye hit and excitement about what had happened.

Although there were no causal connections between Christina's inner experiences, Michael's choice of the white swan as her power animal, and Muktananda's photograph, they clearly formed a meaningful psychological pattern, meeting the criteria for synchronicity, or "acausal connecting principle," as defined by C. G. Jung.

The Making of Brainstorm
Our Hollywood Adventure

I n 1981, Christina and I were approached by Doug Trumbull, a special-effects wizard, who cooperated with Stanley Kubrick on *2001: A Space Odyssey* and created the special effects for the movies *The Andromeda Strain, Silent Running, Blade Runner,* and *Close Encounters of the Third Kind.* Doug was about to direct a Metro-Goldwyn-Mayer science fiction movie, *Brainstorm.* The movie's fascinating plot featured a duo of scientists, computer genius Michael Brace and brilliant brain researcher Lillian Reynolds, who jointly developed a helmet that could record and transmit human experiences.

This device made it possible to tap into the psyche of other people and to record and play back what they saw, felt, and thought. While Michael Brace used the invention to heal his relationship with his estranged wife, Karen, and become once again close to her, other people in the research complex tried to use it for more questionable purposes, exploiting its sexual, commercial, and military potential. The plot took an interesting twist when the hardworking, chain-smoking, and coffee-drinking Lillian experienced a heart attack while working late at night in the laboratory. A curious scientist to the very end, she decided to record the event and managed to put on the helmet and start the machine shortly before her death.

The rest of the plot revolved around the fact that the machine recorded a death experience. Doug's intention was to portray this experience in a way that would use not only the best special effects available at the time, but also scientific information about death and dying amassed by modern consciousness research. He had heard that we had created a slide show portraying a death-rebirth experience called *The Inner Journey*, based on observations from clinical research of psychedelic therapy. He contacted us and asked that we join his team as special consultants for visionary experiences portrayed in the movie. We were very excited because *Brainstorm* had a fascinating subject and a stellar cast. It featured, among others, Natalie Wood, Christopher Walken, Louise Fletcher, and Cliff Robertson. Its producer was John Foreman, known for such movies as *The First Great Train Robbery* and *Butch Cassidy and the Sundance Kid*. The invitation gave us a chance to spend some time in Hollywood and witness the process of moviemaking.

The actors and the crew attended a special slide-illustrated presentation, which I gave for them on the new cartography of the psyche that had emerged from my study of non-ordinary states of consciousness. Most of the images in the slide show depicted experiences from psychedelic therapy, but a few of them came from Holotropic Breathwork sessions of participants in our training and workshops. When Doug Trumbull and John Foreman heard that we had developed a nondrug technique capable of inducing non-ordinary states of consciousness, they asked us if we could make that experience available for their team. Because the central topic of *Brainstorm* was the experience of a non-ordinary state of consciousness, this was a unique opportunity for everybody involved in the production of the movie to get a better understanding of the subject.

Fifteen members of the *Brainstorm* team joined our five-day workshop at Esalen and participated in the Holotropic Breathwork sessions. It was an interesting experience for Natalie to get to know Esalen personally because several years earlier she had starred in making the movie *Bob and Carol and Ted and Alice,* a spoof on Esalen and similar human-potential centers. The Esalen experience certainly lived up to her expectations; when she was the sitter in one of the breathwork sessions, a Mexican work scholar (an Esalen participant who works at the Institute in exchange for attending workshops) breathing near her, stripped naked and stayed that way for the rest of the session. It was not a particularly conspicuous event at Esalen, known for integrated nude bathing in its famous hot springs and in its open swimming pool, but it represented a somewhat unusual experience for our Hollywood friends.

One day, when I sat at lunch with Natalie, I had a chance to find out that she was not a novice as far as non-ordinary states of consciousness were concerned. At one point, she asked me out of the blue: "Stan, are you familiar with a drug called Ketalar?" Ketalar, or ketamine, is a powerful anaesthetic with effects that are quite different from the other substances used to induce anesthesia. It is referred to as a "dissociative anaesthetic," because the patients to whom it is administered do not lose consciousness, but their consciousness detaches from their body to such a degree that they are not aware of what is happening to it. While they are being operated on, they experience fantastic adventures in other domains of reality. They become other people, various other lifeforms, and even inorganic objects, encounter various archetypal figures and discarnate beings, relive past life memories, visit other universes, and have profound mystical experiences.

It turned out that Natalie was given a large intravenous dose of ketamine when she was pregnant with one of her daughters and had to have a Cesarean section. The drug was given to her without any psychological explanation, preparation, or forewarning, which was a common practice among surgeons at that time. In general, surgeons in many countries discontinued using ketamine because of what they called the "emergence syndrome," strange visions reported by their patients recovering from anesthesia. Others limited its use to children and old people, with whom they had fewer difficulties in this regard. Ketamine is still widely used as an anaesthetic by veterinarians.

Natalie had a powerful experience that included a convincing sense that she had left the solar system and visited various extraterrestrial worlds and civilizations. She found this extravagant adventure in consciousness terrifying, overwhelming, and confusing. It was reassuring to her when I told her that such fantastic experiences represented an absolutely normal response to ketamine, because she had occasionally wondered if her strange response to this substance was an indication of latent mental disease.

The Hollywood crew left Esalen very happy with the experience and embarked with great enthusiasm on filming *Brainstorm*. We had a chance to spend several days with them on location in Raleigh, North Carolina, where they found the right kind of building for the futuristic research institute featured in *Brainstorm* and also an ideal house for the residence of Michael Brace and his wife, played by Chris Walken and Natalie Wood, respectively. During our stay in Raleigh, we conducted a breathwork session with Chris Walken, who had not been able to come to Esalen with the rest of the crew.

According to the original arrangement, Natalie wanted to be present as Chris's sitter. This situation would have been similar to the final scene of *Brainstorm*, in which she is present when Chris's character is playing back the last part of the recording of Lillian's death experience. However, shortly after the beginning, Natalie decided to join Chris and have her own experience. At the time when the rest of the crew was experiencing the breathwork at Esalen, Natalie had decided not to do the breathing but to participate as a sitter and observer. Her decision was very understandable considering her celebrity and the public nature of the event. However, she regretted having missed that opportunity, and now she wanted to make up for it. She found the session very useful; it revolved around the death of her father, and she felt that she finally found reconciliation with this very painful part of her life.

When the filming moved to the West Coast, we joined the crew in the Hollywood studios, watching the rehearsals for many of the scenes, the actual shooting, and the review of the "dailies," the footage shot on any particular day. During this time, we had the chance to spend some time with Natalie in her trailer, where she was resting between shoots. She also introduced us to her husband, R. J. (Wagner), who happened to stop by. Much of our discussion during his visit revolved around a subject that, in retrospect, seems uncanny and foreboding in view of the tragic events that followed.

Christina noticed on one of the walls of the trailer a picture of the beautiful yacht that Natalie and R.J. owned. They both loved this boat very much and used it frequently. Sailing was also an important part of Christina's childhood because her stepfather owned a large sailboat and her family spent much time cruising around the Hawaiian islands. Hawaii turned out to be a favorite vacation place for Natalie and R.J., and they knew many of the people who were friends of Christina's stepfather and had played an important role in her own early life. We heard many stories about the $250,000 yacht, its luxurious interior, its desalination equipment, and its various cruises.

To our disappointment, we had to leave Hollywood and could not stay for the last days of shooting. We later heard from the members of the *Brainstorm* crew about the dramatic finale they had experienced on the last day before Thanksgiving. They spent the entire day rehearsing and shooting a powerful scene in which Louise Fletcher's character, Lillian Reynolds, has a heart attack and dies in her laboratory. Louise's performance was excellent and had a very profound impact on the rest of the crew. Watching her for many hours enacting Louise's final agony was a compelling reminder of impermanence and their own finality. At the end of the day, all of them were in a somber and eerie mood.

When the scene of Lillian's death was finally shot to everybody's satisfaction, an important decision had to be made. By that time, all principal photography of *Brainstorm* was finished, with the exception of three scenes. The crew was facing two alternatives. The first one was to take advantage of the long Thanksgiving weekend and finish the remaining scenes of principal photography. In that case, the production of the movie could have moved on to editing of the existing footage and to special effects, the part in which we were most interested and involved. The second possibility was to interrupt the filming, take the weekend off, and complete the shooting during the following week. The opinions were split, and the team members had great difficulty reaching agreement. They finally decided to take a vote; the part of the group opting for the holiday vacation won by one vote. This turned out to be an unfortunate decision for the future of the movie and for Natalie personally.

Natalie and R.J. had plans to spend the weekend on their yacht near Catalina Island, and Natalie invited Chris Walken to share this cruise with them. Only R.J., Chris, and possibly the skipper know what actually happened on the ship. There have been rumors about heavy drinking, inappropriate flirting, jealousy, and fights. What is known is that, at some point, Natalie left the men alone, boarded the dinghy, and tried to reach Catalina Island to spend the night there. She never made it to the shore; her coordination impaired by a high level of alcohol in her blood, she probably fell off the dinghy and drowned. The next morning, her dead body was found floating in the ocean. The newspapers published a photograph showing a man carrying her body out of the water; this picture showed an had resemblance to a similar scene from Natalie's movie *Eyes of Laura Mars*.

Natalie's death shocked her family, friends, acquaintances, and fans. Her tragic demise also proved detrimental for *Brainstorm*. Three scenes of principal photography, all featuring Natalie, remained unfinished, and the MGM officials considered this to be a certain kiss of death for the movie. They decided to scrap the project and to collect fifteen million dollars from Lloyd's of London, by whom the movie was insured. Doug Trumbull was desperate and tried to save *Brainstorm* at all costs. He promised Lloyds of London that he would find ways of finishing the movie if they paid him three million dollars, and they accepted.

The movie got finished, but was severely compromised. Doug did not really succeed in bridging the gap caused by the missing scenes and did not create a smooth yarn. Perceptive viewers had no difficulty noticing logical inconsistencies in the movie. But the crisis caused by Natalie's tragic death had the most detrimental influence on the special effects, the visionary sequences that we were working on. As a result of what had happened, there were not sufficient funds available to do what Doug and ourselves planned and would have liked to do.

The *Brainstorm* project was an exciting attempt to use the best special effects available at the time and portray the death experience in a way that would reflect our scientific knowledge about it. Unfortunately, this effort ended tragically when, instead of being represented artistically in a symbolic way, death struck in reality and destroyed the project. Shooting *Brainstorm* was an extraordinary experience. It left us with a strong desire to try again and more successfully sometime in the future to bring the visionary states to the big screen.

The fantastic progress in special effects brought about by digital technology opened up new and undreamed of possibilities in this regard. I am convinced that combining today's superb imaging skills with the knowledge amassed by transpersonal psychology and consciousness research would make it possible not only to portray spiritual experiences, but also induce them in the audiences.

THE WATERCOURSE WAY

Meetings with President Václav Havel

O ne of the most remarkable features of deep experiential work using non-ordinary states of consciousness is the effect it has on our way of life and on the strategy we use in dealing with challenges and projects. The model offered in this regard in technological societies is to define the goal we want to achieve and pursue it with focused energy and unswerving determination. This includes identifying and removing the obstacles that stand in the way and fighting potential enemies. The life of an individual following this recipe resembles a wrestling or boxing match.

I have worked with many people who were able to gain insight into the psychological forces underlying this strategy and to transcend it. They discovered that this approach to existence reflects the fact that we have not overcome the imprint that the trauma of our birth has left in our psyche and that we are separated and alienated from the spiritual domain. Our striving for external achievements is a projection of a deeper and much more fundamental drive to psychologically complete the birth process and to make a spiritual connection. There is no end to our hunger for external conquests because we cannot get enough of what we do not really want and need.

For those individuals who reached this insight, life dominated by pursuit of material goals appears to be a "treadmill" or "rat-race" type of existence that does not and cannot really bring satisfaction. From this new perspective, this strategy of life is unsuccessful, even if we achieve the goals we pursue.

Responsible and systematic deep self-exploration can help us come to terms with the trauma of birth and make a deep spiritual connection. This moves us in the direction of what Taoist spiritual teachers call *wu wei*, or "creative quietude," which is not action involving ambitious determined effort, but doing by being. This is also sometimes referred to as the Watercourse Way, because it imitates the ways water operates in nature.

Instead of focusing on a predetermined fixed goal, we try to sense which way things are moving and how we best fit into them. This is the strategy used in martial arts and in surfing. It involves focus on the process, rather than the goal or the outcome. When we are able to approach life in this way, we ultimately achieve more and with less effort. In addition, our activities are not egocentric, exclusive, and competitive, as they are during pursuit of personal goals, but inclusive and synergistic. The outcome not only brings satisfaction to us, but serves also a larger purpose of the community.

I have also repeatedly observed and experienced that when we operate in this Taoistic framework, extraordinary beneficial coincidences and synchronicities tend to occur, which support our project and help us in our work. We come "accidentally" across the information we need, the right people appear at the right time, and the necessary funds unexpectedly become available. The occurrence of such favorable synchronicities is so extraordinary and pervasive that Christina and I learned to use it as a compass for our activities, as an important criterion that we were "on the right track."

I would like to illustrate this by an example from our life that is related to the work Christina and I have done in the international transpersonal movement. In 1977, I founded the International Transpersonal Association (ITA), an organization designed to bridge the gap between modern science and the spiritual vision of the world, between Western pragmatism and ancient wisdom. The ITA was created to encourage and promote all serious efforts to formulate a comprehensive and integrated understanding of the cosmos and of human nature.

Since the ultimate goal of the ITA activities was to create a global network of mutual understanding and cooperation, we missed very much during our international conferences participants from the countries beyond the Iron Curtain, who were not at that time allowed to travel abroad and did not have the financial means to join us. When the situation in the Soviet Union changed and Mikhail Gorbachev declared the era of "glasnost" and "perestroika," it suddenly seemed plausible that the next ITA meeting could be held in Russia. When Christina and I were invited to Moscow as official guests of the Soviet Ministry of Health, we used our visit to explore the possibility to hold such a conference in Russia. We tried really hard, but without success; the situation seemed too unstable and volatile to take chances.

In November 1989, I was conducting Holotropic Breathwork outside of California. I received a call from Christina, who asked me if I knew what was happening in my native country. Our training was very intense and featured three sessions a day. We were deeply immersed in the process, and none of us had time or interest to watch the TV or follow the news. Christina informed me that the Prague Velvet Revolution was underway and that the Czechoslovakian Communist regime would very likely fall. "Wouldn't it be great?" she said. "We could hold the next ITA conference in Prague." A few weeks later, Czechoslovakia was a free country, and the ITA board decided to hold its next meeting in Czechoslovakia.

Because I was born in Prague, it seemed only logical to send me to Czechoslovakia as an envoy to find the site and prepare the ground for this conference. However, the years I had spent in my native country turned out to be much less of an advantage than we expected. I left Czechoslovakia at the time of a major liberalization movement aimed at creating "socialism with a human face." In 1968, when the Prague Spring was brutally suppressed by the invasion of Czechoslovakia by the Soviet army, I was in the United States on a scholarship at the Johns Hopkins University in Baltimore. After the invasion, I was ordered by Czech authorities to return immediately, but decided to disobey and stay in the United States.

As a result, I was not able to visit my native country for more than twenty years. During this time, I could not maintain open contact with my friends and colleagues in Czechoslovakia. It would have been politically dangerous for them to exchange letters or telephone calls with me because my stay in the United States was considered illegal. Because of my long absence, I lost all my connections except for my close relatives, was not familiar with the new situation, and did not have any idea where to start.

My mother met me at the Prague airport, and we took a taxi to her apartment. After we had spent some time together and caught up with each other, she left the apartment to visit a neighbor and run a few errands. Alone in the apartment, I sat down in an armchair, had a cup of tea, and reflected about my mission. I contemplated the situation for about ten minutes but was not getting very far. Suddenly, my train of thought was interrupted by a loud ringing of the doorbell. I answered the door and recognized Tomáš Dostál, a younger psychiatrist colleague of mine who, in the old days, used to be my close friend. Before my departure for the United States, we shared some explorations of non-ordinary states of consciousness by sitting for each other in our psychedelic sessions. Tomáš had heard from an acquaintance of his about my visit to Prague and came to welcome me.

I found out to my astonishment that, just as Tomáš was leaving his apartment, his home telephone rang. It was Ivan Havel, a prominent researcher in artificial intelligence and the brother of the Czech president Václav Havel. He was also the leader of a group of progressive scientists that during the Communist era had held secret underground meetings exploring various new avenues in Western science. They were particularly interested in the new paradigm thinking, consciousness research, and transpersonal psychology. Ivan Havel and Tomáš had been classmates in the *gymnasium* (Czech equivalent of high school) and remained close friends ever since. Tomáš had been a frequent guest in the Havel household and also personally knew Ivan's brother Václav.

Ivan Havel's group had heard about my work in the lecture of a friend of mine, Soviet dissident Vassily Nalimov. Vassily was a brilliant Russian scientist who had spent eighteen years in a Siberian labor camp. Christina and I had invited Vassily and his wife, Zhanna, as our guest to the ITA conference in Santa Rosa, California, and had become good friends with them. The title of one of Vassily's books, *Realms of the Unconscious*, was very close to the title of my first book, *Realms of the Human Unconscious*. Vassily included in his book an extensive report about my psychedelic research, and he also discussed my work at length in his lecture for the Prague group.

As a result of Vassily's talk, the Prague group became interested in having me as a guest lecturer. Ivan Havel knew that Tomáš and I were old friends and called him to inquire whether he had my address or telephone number and would be able to mediate contact between the Prague group and me. To his surprise, Tomáš told him that I happened to be visiting Prague and that he was about to walk out of his apartment to pay me a visit. Such a very unlikely concatenation of events seemed to be enough of a sign that we were "surfing," rather than "paddling against the stream." Encouraged by this portentous development of events, Christina and I decided to go ahead with the project.

This spectacular set of coincidences greatly facilitated my role as envoy for the ITA conference. It took me only ten minutes in unfamiliar circumstances to find the ideal contact and support for our future meeting—a group of highly competent academicians connected to the university system who were vitally interested in the subject of the planned conference. By the same token, I also found access to the head of the state, who happened to be an enlightened and deeply spiritually oriented politician open to the transpersonal perspective. The conference was held in 1993 in Prague's Smetana Concert Hall and the Municipal House under the auspices of President Václav Havel.

President Havel was an ideal guest of honor for an ITA conference. He was not a run-of-the-mill politician, but somebody who was much more frequently referred to as "statesman," a head of state with a broad, spiritually based global vision. A well-known playwright, he did not become president as a result of years of struggle for political power, but was somebody who very reluctantly accepted the nomination, responding to an urgent plea of the Czech people. He practically went to the Prague Castle directly from the Communist prison. One of the first things he did after inauguration was to acknowledge His Holiness the Dalai Lama as the head of Tibet and invite him for a visit. He also made a serious attempt to stop all Czechoslovakian production of weapons. Wherever he went, he impressed his audiences by his eloquent call for spiritually based democracy and global solidarity.

Unfortunately, the beginning of the ITA conference happened to coincide with a severe crisis threatening the future of Czechoslovakia. The eastern part of the country, Slovakia, had decided to split from the two western parts, Bohemia and Moravia. On the day the conference started, the Czechoslovakian government had an emergency meeting dealing with the crisis that lasted until three o'clock in the morning. President Havel, who was scheduled to introduce the conference and welcome the guests, was unable to come and had to send an envoy with a personal message instead. In spite of this complication, this conference, including for the first time our colleagues from Eastern Europe, proved to be very successful. It turned out to be one of the most frequently talked-about events in ITA's history.

Our disappointment at President Havel's absence at the ITA conference was outweighed by our opportunity to spend some private time with him. During our next visit to Prague, he invited us for a personal audience in the Prague Castle. He expressed keen interest in transpersonal psychology, its history, and main representatives. The idea of achieving a synthesis of the modern scientific worldview and a spiritual vision of the world clearly fascinated him. He was particularly eager to discuss the implications of transpersonal thinking for politics and economy. For Christina and me, the two-and-a-half hours we spent in his presence have become an unforgettable experience.

UNDER THE SPELL
OF SATURN
The Death of My Mother

The schedule for my lectures, workshops, and seminars in different parts of the world is typically arranged in cooperation with the individuals or institutions that host and organize these events. In most instances, I have very little to do with the choice of the themes, except for offering a list of possible titles of my presentations with brief abstracts. This was also the case when the schedule and itinerary for my European trip in the fall of 1992 was being created. I should mention that the schedule and itinerary for my lecture tours is usually done at least a year or a year-and-a-half before the actual journey.

My European tour began with a six-day training module in Holotropic Breathwork and transpersonal psychology in Findhorn, Scotland. The topic for this module was suggested by Cary Sparks, the director of our Holotropic Breathwork training; it was "Death and Dying: Psychological, Philosophical, and Spiritual Perspectives." The reason for this choice was primarily the fact that a module with this theme was on the list of optional modules for our training and had not been offered for some time.

My plan was to do some sightseeing in England following this training module before going to Germany to conduct a weekend seminar in Munich. The German seminar was organized by Brigitte Ashauer, a dear friend and certified Holotropic Breathwork facilitator. She had chosen for it the title of my book *The Human Encounter with Death*, a subject that she was very interested in and one that she thought would also be interesting for German audiences.

It just so happened that the European Association of Humanistic Psychology had planned its annual meeting for the week following my Munich seminar and its site was Garmisch-Partenkirchen, a city not far from Munich. The organizers found out that I would be in the area at the time of their meeting, and they asked me to come to Garmisch-Partenkirchen on the Monday following the Munich seminar and do a keynote lecture and a workshop at their conference. I agreed to come and asked them what topic they would like me to address. "You have done psychedelic therapy with terminal cancer patients, and there will be many doctors among our participants. It would be great if you could focus on that subject," was the answer.

As the tour actually began, some unexpected developments profoundly changed my original plans. While at Findhorn, I received a phone call from Jill Purce, the editor of the Thames and Hudson Art and Imagination series of high-quality paperbacks with spiritual orientation. In earlier years, Christina and I had contributed a volume to this series entitled *Beyond Death: The Gates of Consciousness*. At the time, I was working on another volume for the same series, called *Books of the Dead: Manuals for Living and Dying*. It was a study of the ancient manuals on death and dying—the Tibetan *Bardo Thödol*, the Egyptian *Pert Em Hru*, the Aztec *Codex Borgia*, the Mayan *Ceramic Codex*, and the European *Ars Moriendi*. Jill told me on the phone that to meet the publishing deadline, it was essential to finish the work on the book within a few days. She urged me to give up my plans for sightseeing in England and come to London immediately, which I did.

I spent the next five days in a small office in the Thames and Hudson headquarters in London, working from early morning until late at night on the spreads for my forthcoming book, arranging the pictures and the corresponding captions. All this time, I was surrounded by images of eschatological mythology—Tibetan wrathful deities, Egyptian guardians of the gates of the underworld, Mesoamerican death gods and chthonic menagerie, scenes of judgment of the dead, and angels and devils fighting for the souls of the deceased. I finished the work just in time to catch my plane to Germany.

As a result of this unexpected change of plans, I spent practically without interruption almost two weeks fully immersed in the subject of death—six days of the training module in Findhorn, five days of working on the *Books of the Dead* in London, and two days of the German weekend seminar. When I finished the Munich seminar and was resting in bed in my hotel, ready for a good night's sleep before my departure for the Garmisch-Partenkirchen conference, I received a shocking phone call that brought another unexpected element into my European trip.

It was the secretary of my brother, Paul, calling from his office at the Royal Psychiatric Hospital in Canada; she had just received the news from Czechoslovakia that my mother had suddenly died in her apartment in Prague. This was completely unexpected because my mother enjoyed good health in spite of her advanced age of eighty-six years. As we found out later, she had conducted a Holotropic Breathwork session a week before she died, and at 11:30 a.m. on the day of her death talked on the phone with two close friends, a husband and wife, and invited them for dessert after lunch. When they arrived two hours later, she was already dead.

Paul's secretary gave me a phone number for Paul, who was staying at the time in a hotel in Berlin. I had to decide whether or not I would go ahead with my speaking engagement in Garmisch-Partenkirchen; the organizers expected over 700 participants, and I had a significant role in the program. After some deliberation, Paul and I decided that I would meet my commitment, while Paul would make all the necessary arrangements for the funeral in Prague. In turn, I would stay in Prague and take care of everything that was necessary to do after the funeral. Paul had to leave almost immediately because he had important commitments in Canada.

I gave my keynote and did the workshop on death and dying at the Garmisch-Partenkirchen conference. There was no late flight from Munich to Prague that evening, and I had to take an overnight train. I arrived in Prague in the morning, after spending the night in my roomette, and took a taxi to the funeral, where I had the last chance to see my mother before she was cremated. In the afternoon, we had a memorial service involving relatives, friends, and acquaintances, where we shared memories and told stories about my mother.

On the following four days, I had, with great help from Christina, who in the meantime had arrived in Prague from California, the sad task of going through all of my mother's belongings and deciding what to do with them. This was for me a time of deep reminiscing and mourning. Because of her war experience, my mother found it very difficult to dispose of things that had outlived their usefulness. Her apartment thus harbored a rich collection of clothes, hats, purses, jewelry, and other items from various periods of her life. Many of them had a distinct scent and were for me loaded with memories. Going through this stuff involved a lot of emotional letting go and felt like a major completion and the end of an era.

When I later discussed with my brother, Paul, this extraordinary accumulation of synchronicities in my life, he added another interesting piece of information to this already rich mosaic. As I mentioned earlier, at the time of our mother's death, I was in Munich and Paul was in Berlin. This was only the second time in twenty-five years that both of us were in Europe at the same time since the time of our emigration from Czechoslovakia. It turned out that on the day of mother's death, he was presenting in Berlin the data of his research on mortality of manic-depressive patients, the work for which his group later received an award from the American Suicidology Society in New York City.

It is interesting to look at the above concatenation of events from an astrological perspective. Astrologers would associate much of what I described earlier with the planetary archetype of Saturn, often called the Great Malefic. In its negative aspect, Saturn represents impermanence, aging, death, ending of things, loss, mourning, and depression. Mythologically, Saturn is a Roman deity often identified with the Greek Kronos, Father Time, and the Grim Reaper. Astrologers talk about archetypal cycles of Saturn that last twenty-eight to thirty years. This is the time that it takes Saturn to complete its orbit around the sun and return to the place where it was at the time of our birth. The times of Saturn returns are typically times of major endings and completions.

I visited Prague twice before during my second Saturn return. The first time, my visit coincided with the celebration of the seventieth anniversary of the founding of Czechoslovakia (in 1918). The large pedestrian zone (Na příkopech), adjacent to the famous Wenceslas Square, was at that time lined with two rows of tall cylindrical pillars covered with enlarged newspaper clippings from various periods of Czechoslovakia's history. They were arranged chronologically, so that walking by them and reading the texts, I was literally reviewing and reliving the most significant times of my life.

The reason for my second visit, in June 1992, was the International Transpersonal Conference entitled "Science, Spirituality, and the Global Crisis: Toward a World with a Future," of which Christina and I were the program coordinators. This was a major closure and completion for me. In the 1960s, I began my independent research with psychedelics in Prague, and now, thirty years later, I was bringing to Prague transpersonal psychology and Holotropic Breathwork, the fruits of many years of this work. The three weeks of immersion in death, from the beginning of the Findhorn training to the end of my stay in my mother's apartment in Prague, seemed like an integral part of my second Saturn return and its completion.

BLESSING OF THE GODS

Don José Matsuwa and the Huichol Rain Ceremony

During the early years of our stay in Big Sur, California, we connected with Prem Das, a young American from San Jose, who stopped
at Esalen to sell artifacts of Huichol Indians from north-central Mexico.
They were all inspired by the Huichols' psychedelic visions during peyote
ceremonies and included exquisite yarn paintings depicting mythological
motifs, carved wooden animals and gourds decorated with intricate bead
designs, God's eyes, and prayer arrows. He also brought richly embroidered
shirts, pants, dresses, belts, and bracelets. At the time when Prem Das came
to Esalen, he lived in Mexico, in a Huichol village near Tepic, the capital of
the state Nayarit, and was apprenticing with Don José Matsuwa, an extraordinary centenarian shaman.

As we found out, Prem Das had a very interesting spiritual history. When he
was eleven years old, he participated in a research study conducted in the Laboratory of Hypnosis Research at Stanford University by Ernest R. Hilgard. Although
Hilgard's intention was simply to study hypnotizability in children, Prem Das had
during one of the sessions a powerful mystical experience that awakened in him a
deep interest in the spiritual quest. In his late teens, he traveled to India and studied Agni Yoga with Haridas Baba, a famous guru known among others for his vow
of silence. It was Haridas Baba who gave him the name Prem Das.

After his return to the United States, Prem Das traveled to Mexico, and during his visit to Tepic he saw a Huichol yarn painting depicting the journey of

the shaman, or *mara'akame,* to the solar realm. The path of the shaman on the painting was punctuated by seven flowers and reminded Prem Das strongly of the yogic system of the chakras. Fascinated by what he saw, he decided to trace the painting to its source, convinced that the people who had made the painting had to have a belief system similar to Kundalini yoga. His quest took him to a Huichol village, where he discovered Don José and was accepted as his apprentice. The main spiritual vehicle of the Huichols and Don José's principal teaching tool was ingestion of peyote, a psychedelic cactus with the botanical name *Lophophora williamsii* or *Anhalonium lewinii.*

Prem Das described to us the tragic situation of the Huichol Indians. These people, descendents of the Aztecs, lived in small communities scattered through the canyons and valleys of the rugged mountains of the Sierra Madre in the states of Jalisco and Nayarit. They lived off the land, cultivating corn, beans, and chili peppers on the steep mountain slopes. The Huichols were representatives and guardians of an old pre-Hispanic tradition of their remote past, which they had been trying to preserve and protect against various external onslaughts. They called themselves Wixalika, or Healers, and believed that conducting proper ceremonies was essential in order to heal the Earth and keep nature in balance. The Huichols had successfully withstood the invasion of the Spanish conquistadores and now they were trying to keep their culture alive in spite of the ever-increasing encroachment of their Mexican neighbors.

In the 1970s, the Mexican government, determined to integrate all indigenous peoples into mainstream society, opened schools, clinics, and agricultural stations to introduce the Huichols to the new ways. Since that time, airstrips had brought small planes carrying tourists and government officials into the most remote areas of the Sierra. Ranchers coveted the high, grassy plateaus on which the Huichols lived and tried to appropriate them as new grazing lands for their increasingly large cattle herds. Christian missionaries and religious zealots had made numerous efforts to convert the "pagans." The young Huichol generation was exposed to the temptations of the consumer society, with its television, transistor radios, motorcycles, and alcoholic beverages.

Modernization of the Mexican society also seriously interfered with a critical element of Huichol ritual life. The Huichols had traditionally obtained their main sacrament peyote in an annual pilgrimage to Wirikuta, or the Land of Flowers, their spiritual home located at the western edge of the Catorce mountain range. This three-hundred-mile journey used to be made on foot, and the first-timers had to walk it blindfolded. According to a millennia-old story, Wirikuta was the land where the Huichols were created and where their ancestors witnessed from Cerro Quemado, the Burnt Hill, the birth of the sun; this was also where the first deer hunt took place.

The Huichols believed that peyote grew in the footprints of the Deer Spirit Kauyumare and they obtained the sacred cactus by imitating a deer hunt. During the pilgrimage to Wirikuta, they ingested peyote ritually and they collected a sufficient supply to last them for the entire year. Private ownership of land and a system of fences now compromised the numinosity of this event by forcing them to use trucks and the highway system for this journey.

The last onslaught of the industrial civilization had been detrimental for the village where Prem Das lived. Since time immemorial, the staples of the Huichols had been corn and beans, a combination that constituted a perfectly balanced diet. To increase the production of corn, the Mexican government introduced into Huichol land herbicides that made the land incapable of growing any crops other than corn and forced the Huichols to buy beans on the market. When the price of beans suddenly tripled, this staple became unavailable to them. The undernourished Huichol children were now showing a variety of health problems related to this deficiency.

Having heard this, we decided to help the Huichols to survive and to preserve their culture and their spiritual life. With Prem Das's help, we established a connection with Huichol shamans and their artists, a liaison that turned out to be mutually beneficial. Prem Das regularly brought from Mexico his teacher, Don José, and other shamans as guest faculty in our monthlong seminars. They regularly carried with them large amounts of stunning Huichol artifacts, which were articles highly valued by the Esalen community, by workshop participants, and by visiting guests. This exchange represented extraordinary enrichment of our program and generated enough money to provide the necessary supply of beans for the Huichol village.

For us, the greatest benefit of this enterprise was the opportunity to meet Don José, a venerated Huichol shaman or mara'akame, and to spend some time with him. During his visits to Big Sur, Don José regularly stayed as a guest in our house. He was one of the most extraordinary spiritual teachers and human beings we have ever met. Don José was more than one hundred years old at the time we first met him. He had only one arm, having lost the other one as a young boy in a fishing accident. A machete injury had cost him the loss of two fingers on his remaining hand. And yet, he personally harvested every year five tons of corn and believed that the best guarantee for good health and longevity is to produce sufficient amounts of sweat every day. His vitality was astonishing; he walked up and down the mountains with such a speed that Prem Das, a young and athletic man in his late twenties, could hardly keep up with him. Despite his age, he showed active interest in sex and repeatedly made advances to women in our groups.

The all-night ceremonies with Don José were truly unforgettable events. He attended them wearing a large hat and his Huichol costume, both richly embroidered and decorated with intricate geometric designs and sacred symbols of his tribe—Deer Spirit Kauyumari; Great-grandfather Fire Tatewari; peyote cactus Hikuri; the double-headed eagle, representing the shaman capable of seeing in all directions; and many others. Don José always ingested before the ceremony the button (or bud) of a large peyote cactus that helped him to transcend the limits of ordinary sense perception and to "see with the mind's eye and the heart of the Great Spirit the interconnectedness of all things, seen and unseen."

In spite of the impressive amount of peyote he had ingested, Don José performed all the ritual activities and healing interventions with impeccable precision, holding his prayer arrow with eagle and turkey feathers in his three remaining fingers and carrying for hours a sweet and haunting sacred chant. Prem Das accompanied him either with rhythmic compelling beats of his drum or playing a handmade wooden string instrument. The group joined in by adding the energetic sounds of Huichol rattles made of gourds and dry beans. Don José had an inimitable capacity to balance the sacred and the earthy. While the drumming and chanting was happening, he was very serious and created a solemn and numinous atmosphere in the room, but, during the breaks, his very mischievous trickster side took over. He laughed out loud and exchanged with Prem Das hilarious and often dirty jokes.

The most extraordinary and memorable ceremony we have experienced with Don José took place in the Big House at Esalen in the late 1970s, in the middle of a catastrophic California drought that lasted several years. During this entire time, the water shortage was critical. The agriculture in California was seriously threatened, and people living in expensive houses were unable to flush their toilets and wash their dishes. As the ceremony was beginning, one of the participants jokingly suggested: "Don José, there is a terrible drought in California; maybe we should make a rain ceremony." Everybody in the group took it as a joke, except for Don José. After a short period of deliberation and to everybody's surprise, he agreed.

For those of us who did not understand Don José's chanting in the Huichol language, the ceremony seemed to resemble others we had done in the past. There was continuous drumming, chanting, and music all through the night, with the exception of a few breaks. In the middle of the ceremony, Prem Das led the group in the Huichol Deer Dance, during which we moved around the room in a stylized way combining forward steps with rotations of our bodies along the vertical axis. At dawn, Don José took out of his medicine bag a large abalone shell and a rabbit's tail and invited us to go with him down to the ocean to receive *limpieza,* or purification, and give offerings to the ocean as a thanksgiving for a good ceremony.

We walked out of the Big House to the cypress-covered cliffs of the stunning Big Sur coast, still experiencing the "afterglow" of the ceremony. The view of the Pacific Ocean in the morning light was breathtaking and overwhelming. As the entire group stood there motionless, staring at this spectacular panorama, somebody noticed that it had started to drizzle. "Incredible ... unbelievable ... fantastic ... " were people's comments about what in the middle of a disastrous drought seemed like a miracle. But Don José remained calm. "It is *kupuri*, the blessing of the gods," he said. "It always happens; it means we did a good ceremony."

As we walked down the stone steps to the ocean, the drizzling rapidly turned to a shower. Don José reached the ocean shore and stood on a flat rock, about ten feet above the water line. He placed his offering on the surface of the rock near his feet and started to chant. The ocean was very calm that day, but, after a few minutes of his prayer, as we all watched in astonishment, a single giant wave formed on its surface and moved rapidly toward the rock on which Don José stood. This massive body of water reached the rock with tremendous force, but it formed at its end a spiral crest that gently swept the offerings from the rock without spraying Don José's feet. There was no doubt in anybody's mind that the extraordinary *mara'akame* had interacted with the ocean as a living being and that it responded to him by receiving his offerings.

Don José filled his abalone shell with ocean water and, dipping his rabbit tail into it, blessed and purified one group member after another as we were standing there in a line. By that time, it was literally pouring, and we were all soaking wet, receiving limpieza of another kind. When we climbed back up the hill, we all danced in the rain on the lawn in front of the Big House around a beautiful eucalyptus tree, some people after taking off all their clothes. This might seem somewhat unusual behavior to an average American, but in Esalen, known for its cult of bodywork and integrated bathing, it seemed quite natural. We were astonished by what we just had experienced, and the mood in the group was ecstatic.

When we later related this experience to Joseph Campbell, he shared with us a similar story from his own life. Several years earlier, he had been invited as a guest to a rain ceremony on the Navajo reservation in New Mexico. Like our own ceremony, it took place during a severe drought. When they arrived at the ritual site and the ceremony began, the sky was blue and there was not a single cloud in sight. Joseph confessed that he felt very amused by the vain effort of the Navajo shaman, who carried on with great determination what seemed like a silly and foolish activity. Seemingly ignorant of all the odds he was against and with everybody watching, he kept chanting and beating his drum. But then dark clouds started to gather on the horizon, and they traveled rapidly in their direction. And, before the ceremony was over, they all were soaking wet.

When I later thought about the native belief in such ceremonial magic, I had to admit that the positive result of the rain ceremonies should not surprise us. The people in native cultures might not be technologically advanced, but they are not stupid. It is hard to imagine that they would continue venerating shamans who would conduct one ceremony after another without being able to show any results. For the tradition of rainmaking ceremonies to continue, they have to be successful in a significant number of cases. That does not mean that the relationship has to be causal in the sense that the shaman is actually making the rain. We have seen in other stories in this book the significant role that, on occasion, the principle of synchronicity plays in the universal scheme of things.

SRI YANTRA IN THE
OREGON DESERT

UFO Visit or a Spectacular Hoax?

I n 1989, Christina and I organized a conference of the International Transpersonal Association (ITA) in Eugene, Oregon, entitled Mystical Quest, Attachment, and Addiction. As it turned out, this event became a focus of some interesting synchronistic happenings. At the time of this conference, I was deeply immersed in the study of UFO sightings and of experiences of alien encounters and abductions. My interest in this subject was prompted by my observations of UFO abduction experiences in psychedelic sessions of my clients, in sessions of Holotropic Breathwork of participants in our workshops and training, and during spiritual emergencies of the people I worked with. My personal encounter with what seemed to be alien intelligence during a ketamine session in Rio de Janeiro contributed to my interest in this area.

Since Kenneth Arnold's first sighting of disk-shaped "unidentified flying objects" in 1947 near Mt. Rainier in Washington, the UFOs and various forms of encounters with and abduction by alien visitors have belonged to the most enigmatic and controversial phenomena of modern times. As a result of my personal observations and study of UFO literature, I realized very quickly that the attitude of mainstream scientists toward this phenomenon was simplistic and inadequate. Like experienced UFO researchers, such as Jacques Vallée and Allen Hynek, I came to the conclusion that we are dealing here with observations that represent true "anomalies" and seriously challenge our established concepts of reality.

I became convinced that the two alternative explanations offered by materialistic science—hallucinations of psychotic individuals and misperception and misinterpretation of some natural or human-made objects—were painfully inadequate efforts to capture the nature of these enigmatic experiences. I also felt that it was very unlikely that we were dealing with actual visits of physical extraterrestrial beings. We have enough information about the planets of our solar system from unmanned probes to know that they are unlikely habitats for such visitors. And the next possible point of origin of such interstellar journeys would be Proxima Centauri, separated from us by 4.2 light-years. Spacecraft from such destinations would have to travel at a speed approaching or exceeding the velocity of light or use interdimensional travel through hyperspace.

I concluded that the UFO experiences were phenomena *sui generis*, anomalous events that represented a radical challenge to mainstream scientific paradigms and required a radically different explanation. I read with great interest C. G. Jung's book *Flying Saucers: A Modern Myth of Things Seen in the Skies* (Jung 1964). In it Jung reviewed accounts of UFO-like visions reported throughout human history and suggested that these experiences were manifestations that had their origin in the imaginal world of the collective unconscious. According to him, they were thus neither hallucinations nor perceptions of material reality, but belonged to the twilight zone between consciousness and the world of matter. Jung thus relegated the UFO phenomena into the realm of consciousness research and transpersonal psychology. I found his argument very convincing and saw it as a justification of my own interest in this area.

We had scheduled our training for facilitators of Holotropic Breathwork in such a way that it immediately preceded the Eugene conference. Because the training took place at Hollyhock Farm on Cortez Island in the Vancouver Bay, I was able to incorporate both destinations into one airplane itinerary. The chain of synchronicities started when I was flying from San Francisco to Seattle on the way to Cortez Island. I was reading Whitley Strieber's book *Communion* (Strieber 1987), describing his experiences of encounters with extraterrestrial beings. One of the four-hundred-some pages of this paperback, located in the middle of the book, gave general information about UFOs; the rest was about Strieber's personal experiences.

Just as I was reading the sentence describing the first sighting of UFOs by Kenneth Arnold near Mt. Rainier, I heard the captain's voice, bringing to our attention that the majestic snowcapped mountain on our right was Mt. Rainier. I found the timing quite impressive, considering that Mt. Rainier was mentioned just once in the entire book. We landed in Seattle, and a taxi took me to the harbor, where I boarded a small seaplane for a spectacular flight over the hundreds of little islands of the Vancouver Bay to Cortez Island. The first person I saw when I arrived at Hollyhock Farm was John Mack, a well-known Harvard psychiatrist and psychoanalyst who was participating in our training.

"Stan, I have to talk to you," was the first thing John said after we greeted each other. "You were absolutely right. I have been looking into the UFO abduction experiences, and it's fascinating stuff!" John was referring to a discussion we had had earlier that year at Pocket Ranch in Geyserville, California, about a paper by Keith Thompson entitled "Angels, Aliens, and Archetypes," which Christina and I decided to include in our book *Spiritual Emergency*. In this paper, Keith compared the situation of the UFO abductees to that of the initiates in Aboriginal rites of passage.

At the time of our discussion at Pocket Ranch, John was very skeptical, and I tried to convince him that the UFO phenomenon represented a serious challenge to the existing paradigm in psychiatry and that it deserved serious investigation. Hearing John's comment, I was very curious about what had transpired in the meantime that forced him to change his attitude. We sat down by the ocean, and he described to me that Blanche, one of his fellow trainees, had taken him to see her New York friend Bud Hopkins, a dedicated UFO researcher. John, a rigorous but honest and open-minded scientist, was very impressed by the evidence Bud presented to him.

Bud had reports from many hundreds of abductees from different parts of the world, most of whom had no contact with each other. Some of them were from remote parts of the world and involved people who were illiterate. And yet, there was great similarity between the narratives of the abductees, often involving details such as the mechanics of the abductions, specific physical features of the aliens and spacecraft, mysterious symbols decorating the walls of the extraterrestrial spaceships, and the nature of the procedures to which the abductees were exposed. John, inspired by this visit, started his own independent research and was becoming increasingly impressed and fascinated by what he was finding.

I should mention here that in the following years John published his findings in the books *Abductions* (Mack 1994) and *Passport to the Universe* (Mack 1999). His research got extensive coverage in the press and gained John appearances on all the major American TV talk shows. The resulting controversy almost cost John his tenure at Harvard, and the legal procedure involved consumed a significant part of his advance royalties. After winning the lawsuit with Harvard, John started PEERS, an organization for the study of "anomalous phenomena," observations challenging the current scientific paradigm. In September 2004, John's life was terminated by a tragic accident; during his visit to a London conference he was killed by a drunken truck driver while crossing a street.

In our Hollyhock training, the discussions about alien abductions soon spread among the participants and continued for the rest of our stay in Cortez Island. This situation culminated when Anne and Jim Armstrong, our guest faculty for this training module, arrived on the scene. Anne was known for her capacity to channel psychic information on any particular topic, whether it involved people's personal lives, cultural phenomena, human history, or scientific problems. Under the circumstances, the group made a unanimous decision to ask Anne for a reading on the UFO phenomenon. In a reading that lasted over an hour, Anne was able to offer an interesting perspective and many unique insights concerning flying saucers, extraterrestrials, and alien abductions.

When the training ended, Christina and I flew to Seattle to launch the ITA conference. On the second day of the meeting, the *Oregon Herald* published an astonishing report about a discovery an airplane pilot had made in the Oregon desert. Flying across this vast plain, he had noticed a remarkable design carved in the desert floor. It turned out to be a perfectly executed Sri Yantra, the most sacred symbol of Tantra, one of the most ancient Indian spiritual traditions. The image was gigantic, covering an area the size of four football fields!

Yantra is a Sanskrit word that means "aid" or "tool." Yantras are abstract diagrams, images of various deities composed entirely of primal geometric forms—points, lines, circles, triangles, squares, and stylized lotus blossoms. These forms are juxtaposed, intersected, combined, and harmonically arranged. According to Tantraraja Tantra, there are 960 yantras, each representing a different deity or a specific aspect thereof. Sri Yantra, the most ancient and celebrated of these yantras, is composed of nine intersecting triangles, four oriented upward, five downward. It represents the union of Shiva and Shakti, the cosmic field in creation, and different stages of Shakti's descent into manifestation.

In the middle of the intersecting triangles is *mahabindu,* a point representing simultaneously the source of creation and the transcendence of all polarities and final integration at the end of the spiritual journey. The intersecting triangles are surrounded by concentric circles decorated with stylized lotus petals. The outer layer of this intricate diagram is a square with *T*-shaped gates on each of its sides. This elaborate and complex spiritual symbol was executed in the Oregon desert with mathematical precision and on a colossal scale. The furrows forming it were exactly four inches deep and absolutely even throughout the diagram.

When people responding to the pilot's report arrived on the scene, they were astonished when they discovered that the desert surface all around the design was absolutely pristine and intact. There were no imprints of tires or footprints leading to it. The writer of the newspaper article concluded after doing some research that to replicate this work on the same scale and with the same precision would cost about $100,000. The origin and purpose of this remarkable project was a mystery and, to my knowledge, has remained so until this very day. The article mentioned the obvious parallel to the crop circles appearing mysteriously in the fields of various parts of Europe and added that the prevailing popular belief was that the Sri Yantra in the Oregon desert was the work of extraterrestrial visitors.

This was the culmination of a series of instances in my life involving UFOs and aliens. However, for Christina and myself, this event had also an interesting personal dimension. During our darshans with Swami Muktananda, he often referred to us mischievously in a tongue-in-cheek fashion as Shiva and Shakti. And just at the time when the two of us launched a large international conference, a sacred symbol representing Shiva and Shakti manifested in a nearby desert. While we ourselves tended to interpret similar happenings in terms of Jung's concept of synchronicity, there were people in the Siddha Yoga movement who liked to see Baba as a cosmic puppeteer. They believed that he consciously and deliberately staged auspicious events in the lives of his devotees. A few of them who participated in the conference saw the manifestation of Sri Yantra in the desert as Baba's work. They came to us individually to share their belief that it was without any doubt an expression of his blessing for the conference.

A LESSON IN FORGIVENESS

Peyote Ceremony with Potawatomi Indians

As a psychiatrist dealing on a daily basis with emotional problems that plague human life, I became keenly aware of various destructive and self-destructive patterns that are being passed like a curse from one generation to another throughout history. The traumas that the parents experience during their own development in the family of origin leave them emotionally wounded and unable to function adequately in the role of husbands, wives, fathers, and mothers. As a result, they inflict emotional wounds on their offspring. To break this vicious circle is one of the major challenges of modern psychology and psychiatry.

A similar pattern of a higher order operates on the collective level and poisons relations between entire countries and nations. Unbridled violence and insatiable greed, two dangerous flaws of human nature, have in the past engendered innumerable bloody wars and revolutions and created immense suffering. The memory of the pain and injustice inflicted by various historical enemies survives in the collective consciousness of nations for centuries and colors their present attitudes and relations with each other. Unresolved and unforgiven harms and injuries keep breeding new violence.

In the unfolding of human history, the roles of various nations and their relationships keep constantly changing in a rather capricious way. On the surface, alliances and internecine encounters come and go, but the memories of the deep wounds and the resulting prejudices remain. During World War II,

Germany, Japan, and Italy, the "Axis powers," were enemies of the United States, while the Soviet Union was an important ally. After the war, the political landscape changed dramatically. Japan and Italy became friendly countries and the Soviet Union an archenemy. The situation with Germany was more complicated; West Germany now was an ally and East Germany became a member of the hostile camp.

In the twentieth century, the main challenge for Great Britain and France was Germany, and they maintained a relatively decent relationship with each other. However, a few centuries earlier, they were sworn enemies. At one point of history, the major challenge for England was Spain and for Russia, France: Spain was at war with Holland, Russia's enemy was Sweden, and so on. Having experienced as a child and teenager the horrors of the German occupation of Czechoslovakia and in my later years the ruthless Stalinist regime imposed on us by the Soviet Union, I have strong personal feelings about this problem.

Since my early childhood, I have always hated borders and everything that belonged to them—the towers with submachine guns, barbed-wire fences, mine fields, and the soldiers and dogs that guarded them. This aversion extended even to more civilized forms of frontiers in the free world and their custom officers, visas, and tolls. I have often dreamed about a United States of Europe, about a future when all European nations would live in peaceful coexistence. Later in my life, this vision broadened to include the entire planet. I like to imagine a future when humanity will overcome all racial, sexual, national, cultural, political, and economic divisions and create a global community. However, I am sufficiently aware of the complexity of the problems involved to realize that this is not a very plausible scenario for our planet.

After this somewhat pessimistic introduction, I would like to relate an episode from my life that gave me some hope in a better future for us all in spite of the grim overall situation. It was an experience of profound healing and transformation that occurred many years ago in a group of people with whom I shared a nonordinary state of consciousness. Although it happened more than thirty years ago, I still feel very moved and tearful whenever I think and talk about it. This event showed me the depth of the problems we are facing in our world, where for many centuries hatred has been passed from one generation to another. However, it also gave me hope and trust in the possibility of lifting this curse and dissolving the barriers that separate us from each other.

In the late 1960s and early 1970s, I participated in a government-sponsored research program at the Maryland Psychiatric Research Center in Baltimore, exploring the potential of psychedelic therapy. One of our projects at the center was a training program for mental health professionals. It made it possible for psychiatrists, psychologists, social workers, and priests doing pastoral counseling to have up to three high-dose LSD sessions for educational purposes. One of the participants in this program was Kenneth Godfrey, a psychiatrist from the VA hospital in Topeka, Kansas. Ken was one of the pioneers of psychedelic research himself, conducting sessions with his clients, but he did not have in his program provision for his own sessions. I was his guide in the three psychedelic sessions he had in our institute, and, in the process, we became very close friends. Ken and his wife were both Native Americans and had a very deep connection with the spiritual tradition of their people and with the elders of their tribe.

When I was still in Czechoslovakia, I read about the Native American Church, a syncretistic religion combining Indian and Christian elements and using as a sacrament the Mexican psychedelic cactus peyote. I became very interested in having a personal experience of a peyote ceremony, which would make it possible for me to compare therapeutic use of psychedelics with their use in a ritual context. After my arrival in the United States, I was looking for such an opportunity, but without success.

During our final discussion after Ken's third LSD session, it crossed my mind that he might have some contacts with the Native American Church and could help me find a group that would allow me to participate in their peyote ceremony. Ken promised to explore this issue with John Mitchell, a well-known Potawatomi "road chief," or leader of sacred ceremonies, who was his close friend. Several days later, Ken called me on the phone and had some good news. John Mitchell had not only invited me as a guest to his peyote ceremony, but offered that I could bring along several other people from our staff.

The following weekend, five of us flew from Baltimore to Topeka. The group consisted of our music therapist Helen Bonny, her sister, psychedelic therapist Bob Leihy, professor of religion Walter Houston Clark, and me. We rented a car at the Topeka airport and drove from there deep into the Kansas prairie. There, in the middle of nowhere, stood several teepees, the site of the sacred ceremony. The sun was setting, and the ritual was about to begin. But before we could join the ceremony, we had to be accepted by the other participants, all of whom were Native Americans. We had to go through a difficult process that resembled a dramatic encounter group.

With intense emotions, the native people brought up the painful history of the invasion and conquest of North America by white intruders—the genocide of American Indians and rapes of their women, the expropriation of their land, the senseless slaughter of the buffalo, and many other atrocities. After a couple of hours of dramatic exchange, the emotions quieted down and, one after the other, the Indians accepted us into their ceremony. Finally, there was only one person who had remained violently opposed to our presence—a tall, dark, and sullen man. His hatred toward white people was enormous.

It took a long time and much persuading from his peers, who were unhappy about further delays of the ceremony, before he finally and reluctantly agreed that we could join the group. Finally, everything was settled, at least on the surface, and we all gathered in a large teepee. The fire was started and the sacred ritual began. We ingested the peyote buttons and passed the staff and the drum. According to the Native American custom, whoever had the staff could sing a song or make a personal statement; there was also the option to pass.

The sullen man, who was so reluctant to accept us, sat directly across from me, leaning on a pole of the teepee. He radiated anger and hostility, and it was obvious to everybody that he was sulking. While all other participants wholeheartedly participated in the ceremony, he remained detached and aloof. Every time the staff and the drum made the circle and came to him, he very angrily passed them on. My perception of the environment was extremely sensitized by the influence of peyote. This man became a sore point in my world, and I found looking at him increasingly painful. His hatred seemed to radiate from his eyes like bright laser beams that were consuming me and filling the entire teepee. He managed to maintain this recalcitrant attitude throughout the ceremony.

The morning came, and, shortly before sunrise, we were passing the staff and the drum for the last time. It was an opportunity for everybody to say a few final words about their experiences and impressions from the night. Walter Houston Clark's speech was exceptionally long and very emotional. He expressed his deep appreciation for the generosity of our Native American friends, who had shared with us their beautiful ceremony. Walter specifically stressed the fact that they had accepted us in spite of everything *we* had done to them—invaded and stolen their land, killed their people, raped their women, and slaughtered the buffalo. At one point of his speech, he referred to me—I do not remember exactly in what context—as "Stan, who is so far from his homeland, his native Czechoslovakia."

As soon as Walter uttered the word Czechoslovakia, the man who had resented our presence all through the night suddenly became strangely disturbed. He got up, ran across the teepee, and threw himself on the ground in front of me. He hid his head in my lap, crying and sobbing loudly. After about twenty minutes, he quieted down, returned to his place, and was able to talk. He explained that the evening before the ceremony he had seen us all as "pale faces" and thus automatically enemies of Native Americans. After hearing Walter's remark, he realized that, being of Czechoslovakian origin, I had nothing to do with the tragedy of his people. The Czechs certainly were not notorious as raiders of the Wild West. He thus hated me through the sacred ceremony without justification.

The man seemed heartbroken and desolate. After his initial statement came a long silence, during which he was going through an intense inner struggle. It was clear that there was more to come. Finally, he was able to share with us the rest of his story. During World War II, he had been drafted into the American Air Force, and several days before the end of the war he personally participated in a rather capricious and unnecessary American air raid on the Czech city Pilsen, known for its world-famous beer and the Skoda automobile factory. Not only had his hatred toward me been unjustified, but our roles were actually reversed; he was the perpetrator, and I was the victim. He invaded my country and killed my people. This was more than he could bear. He came back to me and kept embracing me, begging my forgiveness.

After I had reassured him that I did not harbor any hostile feelings toward him, something extraordinary happened. He went to my Baltimore friends, who all were Americans, apologized for his behavior before and during the ceremony, embraced them, and asked them for forgiveness. He said that this episode had taught him that there would be no hope for the world if we all continued to carry in us hatred for the deeds committed by our ancestors. And he realized that it was wrong to make generalized judgments about racial, national, and cultural groups. We should judge people on the basis of who they are, not as members of the group to which they belong.

His speech was a worthy sequel to the famous letter attributed to Chief Seattle, in which he addresses European colonizers. He closed it with these words: "You are not my enemies; You are my brothers and sisters. You did not do anything to me or my people. All that happened a long time ago in the lives of our ancestors. And, at that time, I might actually have been on the other side. We are all children of the Great Spirit; we all belong to Mother Earth. Our planet is in great trouble, and if we keep carrying old grudges and do not work together, we will all die."

By this time, most people in the group were in tears. We all felt a sense of deep connection and belonging to the human family. As the sun was slowly rising in the sky, we partook in a ceremonial breakfast. We ate the food that throughout the night had been placed in the center of the teepee and was consecrated by the ritual. Then we all shared long hugs, reluctantly parted, and headed back home. We carried with us the memory of this invaluable lesson in interracial and international conflict resolution that will undoubtedly remain vivid in our minds for the rest of our lives. For me, this extraordinary synchronicity experienced in a non-ordinary state of consciousness foments feelings of hope that, sometime in the future, a similar healing could happen in the world on a large scale.

PART 2

TRAILING CLOUDS OF GLORY

Remembering Birth and Prenatal Life

A mong the most frequent experiences occurring in holotropic states of consciousness of different origin are episodes of psychological regression to birth, during which one relives with extraordinary intensity all the emotions, physical sensations, body postures, and other aspects of this process. The strong representation of birth in our unconscious psyche comes as a great surprise for mainstream psychologists, psychiatrists, and neurophysiologists because it challenges their deeply ingrained assumptions about the limits of human memory. However, closer examination reveals that these assumptions are unfounded beliefs that are in sharp conflict with scientific facts.

According to the traditional psychiatric view, only birth that is so difficult that it causes irreversible damage to the brain cells can have psychological and psychopathological consequences. It is well known that extended exposure to oxygen deprivation associated with difficult and long delivery can cause psychiatric problems, primarily mental retardation or hyperactivity. There also exist studies linking criminal recidivism with a history of long, difficult, and complicated birth with high degrees of asphyxia. Viral infections during mother's pregnancy and obstetric complications during birth, including long labor and oxygen deprivation, are among the few consistently reported risk factors for schizophrenia. But, surprisingly, academic psychiatrists tend to interpret these finding only in terms of physical damage to the brain and do not consider the possibility that pre- and perinatal insults, whether or not they damage the brain cells, also have a strong psychotraumatic impact on the child.

The cerebral cortex of the newborn is not fully myelinized, which means that its neurons are not completely covered with protective sheaths of a fatty substance called *myelin*. This is usually offered as an obvious reason why birth is psychologically irrelevant and why the experience of it is not recorded in memory. The belief of mainstream psychiatrists that the child is not conscious during this extremely painful and stressful ordeal and that the birth process does not leave any record in the brain not only contradicts clinical observations, but also violates common sense and elementary logic.

It is certainly hard to reconcile such an assumption with the fact that widely accepted psychological and physiological theories attribute great significance to the early interaction between the mother and the child. This includes such factors as eye contact between the mother and the infant immediately after birth ("bonding"), loving physical contact, and the quality of nursing. It is well known that "imprinting" of these early experiences has critical influence on the relationship between the mother and the child in the future and on the emotional well-being of the individual for the rest of his or her life. The image of the newborn as an unconscious and unresponsive organism is also in sharp conflict with the growing body of literature describing the remarkable sensitivity of the fetus during the prenatal period.

The denial of the possibility of birth memory, based on the fact that the cerebral cortex of the newborn is not fully myelinized, does not make any sense, considering the fact that the capacity for memory exists in many lower life forms, which do not have a cerebral cortex at all. The assertion that the memory of birth would require a myelinized neocortex becomes absurd and ridiculous if we compare it with the fact that the Swedish physiologist Eric Kandel was awarded the 2000 Nobel Prize in medicine for his study of memory mechanisms in the sea slug *Aplysia*, an organism with only a small number of nerve cells that is many rungs lower on the evolutionary ladder than the newborn infant. Moreover, it is well known from biology that certain primitive forms of protoplasmic memory exist even in unicellular organisms.

It is certainly surprising to find such blatant logical contradictions in the context of scientific thinking, which takes great pride in the rigor of its logic. It is hard to find any other explanation for the above discrepancies than the profound emotional repression to which the memory of birth is subjected. The amount of emotional and physical stress and pain involved in childbirth clearly surpasses those of any postnatal trauma in infancy and childhood discussed in psychodynamic literature, with the possible exception of extreme forms of physical abuse. It is understandable that it is subjected to a strong psychological repression and denial.

In the second half of the twentieth century, psychedelic researchers and clinicians exploring various forms of experiential psychotherapy amassed convincing evidence that biological birth is the most profound trauma of our lives and an event of paramount psychospiritual importance. It is recorded in our memories in miniscule detail down to the cellular level, and it has far-reaching effects on our psychological development. Once we overcome our psychological resistance to confronting this painful and terrifying aspect of our personal history, it appears not only possible but very logical that an event of such magnitude is recorded in the unconscious psyche and that the memory of it can be brought into consciousness and relived.

The conceptual challenges increase exponentially as the regression in holotropic states continues further and reaches early stages of embryonal life and even the moment of conception. As we approach the beginning of life, the nervous system becomes increasingly immature and primitive, until it disappears altogether. And yet, there exists ample empirical evidence for the existence of memories from the dawn of our individual existence. We are then left with cellular memory as the only candidate for the material carrier of information.

In the following text, I will illustrate reliving of birth, intrauterine existence, and conception with a few examples drawn from psychedelic therapy and sessions of Holotropic Breathwork.

THE CHALLENGES
OF NOON DELIVERY

The Story of Leni

To protect the privacy of my clients, I refer to them in my writings by fictional first names, which is a common practice in psychiatric literature. In this story I can make an exception, because its protagonist, the late Leni Schwartz, shared this story in her book *World of the Newborn* (Schwartz 1981). I first met Leni and her husband, Bob, who later became close and dear friends of mine, in 1971, when they attended one of my lectures in Miami, Florida. At the time when I sat for Leni's LSD sessions, she was fifty years old and was an extremely gifted interior architect. The experiences that I am going to describe inspired her to study psychology and get a Ph.D. degree. Her dissertation, entitled *Bonding Before Birth,* was based on a longitudinal study of several couples, whom she followed in weekly group sessions from the time they had conceived a child to the time of the respective deliveries and beyond the birth of their offspring.

One of Leni's high-dose LSD sessions took her deeply into the memory of her biological birth. She spent over two hours experiencing what I call the second basic perinatal matrix, or BPM II, the initial stage of delivery when the uterus contracts but the cervix is not yet open. This is one of the most difficult and challenging experiences one can have in holotropic states of consciousness. It typically involves agonizing feelings of emotional and physical suffering and a sense of no exit—a conviction that there is no escape from this situation and that it will never end. The most profound encounters with this matrix can take the form of being in hell, complete with visions of devils and infernal landscapes.

Later in the session, the experiences shifted to what I call the third basic perinatal matrix, or BPM III. This is the experience of the next stage of delivery, involving the struggle of the fetus in the birth canal after the cervix is sufficiently dilated and open. This experience involves among others powerful clashing energies, images of violent destructive and self-destructive scenes, and strange sexual arousal manifesting in a rich spectrum of deviant erotic imagery. If brought to successful completion, this stage culminates in an experience of psychospiritual death and rebirth.

However, this is not what happened in Leni's session. After a long episode of determined struggle to be born, she suddenly felt enveloped by ominous darkness and had a sense of being engulfed and trapped. Her hope that she could succeed in freeing herself from the clutches of the birth canal all but vanished, and she found herself back in a no-exit situation. The effects of the drug gradually subsided, and she did not reach a resolution of her difficult predicament. The session left her with a feeling of discouragement and a pessimistic outlook on her life.

We decided to wait a week and schedule another session to reach a closure for this unsatisfactory experience. A week is about the time it takes after the administration of LSD to overcome the ensuing pharmacological tolerance toward another dose of the same substance. Leni's next LSD session started again with an intense experience of BPM II with feelings of hopelessness and no exit. However, this did not take long, and all her discomfort suddenly disappeared as if by magic. She was flooded by a golden light of extraordinary brilliance that had a numinous quality. This was accompanied by an overwhelming sense of liberation and psychospiritual rebirth. This time her experience completely avoided the elements of the third perinatal matrix; there was a rapid transition from the deepest pit of despair and darkness into the ecstatic rapture of rebirth.

Puzzled by this strange sequence of events and seeking some understanding, Leni decided to call her mother and inquire about her birth. She did it after some hesitation, because her mother was very conservative and old-fashioned, and Leni knew that discussions of this kind were not easy for her. For example, she had not discussed anything related to sex with Leni until Leni was an adult and got married. And she certainly had not ever mentioned anything related to her own pregnancy and Leni's delivery. Leni did not dare to mention to her mother that she had had an LSD session; she told her that she had had a "hypnotic regression" during which she had connected with a memory of what felt like her birth. However, as we had agreed in advance, she did not share with her mother any specifics concerning the content of her session.

Her mother's story threw some extraordinary light on Leni's experience. She shared with Leni that she had been inexperienced because this was her first pregnancy and childbirth and had not known what to expect. She was surprised and astonished by the intensity of the experience, but everything seemed to be going fine. And then something unexpected happened. The obstetrician and the nurse attending to her delivery announced that it was noontime, and they were going to take a break and "grab a sandwich." The obstetrician asked her to cross her legs and wait for them to come back.

Leni's mother, being an obedient patient, did not raise any objections and complied with the instructions. Fighting intense labor pains, she held her legs firmly together, awaiting the return of her caretakers. When the doctor and the nurse returned from their lunch break, all they had to do was to give her the permission to uncross her legs. When she did, Leni was literally propelled from the birth canal into the light of the day. After the telephone call with her mother, Leni shared with me this unexpected explanation for the unusual course of events in her sessions, adding another striking example to my long list of birth memories, the veracity of which could be independently validated.

THE SCENT OF
FRESH LEATHER
The Story of Kurt

The second example is from a Holotropic Breathwork session of Kurt, a psychologist who participated in our European training. In the second half of his session, Kurt experienced a very deep regression and got so involved in the reliving of his birth that he had to be held down by five people because he was moving forcefully into the spaces of other people around him. He charged repeatedly with his head and turned in a spiral fashion from his back to his belly and back again. After an intense struggle, the session ended with an extraordinary breakthrough. He felt reborn and emotionally liberated.

During the sharing group, we were able to reconstruct what had happened during the session. Kurt reported that, at the beginning of his session, he identified with a scaly, wormlike creature and got involved in a number of slithering movements. Suddenly, he felt on his feet and his body sensations that he experienced as bothersome and confining. He began to fight against them, at first lightly and later with increasing strength and effort. This intensified gradually to such an extent that he was sure he was fighting for his life. He was determined never to give up, even if the entire world were against him. With loud screaming and combining strength with various tricks, he fought desperately against his powerful foes.

As we were holding him down, he was not able to distinguish the inner from the outer, in spite of the fact that I kept repeating that we were not his enemies, that we were helping him to get through. It took some time before he reached some critical insight and was able to identify this struggle as the reliving of his birth. The feeling of helplessness kept triggering in him intense resistance and determination, never resignation. He shared with us that a similar pattern had also often manifested in his everyday life. After a long struggle, Kurt's hectic movements and loud screams eventually reached a culmination point and then abruptly subsided. He stopped fighting and moved into a phase of deep relaxation.

At this point, he decided to sit up, open his eyes, and look around. I told him it was too early and asked him to lie down and go back into the experience. A sudden realization flashed through his mind; he remembered that he had been told that his birth was premature. In that context, my comment about it being early seemed to make sense. He lay down again and covered himself with a blanket. As he was lying there curled up in a fetal position, he had the feeling that this might help him to make up for all the lost time in the womb. He found that very gratifying and beautiful, and felt contented and happy. Suddenly, he noticed to his great surprise a very intense and distinct smell of fresh leather. He smelled it again and again and found it extremely pleasant.

At the end of the session, Kurt was in a state of complete relaxation, a condition that was unfamiliar to him from his everyday life. He was normally very driven and enjoyed tackling difficult challenges and crises. He shared with the group that he was very unhappy if there were no problems in his life and adversaries against whom to fight. Then he focused on the strong and intense smell of leather, which had been such an important part of his session. He felt that this scent was somehow closely connected with his comfortable and relaxed state and kept repeating that it was the most striking and remarkable aspect of his experience. He had absolutely no idea how to account for it and found the whole situation utterly puzzling.

During the group sharing, he asked me for an explanation of why the smell of fresh leather might be such a significant part of his birth experience. I told him that fresh leather, or the smell of it, was not a typical symbolic concomitant of birth and that this was the first time I had heard anything like that. I suggested that it had to be somehow related to the actual circumstances of his delivery. However, we were not able to figure out how something like this was possible. Kurt could not stand the uncertainty, and later that evening called his mother to discuss his birth.

It turned out that during her pregnancy his mother worked in a leather shop. On the day of his birth, she stayed at work until late at night, sewing Tirol leather pants (lederhosen) on her lap. Like Leni's mother, she was inexperienced because Kurt was her first child. The labor was not expected to start and when her water broke, she misinterpreted it as a problem with her urinary bladder. When she realized what was happening, Kurt was already on his way.

The delivery was rather fast, and Kurt was born on the floor near the unfinished pair of leather pants, surrounded by the smell of fresh leather, which permeated the entire workshop. Also, his early postnatal life was closely connected to the smell of fresh leather because his mother resumed her work on leather pants at home shortly after his delivery. This significant detail convinced Kurt, as well as the group, that his experience of birth was an authentic memory.

THE VISION OF THE OLD OAK TREE

The Story of Anne-Marie

This third account of a birth experience is even more extraordinary than the first two because it suggests the possibility of transmission of visual images from the mother to the fetus. It involves Anne-Marie, a thirty-year-old anthropologist, who relived her birth in a high-dose LSD session. Although it was generally recommended to stay during most of the session in a reclining position with eyes closed, she felt an irresistible urge to get up and pace around at a fairly high speed. For a while, she was also laughing hilariously and uncontrollably without knowing why. When she finally was able to lie down, the experience culminated very rapidly, and she experienced the moment of her birth. As she was emerging from the birth canal, she had a vision of a beautiful giant oak tree.

None of this made much sense, and Anne-Marie decided, like many others who have relived their birth memories with some specific details, to call her mother and find out about her delivery. Anne-Marie was from a very conservative family; her mother was very puritanical and had always tried to avoid discussions related to sex. This was the first time that they had ever had a discussion about her birth. Although her mother was somewhat reluctant to go into much detail, her account threw some interesting light on Anne-Marie's LSD experience. She described that she was very scared and nervous in the birthing room and had to pace around much of the time to deal with her tension. She also confirmed that the doctor had given her a big dose of nitrous oxide, often referred to as "laughing gas" because it caused uncontrollable laughter.

The delivery was not going very well, and she overheard the discussion of two interns, one of whom said: "This mother doesn't know how to push; she better learn fast, or we'll lose her or the child." She panicked and was determined to push with all her strength and energy. At that point, a vivid memory from her childhood suddenly emerged into her consciousness. She remembered that, as a little girl, she had spent a lot of time near a beautiful oak tree that grew in the vicinity of their home. She often lay by the tree with her legs leaning against its trunk. As she was pushing during the final stage of her labor, she imagined that she was pressing with her legs against this oak tree the way she used to in her childhood.

At the moment when Anne-Marie was born, her mother was thus envisioning an oak tree; it was the same image that emerged during the time when Anne-Marie relived her own birth. If we tried very hard, we might be able to come up with some materialistic explanation for the laughing and possibly the pacing around. However, the transmission of the mental image of the oak tree suggests that we have to seek a radically different mechanism for the birth memories, one that does not require a material substrate.

PRENATAL VISIT TO THE
ANNUAL VILLAGE MART

The Story of Richard

The next story takes us further back in time, to the period of advanced pregnancy immediately preceding delivery. It involves Richard, a bright and attractive young man, who was admitted to the open ward of the Psychiatric Research Institute in Prague because of severe chronic depression. He had made repeated suicide attempts and tried to castrate himself with large dosages of estrogen to combat his strong homosexual impulses. After unsuccessful therapy with traditional methods of psychiatric treatment, he volunteered for the program of psychedelic therapy.

In one of his sessions, Richard had what appeared to be an authentic intra-uterine experience. His body image changed into that of a fetus, which was, of course, very different from his adult body image. He felt very small, and his head felt disproportionately large compared to his body and his extremities. He felt immersed in fetal liquid and connected with his mother by the placenta and the umbilical cord. He was aware of the blood circulating between them and bringing into his body life-giving nourishment. This was associated with wonderful feelings of bliss and symbiotic unity with his mother. He felt that the blood flowing between them was a mysterious and magical fluid that was creating a sacred bond.

While he was experiencing this, he distinctly heard two sets of heartbeats with different frequencies that were merging into one undulating acoustic pattern. This was accompanied by peculiar noises that he identified after some deliberation as sounds produced by the blood gushing through the pelvic arteries of his mother. There were also occasional hollow and roaring sounds that sounded like the movements of gas and liquid through the intestines adjacent to the uterus. On the basis of various experiential clues and with the use of adult judgment, he was able to conclude that he was a mature fetus in an advanced stage of pregnancy, shortly before delivery.

His peaceful and blissful condition was suddenly interrupted by strange noises coming from the outside world. They had a very unusual echoing quality, as if they were resounding in a large hall or coming through a layer of water. The resulting effect reminded him of special sound effects in certain modern recordings that technicians create through electronic means. He finally concluded that the abdominal and uterine walls and the fetal liquid were responsible for this effect and that this was the way in which external sounds reach the fetus.

He tried very hard for quite a while to identify what these sounds were and what was their source. After some time, he could distinguish two separate kinds of sounds that were merging together. He recognized that some of them were unmistakably human voices that were yelling and laughing. They were punctuated in irregular intervals with what seemed to be sounds of trumpets. Suddenly, the idea came to him that these had to be the sounds of the annual fair, held each year in his native village two days prior to his birthday. After having put together the above pieces of information, he concluded that his mother must have attended this fair in an advanced stage of pregnancy.

When I asked Richard's mother about the circumstances of his birth, without telling her about his LSD experience, she volunteered among other things the following story. In the relatively dull life of her native village, the annual fair was an event providing rare excitement. Although she was in a late stage of pregnancy, she would not have missed this opportunity for anything in the world. In spite of strong objections and warnings from her own mother, she left home to participate in the festivities. According to her relatives, the noisy environment and turmoil of the mart precipitated Richard's delivery. Richard denied ever having heard this story, and his mother did not remember ever having told it to him.

WINNING THE SPERM RACE

Experiencing the Cellular Level of Consciousness

As we continue back in time, the accounts of prenatal experiences in holotropic states of consciousness become increasingly fantastic and harder to believe. And yet, they sometimes bring new information that can be later verified. I remember attending a fascinating presentation of the Australian therapist Graham Farrant at the conference of the Association of Pre- and Perinatal Psychology in San Diego, California. During his lecture he showed a videotape of his session of primal therapy, in which he relived his conception.

To his surprise, Graham experienced in his session that being the sperm, he did not attack and penetrate the passive ovum, as it was at the time taught in medical schools, but that the ovum cooperated by sending out an extension of its cytoplasm and engulfing him. As Graham was showing the videotape of his session, we could see on a split screen the very first film ever made of actual human conception, shot in the Karolinska Institute in Stockholm by Leonard Nielson with the use of an electron microscope four years after his experience. While Graham kept describing on the videotape what he was experiencing, we could see that the film confirmed his experiential insights.

The following is an excerpt from a high-dose LSD session of a young psychiatrist, in which he describes his convincing identification with the sperm and the ovum on a cellular level of consciousness. Having experienced the sperm race and the fusion of the two germinal cells during conception, he relived the cellular divisions of the fertilized egg and the entire embryonal development to a mature fetus:

"My consciousness became less and less differentiated and my body image underwent a radical change. It seemed that I became some primitive organism, like an amoeba. I started experiencing strange excitement that was unlike anything I had ever felt in my life. I realized that I was involved in a hectic super-race following some chemical messages, which had an enticing and irresistible quality. A part of me, located somewhere where my spine used to be, was generating rhythmic pulses, which seemed to be propelling me through space and time toward some unknown goal. I had only a vague awareness of the final destination, but the mission appeared to be of utmost importance. After some time, I began to suspect to my surprise that I had become a spermatozoid and that the mysterious regular pulses were coming from its pacemaker. They were stimulating a long flagella, which was undulating and propelling me forward.

"Using my adult intellect, I concluded that the goal that I was so eagerly pursuing was to reach the egg and impregnate it. In spite of the fact that this scenario seemed absurd and ridiculous to my scientific mind, I could not resist the temptation to get fully immersed and absorbed in this race with great seriousness and investment of energy. Experiencing myself as a spermatozoid competing for the egg, I was aware of the complexity of all the factors involved. What was happening had the basic characteristic of the physiological process as it is taught in medical schools. However, there were many additional dimensions, which were far beyond what I knew intellectually and what my fantasy might have been able to conjure in my ordinary state of consciousness.

"This sperm cell that I had become appeared to be an intricate microcosm, a universe in its own right. I sensed the biochemical processes in the nucleoplasm and envisioned the chromosomes and even the molecular structure of the DNA. The primordial archetypal makeup of the DNA molecules was interspersed with holographic images of various life forms. The physiochemical configurations seemed to be intimately linked with primordial phylogenetic imprints, ancestral memories, myths, and archetypal images, all coexisting in the same infinitely complex matrix. Biochemistry, genetics, natural history, and mythology seemed to be inextricably interwoven and were just different aspects of the same intricate cosmic fabric. The sperm race also seemed to be governed by some external forces determining its final outcome. I sensed that they had something to do with history and with the stars and concluded that they represented mysterious karmic and astrological influences.

"At some point of this race I also identified with the ovum. My consciousness was oscillating and alternating between that of a sperm heading toward its destination and that of the egg, with a vague but strong expectation of a highly desirable and important event. The excitement of this race was building up every second, and its hectic pace eventually increased to such a degree that it seemed to resemble the flight of a spaceship approaching the speed of light. Then came the culmination in the form of triumphant implosion and ecstatic fusion of the sperm with the egg. At this point, the two split units of consciousness came together, and I was both germinal cells at the same time.

"Strangely enough, both the sperm and the ovum seemed to experience the same event as individual success, as well as joint triumph. Both of them achieved their missions—the sperm that of reaching and entering the ovum, and the ovum receiving and incorporating the sperm. A single act involving two participants thus resulted in victory and total satisfaction of both of them. I felt that this win-win situation represented an ideal model, not only for cooperation of the male and female in adult sexual activities, but also for interpersonal relations in general. The task seemed to be to arrange the circumstances in such a way that all involved parties would reach satisfaction and experience the positive outcome as their personal success.

"After the fusion of the germinal cells my experience continued at the same rapid pace as the sperm race. In a condensed and greatly accelerated way, I relived the entire embryogenesis following conception, from the fertilized egg through the first cellular division, morula, blastula, and beyond it, to a fully developed fetus. I had full conscious awareness of the biochemical processes, cellular divisions, and tissue growth involved in this process. There were numerous tasks to be accomplished, challenges to be faced, and critical periods to be overcome. I was witnessing and experiencing the differentiation of tissues and formation of new organs. I became the branchial arches, the pulsating embryonic heart, columns of liver cells, the intestinal mucous membrane, and many other parts of the developing organism. This explosive embryonic growth was accompanied with tremendous release of energy and golden light. I felt that I was experiencing the biochemical energy involved in the precipitous growth of cells and tissues.

"At one point, I had a very distinct feeling of having completed my fetal development. This was again experienced as a great accomplishment—individual success, as well as triumph of the creative force of nature. When I returned to my usual state of consciousness, I was convinced that this experience would have a profound lasting effect on my self-esteem. No matter what my further life trajectory would be, I had already accomplished two quite extraordinary feats just by completing my incarnation: I had won a race featuring hundreds of millions of competitors and completed successfully the challenging task of embryogenesis. Although the scientist in me was amused by this silly reasoning and responded to it with a condescending smile, the emotions behind it were strong and convincing."

PART 3

REVISITING HISTORY

Farther Reaches of Human Memory

As soon as I came to terms with the fact that in holotropic states of consciousness it was possible to gain access to memories of biological birth and embryonal life, I encountered an even more fundamental conceptual challenge. On a number of occasions, my clients reported that they had experienced in psychedelic sessions episodes from the lives of their ancestors, who had lived long before they themselves were conceived. Others experienced episodes from other historical periods and other geographic areas, but without the feeling of a biological link to the protagonists of these sequences. The experiential identification often involved people belonging to other racial groups.

These ancestral, racial, and collective memories often contained accurate historical and cultural information that by far transcended the actual intellectual knowledge of the people who experienced them. They accurately portrayed costumes, weapons, architecture, rituals, and other aspects of life in the historical periods and countries involved, with many specific details. All this seemed to indicate that these experiences were not fantasies, symbolic elaboration of some current problems, or products of brain pathology, as they are usually seen by mainstream psychiatrists, but unique and fascinating phenomena *sui generis*. These observations brought strong supportive evidence for the existence of a collective unconscious, as described by C. G. Jung.

Validation of these experiences and proof of their authenticity required confirmation of the information conveyed and demonstration that my clients had not acquired it through the conventional channels. And this, naturally, was not an easy task. Many of the events portrayed in these experiences had taken place a long time ago and in foreign countries. Sometimes the information that they contained was not sufficiently concrete and specific. Other times it was very precise and detailed, but there existed no archives or other kind of sources necessary for its validation. However, once in a while it happened that an experience had all the necessary criteria for verification—clear and unambiguous information, adequate sources for independent research and assessment of its accuracy, and a reasonable guarantee that the individual had not acquired it through the conventional channels. In the following text, I will describe a few examples of remarkable instances of this kind that I have encountered over the years.

Episode from the Russo-Finnish War

The Story of Inga

The first of these stories involves Inga, a young woman from Finland who attended one of our workshops in Stockholm. Her Holotropic Breathwork session was very powerful and revolved around her biological birth. As she was reliving the struggle in the birth canal, the stage of delivery to which I refer as the third basic perinatal matrix (BPM III), her experience opened up into scenes portraying aggression and killing in various types of war. This connection between perinatal experiences and images of violence from the collective unconscious is characteristic and frequent. However, one of these scenes was unusual and different from the others.

She experienced herself as a young soldier participating in a battle of the Russo-Finnish War that had taken place at the beginning of World War II, fourteen years before she was conceived. To her great surprise, she suddenly realized that she actually became her father and experienced this battle from his point of view. She was fully identified with him and felt his body, his emotions, and his thoughts. She could also perceive very clearly what was happening in the environment around her. At one moment, as she/he was hiding in the forest behind a birch tree, a bullet came and scraped her/his cheek and ear.

The experience was extremely vivid, authentic, and compelling. Inga did not know where it came from and what to make of it. Intellectually, she knew that her father had participated in the Russo-Finnish War, but was sure that he had never talked about the above episode. Finally, after the group discussion following her experience, she concluded that she must have connected with her father's memory of an actual historical event and decided to check it out by telephone.

Inga returned to the group very excited and in awe. When she called her father and told him about her experience, her father was absolutely astounded. What she had experienced was an episode that had actually happened to him in the war, and her description of the scene and of the environment, including the birch tree, was absolutely accurate. He also reassured her that he had never discussed this particular event with her or any other members of the family because the injury was not sufficiently serious to deserve special notice.

THE LITTLE GIRL WITH WHITE PINAFORES
The Story of Nadja

I n this second example, the experience portrays an even earlier ancestral memory. Nadja, a fifty-year-old psychologist, experienced in her LSD training session a very realistic episode from the early childhood of her mother. To her utter astonishment, she suddenly became her mother when her mother was a little girl at the age of three or four, dressed up in a starched, fussy dress and hiding underneath the staircase. She was covering her mouth with her hand and felt anxious and lonely, like a frightened animal. The reason for it was that she had said something very bad and had been severely reprimanded for it. She could not recapture the specifics, but was painfully aware that something very unpleasant and scary had just happened.

From her hideout, she could see a scene with many relatives—aunts and uncles—sitting on the porch of a frame house in old-fashioned dresses characteristic of that time (beginning of the twentieth century). Everybody seemed to be talking, unmindful of her. She had a sense of failure and felt overwhelmed by the unrealistic demands of the adults—to be good, to behave herself, to talk properly, not to get dirty. It seemed impossible to please them, and she felt excluded, ostracized, and ashamed.

Curious what this was all about, Nadja approached her mother to obtain the necessary data about her mother's childhood, something they had never discussed before. Reluctant to admit that she had had an LSD session, of which her conservative mother would have disapproved, Nadja told her that she had

had a dream about her childhood and wanted to know if it was true. No sooner had she started her story than her mother interrupted her and finished it in full accord with the reliving. She added many details about her childhood that logically complemented the episode experienced in the LSD session.

She confessed to Nadja how authoritarian and strict her own mother (Nadja's grandmother) had been and talked about her mother's excessive demands regarding cleanliness and proper behavior. This was reflected in her mother's favorite saying, "Children should be seen but not heard." Nadja's mother then emphasized how lonely she had felt during her whole childhood, being the only girl with two much-older brothers, and how much she craved to have playmates. According to the mother's narrative, Nadja's grandmother used to invite many relatives for family reunions on Sundays and made food for everyone. Her description of the house exactly matched Nadja's LSD experience, including the large porch and the steps leading up to it. She also mentioned the dresses covered by starched white pinafores that were characteristic of her childhood. There were no family photographs capturing this scene, and the house had been torn down before Nadja was born.

RETRIEVING MEMORIES OF THE STOLEN GENERATIONS

The Story of Marianne

The third example of verified ancestral memories involves experiential exploration of family history that reached back several generations. It is the story of Marianne Wobcke, an Australian midwife who participated in our training in Holotropic Breathwork and transpersonal psychology and eventually became a certified practitioner. I am using here her real name because she decided to share her story with the public and presented it in June 2004 at the Sixteenth International Transpersonal Conference in Palm Springs, which I organized jointly with Christina.

Marianne's extraordinary genealogical quest began on her thirteenth birthday, when her parents told her that she was adopted. When she shared this secret at school, she was teased and chose not to mention it again. She also found it very puzzling why so many of her dreams and nightmares, as well as experiences with magic mushrooms and LSD she had had in her adolescence and during her twenties, featured Australian Aborigines. However, it was not until a very intense emotional experience she had as a midwife that she began seriously to ponder her adoptive status.

In April 1991, Marianne began her midwifery training at Toowoomba Base Hospital. Her first delivery involved a full-blood Aboriginal woman from Western Australia whose pregnancy was a result of a rape. Marianne was a student midwife, full of enthusiasm, and in her eagerness to support this woman, she repeatedly invaded her space. Not familiar with the tradition of the Australian Aborigines, she also tried to make eye contact with her, which is something that is forbidden to full bloods.

To protect herself, the woman crouched with her back to Marianne, covering her nose and face with her hands. She was also responding negatively to Marianne's smell; to her Marianne reeked of soap and perfume, which made her feel sick. Finally, responding intuitively to this situation, Marianne stepped back, squatted at a respectable distance from the delivering woman, and granted her the privilege to birth silently without her interference.

The Aboriginal woman's birthing experience, culminating in her abandoning the baby, had a profound impact on Marianne. The baby stayed in the nursery for three weeks while Family Services searched for the mother, who had effectively disappeared. Marianne was deeply moved and strangely infatuated with the infant. She tried to rationalize her reaction by assuming that her maternal instincts had been triggered by witnessing the delivery, but was nevertheless shocked by the intensity of her emotional response. By coincidence, she was on duty the day three elders, all of them grandmothers, arrived at the ward to claim the infant, and she relinquished the baby to them. This triggered in her an intense grieving process that heralded her personal journey into her ancestral heritage.

It was not until this experience, which she had as a beginning midwife, that Marianne started to feel intense curiosity considering her adoptive status. As her parents had never alluded to it again, she was reluctant to approach them with her concerns. Instead of questioning them, she wrote to Family Services. Eventually, she received a parcel in the mail, including a brief outline of her adoptive status, her birth mother's name and age at the time of her birth, and a book called *No More Secrets*. In the following decade, there were times when she gave up on ever unraveling the mystery of her past. On the way, she experienced many disappointments, many trips up dry gullies.

Marianne's quest received a new impetus when she met Mary Madden, a therapist who had trained with us in the United States and was a certified Holotropic Breathwork practitioner. Mary became the facilitator for Marianne's breathwork sessions and eventually her dear friend. With Mary's help, Marianne embarked on a challenging journey of self-exploration during which she had many difficult experiences, some of them in holotropic sessions, others in her dreams and in the course of her everyday life.

Among them were memories of repeated sexual abuse as a child and of being raped by a man who spoke Italian, no English. Marianne was puzzled by these experiences because she was reasonably sure that the events involved did not represent anything from her present lifetime. She started having migraine headaches that seemed to be related to her traumatic birth, involving a forceps. As she was reliving this part of her history, bruises would appear spontaneously on her forehead and body. She was desperately trying to remember if these experiences had actually happened to her and if it was possible that she had blocked them from her consciousness.

At this difficult stage of her self-exploration, Marianne withdrew from her partner, family, and friends. She was confused and disoriented, and temporarily lost all points of reference and the will to live. Retrospectively, she reported that only the loving support of the breathwork community, facilitators, and peers, made it possible for her to survive this crisis. She was convinced that without it, she would have taken her life during this challenging time.

Although she had had very limited connection with the indigenous community up to this point, she had many inner experiences involving the Aborigines, some of them during the breathwork sessions, others in her dreams or spontaneously in her everyday life. She imagined with extraordinary intensity and clarity Aboriginal elders coming to her and showing her practices that strongly enhanced her abilities as a midwife. This inspired her to collaboratively set up, through Blue Care, Queensland's first, partially state-funded, independent midwifery program.

Throughout this time, she had no luck in her search for her birth mother. But she carefully documented her experiences in her journal and drew prolifically the scenes that haunted her. This resulted in a remarkable series of paintings documenting and illustrating her stormy inner process. In 1995, Marianne had her first breakthrough, when Salvation Army Missing Persons Service discovered her grandmother and uncles living in Sydney, and subsequently her birth mother, living in New Zealand. However, her relatives did not want to have anything to do with her, and Marianne was devastated.

Finally, six months later, her birth mother reluctantly wrote to her. The letter was brief and brought unexpected validation for Marianne's experiences. It described her conception as a rape by an Italian man who spoke no English. At the time it happened, Marianne's mother was a teenager from a small town in far north Queensland. She was not only brutally traumatized by the rape, but also shamed and blamed by her parents. After unsuccessful attempts to arrange an abortion, she was sent to a home for unmarried girls.

Following Marianne's birth, a traumatic forceps delivery, her mother never saw or touched her again. She was put on a boat to New Zealand, where she did her best to forget her past and start anew. In her letter, she wished Marianne well and made no further attempts to contact her, in spite of numerous attempts on Marianne's part. However, this was not the end of Marianne's quest. Following this unexpected validation of the circumstances of her conception and birth, her experiences in Holotropic Breathwork continued with renewed intensity.

In one of her sessions, she identified experientially with a full-blood Aboriginal woman who was tied, raped, and beaten at the hands of two uniformed men on horseback. Her two children were taken away from her, and her legs were doused in petrol, set ablaze, and badly burnt. As her process continued, Marianne kept drawing and documenting these episodes in an attempt to maintain her sanity. One day, after a therapy session that again featured an indigenous theme, Marianne called at Mary Madden's suggestion, the directory assistance and made a long-distance phone call to New Zealand. She hoped to make phone contact with her birth mother, and this time her attempt was successful.

In the conversation that followed, Marianne's mother told her that her great-grandmother was a full-blood Aborigine, and she graphically described the sexual, emotional, physical, and spiritual abuse that had defined this woman's life. The mystery seemed to be unfolding at last, and Marianne's hopes were up. However, following this conversation, her birth mother withdrew again and refused further contact. In desperation, Marianne approached Link Up, an Aboriginal organization, to assist her to verify her indigenous status.

They could offer no support without her birth mother's permission. This was not forthcoming, and Marianne's frustration grew.

Marianne's adoptive parents had staunchly supported her through this process, and one day her father gave her a phone number he had discovered by chance. Marianne was able to make contact with Community and Personal Histories, an organization that was willing to investigate her case. Some months later, she received in the mail pages of documentation from 1895 to 1918, detailing the history of her great-grandmother, who was the illegitimate daughter of an elderly bachelor landowner in far north Queensland. He was seeking an exemption from the Aboriginal Protection Act so this half-caste child could be returned to care for him.

This man referred to having taken a full-blood Aboriginal woman as his mistress, which resulted in the conception of two half-caste children. There was also the police report concerning two officers on horseback and their ride in the early 1900s to capture "the gin and her children," who were subsequently sent to the "Nigger camp" and into service. Eventually, Marianne was able to confirm that her great-grandmother's feet were seriously burnt during this episode, just as she had experienced it in her breathwork session.

Marianne was referred to a Stolen Generations' counselor and found the work with him extraordinarily helpful and transformative. In June 2003, a representative of Link Up, an organization responsible for reuniting indigenous families from the Stolen Generations, flew with her to Sydney for a three-day reunion with her grandmother and uncle, Robbie. Words could never adequately express the emotion Marianne experienced as she walked into her grandmother's house. Her grandmother took her in her arms, cried, and turning to her son she said: "At last our baby is home." Marianne found out that when the Salvation Army had made contact with her grandmother years ago she had just suffered a stroke. As she recovered, she did not remember this episode and did not know where Marianne was and how to make contact with her. A deeply spiritual person, she had prayed daily for Marianne to find her way back.

Marianne's birth mother has limited contact with her family, and she still refuses to acknowledge her daughter. But the pain of that rejection is healing with the combined acceptance and love of Marianne's grandmother and uncle, Robbie, who wrote in a recent letter: "I was trying to think of why you have made such a difference in our lives. Then it hit me that you completed our family, when you arrived at your Grandma's door. It was as if finally the circle was closed. We love you dearly." Marianne's heroine's journey has come to an end, and she was finally able to find her home.

ANCESTRAL MEMORY OR PAST-LIFE EXPERIENCE?

The Story of Renata

I n the fourth example, the portrayed situations reach far back in history, to the beginning of the seventeenth century. This case also illustrates extremely well the conceptual challenges associated with the verification of the information involved. The protagonist in this story is Renata, a former client of mine, who came into treatment because of her cancer phobia, which was complicating her life. In her LSD therapy, she relived various traumatic experiences from her childhood and repeatedly dealt with the memory of her birth. In the advanced stage of her self-exploration, the nature of her sessions suddenly changed dramatically. What happened was very unusual and unprecedented.

Four of her LSD sessions brought up almost exclusively material from a specific historical period. She experienced a number of episodes that took place in Prague in the seventeenth century, which was a crucial period in Czech history. After the disastrous battle of White Mountain in 1621, which marked the beginning of the Thirty Years' War in Europe, the country ceased to exist as an independent kingdom and came under the hegemony of the Hapsburg dynasty. In an effort to destroy the feelings of national pride and to defeat the forces of resistance, the Hapsburgs sent out mercenaries to capture the country's most powerful noblemen. Twenty-seven prominent aristocrats were arrested and beheaded in a public execution on a scaffold erected in the Old Town Square in Prague.

During her historical sessions, Renata had an unusual variety of images and insights concerning the architecture of the experienced period and typical garments and costumes, as well as weapons and various utensils used in everyday life. She was also able to describe many of the complicated relationships existing at that time between the royal family and the vassals. Renata had never specifically studied this period of Czech history, nor was she interested in it. I had to go to the library and do historical research in order to confirm that the information Renata reported was accurate.

Many of Renata's experiences were related to various periods in the life of a young nobleman, one of the twenty-seven aristocrats beheaded by the Hapsburgs. In a dramatic sequence, she finally relived with powerful emotions and in considerable detail the actual events of the execution, including this nobleman's terminal anguish and agony. On many occasions, Renata experienced full identification with this individual. She was not able to figure out how these historical sequences were related to her present life, why they emerged in her therapy, and what they meant. After much reflection, Renata finally concluded that she must have relived events from the life of one of her ancestors. All this happened at an early stage of my psychedelic explorations, and I, admittedly, was not quite intellectually ready for this interpretation.

Trying to reach some understanding, I chose two different approaches. On one hand, I spent a considerable amount of time in an effort to verify the specific historical information involved and was increasingly impressed by its accuracy. On the other hand, I tried to use the Freudian method of free associations, treating Renata's story as if it were a dream. I hoped that I would be able to decipher it as a symbolic disguise for some childhood experiences or problems in her present life. No matter how hard I tried, the experiential sequences did not make much sense from a psychoanalytic point of view. When Renata's LSD experiences moved into new areas, I finally gave up, stopped thinking about this peculiar incident, and focused on other more recent and immediate conceptual challenges.

Two years later, when I was already in the United States, I received a long letter from Renata with the following unusual introduction: "Dear Dr. Grof, you will probably think that I am absolutely insane when I share with you the results of my recent private search." In the text that followed, Renata described how she happened to meet her father, whom she had not seen since her parents' divorce, when she was three years old. After a short discussion, her father invited her to have dinner with him, his second wife, and their children. After dinner, he told her that he wanted to share with her something that she might find interesting.

In World War II, the Nazis issued an order requesting all families in the occupied territories to present to German authorities their pedigrees demonstrating the absence of anyone of Jewish origin for the last five generations. This was a very serious issue because failure to prove the "purity" of the family lineage had catastrophic consequences for its members. While conducting this mandatory genealogical research, Renata's father became fascinated by this procedure. After he had completed the required five-generation pedigree for the authorities, he continued this quest because of his private interest.

He was able to trace back the history of his family more than three centuries, thanks to the meticulously kept archives of the European parish houses that had preserved birth records of all the people born in their district for untold generations. He was now able to show Renata the fruit of many years of his investigation, a carefully designed, complex pedigree of their family, indicating that they were descendants of one of the noblemen executed after the battle of White Mountain in the Old Town Square in Prague.

Renata was astonished by this unexpected confirmation of the information she had obtained in her LSD sessions. Having described this extraordinary episode, she expressed her firm belief that "highly emotionally charged memories could be imprinted in the genetic code and transmitted through centuries to future generations." Renata's letter ended with a triumphant "I told you so." She felt that this new, unexpected information provided by her father confirmed what she had suspected all along on the basis of the convincing nature of her experiences—that she had encountered an authentic ancestral memory. As I mentioned earlier, this was a conclusion I was at the time reluctant to accept.

After my initial astonishment concerning this most unusual coincidence, I discovered a rather serious logical inconsistency in Renata's account. One of the experiences she had had in her historical LSD sessions involved the execution of the young nobleman, including all the emotions associated with it. In the seventeenth century, long before the revolutionary breakthroughs of modern medicine, a dead person was not able to procreate. Death would have destroyed all material channels through which any information about the life of the deceased could be transmitted to posterity.

As a result of this realization, the situation got even more complicated than it was before—"the plot got thicker." On the one hand, Renata's experience received a powerful independent validation from her father's genealogical research. On the other, there was no material substrate to account for the storage, transmission, and retrieval of the information involved. However, before we discard the information contained in Renata's story as supportive evidence for the authenticity of ancestral memories, several facts deserve serious consideration.

None of the remaining Czech patients, who had a total of over two thousand sessions, had ever even mentioned this historical period. In Renata's case, four consecutive LSD sessions contained, almost exclusively, historical sequences from this time. And the possibility that the convergence of Renata's inner quest and her father's genealogical research was a meaningless coincidence is so astronomical that it is difficult to take this alternative seriously. We are left with an extraordinary observation for which the current materialistic paradigm has no explanation. It is an example of the observations from modern consciousness research that have recently received the name "anomalous phenomena."

PART 4

HAVE WE LIVED BEFORE?

Reincarnation and the Akashic Record

Among the most interesting phenomena I have encountered in my research of holotropic states of consciousness have been without any doubt past-life experiences. They occurred with extraordinary frequency in psychedelic sessions of my clients, in sessions of Holotropic Breathwork, and in the course of spontaneous psychospiritual crises ("spiritual emergencies") of the people we have worked with. This happened in spite of the fact that I initially did not take the idea of reincarnation and karma seriously and saw it as a product of wishful fantasy of people who could not accept the grim reality of impermanence and death. In addition, these experiences were contrary to the beliefs of the culture I grew up in because the concept of reincarnation is rejected both by mainstream science and by the theologians of our dominant religion. It is one of the rare issues about which materialistic science and Christianity are in agreement.

For many people, the first encounter with past-life experiences happened at the time when they were reliving their birth; for others these episodes emerged independently. These experiences typically took the individuals involved to some emotionally highly charged situations that were taking place in various countries of the world and different historical periods, both recent and remote. The content of these experiences usually came as a complete surprise, and yet, they were accompanied with a strange feeling of déjà vu or déjà vecu: "This is not the first time this is happening to me; I have been here before. I experienced this in one of my previous lives." There also typically was a deep connection between the protagonists and events in these experiences and the individuals' present lives.

I soon became aware of the fact that past-life experiences had many characteristics that made it difficult to dismiss them as childish fantasies. They occurred on the same continuum with accurate memories from adolescence, childhood, infancy, birth, and intrauterine existence, phenomena that could often be reliably verified. They were also often intimately connected with the individuals' emotional and psychosomatic symptoms and with important issues and circumstances in their present lives. When karmic sequences emerged fully into consciousness, they frequently brought illuminating insights into various previously incomprehensible and puzzling aspects of everyday existence of the people involved.

This included a wide variety of psychological problems and interpersonal issues for which traditional schools of psychotherapy failed to provide adequate explanation. I also witnessed repeatedly that past-life experiences led not only to intellectual understanding, but also alleviation or complete disappearance of various difficult emotional and psychosomatic symptoms, as well as resolution of conflicts in relationships with other people. In addition, like the earlier mentioned ancestral, racial, and collective memories, past-life experiences often provided accurate insights into the time and culture involved. In many instances, the nature and quality of this information made it unlikely that these people could have acquired it through the conventional channels.

What follows are several examples of these fascinating experiences that either contained specific information that could later be verified or were associated with remarkable synchronicities. With the exception of the story of Karl, they describe experiences and events related to karma and reincarnation involving me and Christina. They helped me to appreciate the experiential power and convincing nature of these phenomena.

THE SIEGE OF
DÚN AN ÓIR

The Story of Karl

As impressive and convincing as the features of past-life experiences might be, the dream of every researcher in this area is to find cases in which some important aspects of these experiences can be verified by independent historical research. For me such a dream came true when Christina and I met Karl and had the privilege to facilitate his process of deep self-exploration and healing. Karl enrolled in one of our Esalen monthlong seminars after he had done some inner work in a renegade primal therapy group in Canada. It was one of the groups of people who had left the The Primal Institute in Los Angeles after serious disagreements with Arthur Janov.

In the course of primal therapy, these people started having various forms of transpersonal experiences, such as archetypal visions, identification with various animals, and past-life memories. Janov, who had no understanding of the transpersonal domain of the unconscious, was violently opposed to anything related to spirituality and interpreted these experiences as a "cop-out from primal pain." Many people who valued the technique of primal therapy, but could not stand the straitjacket of Janov's conceptual prejudice, left his institute and formed their own groups.

Karl had begun his self-exploration as a member of such a group. After some time, his inner process reached the perinatal level. As he was reliving various aspects of his biological birth, he started experiencing fragments of dramatic scenes that seemed to be happening in another century and in a foreign country. They involved powerful emotions and physical feelings and seemed to have deep and intimate connection with his life; yet none of them made any sense in terms of his present biography. He had visions of tunnels, underground storage spaces, military barracks, thick walls, and ramparts, which all seemed to be parts of a fortress situated on a rock overlooking an ocean shore. This was interspersed with images of soldiers in a variety of situations. He felt puzzled because the soldiers seemed to be Spanish, but the scenery looked more like Scotland or Ireland.

This was the time when Karl came to our Esalen workshop and shifted from primal therapy to Holotropic Breathwork. As the process continued, the scenes were becoming more dramatic and involved; many of them represented fierce combat and bloody slaughter. Although surrounded by soldiers, Karl experienced himself as a priest and at one point had a very moving vision that involved a Bible and a cross. At this point, he saw a seal ring on his hand and could clearly recognize the initials that it bore.

Being a talented artist, he decided to document this strange process, although he did not understand it at the time. He produced a series of drawings and very powerful and impulsive finger paintings. Some of these depicted different parts of the fortress, others scenes of slaughter, and a few of them Karl's own experiences, including being gored by a sword of a British soldier, thrown over the ramparts of the fortress, and dying on the shore. Among these pictures was a drawing of his hand with the seal ring engraved with the initials of the priest's name.

As he was recovering bits and pieces of this story, Karl was finding more and more meaningful connections between various aspects of its plot and his present life. He started suspecting that the drama of the Spanish priest in the remote past might be the source of many of his own emotional and psychosomatic symptoms, as well as interpersonal problems. A turning point came when Karl suddenly decided on impulse to spend his holiday in Ireland. After his return, when he was looking at the slides he had shot on Ireland's western coast, he realized that he had taken eleven consecutive pictures of exactly the same scenery. This surprised him because he did not remember having done it, and the view he had chosen did not seem particularly interesting.

Being a pragmatic man, he took a very rational and analytic approach to this quizzical situation. He looked at the map and reconstructed where he stood at the time and in which direction he was shooting. He discovered that the place that attracted his attention was the ruin of an old fortress called Dún an Óir, or Forte de Oro (Golden Fortress). From the distance he was shooting, it was barely visible with the naked eye, and he had to look hard to find it in the slide. Suspecting a connection between his strange behavior and his experiences from primal therapy and Holotropic Breathwork, Karl decided to study the history of Dún an Óir, looking for any possible clues.

He discovered, to his enormous surprise, that in 1580, a small invasion force of Spanish soldiers landed in the nearby Smerwick Harbor to assist the Irish in the Desmond Rebellion. After being joined by some Irish soldiers they numbered about 600. They managed to garrison themselves within the defenses of the fort at Dún an Óir, before they were surrounded and besieged by a larger English force commanded by Lord Grey. Walter Raleigh, who accompanied Lord Grey, played the role of mediator in this conflict and negotiated with the Spaniards. He promised them free egress from the fortress if they opened the gate and surrendered to the British. The Spaniards agreed to accept this condition and surrendered, but the British did not hold their promise. Once inside the fortress, they slaughtered mercilessly all the Spaniards and threw their bodies over the ramparts into the ocean and on the beach.

In spite of this absolutely astonishing confirmation of the story that he laboriously reconstructed in his inner exploration, Karl was not satisfied. He continued his library research until he discovered a special document about the battle of Dún an Óir. There he found that a priest accompanied the Spanish soldiers and was killed together with them. The initials of the name of the priest were identical to those that Karl had seen in his vision of the seal ring and had depicted in one of his drawings.

The Karmic Triangle

Time Travel to Ancient Egypt

In 1967, at the time of my immigration to the United States, I was struggling with the problem of past incarnation experiences. I had witnessed them repeatedly in my clients and was impressed and puzzled by the amount and quality of information that was revealed when they surfaced into consciousness. This information involved social structure, ritual and spiritual life, as well as costumes, weapons, and battle strategies of the cultures and historical periods that formed the context of these experiences. The knowledge that these karmic episodes provided by far transcended the intellectual level and educational background of my clients.

I was also deeply impressed by the connections between certain important aspects of these karmic experiences and my clients' everyday lives—their emotional and psychosomatic problems, difficulties in interpersonal relationships, strange and unexplainable idiosyncrasies or attractions, and reactions to certain people and situations. Even more remarkable was the therapeutic impact that such karmic experiences had when they were fully relived and integrated.

In spite of all this impressive evidence, I found it impossible to accept that we were dealing here with an authentic phenomenon. The conceptual barrier involved was of a qualitatively different level than the one that stood in the way of accepting the capacity of the brain of the newborn to register the ordeal of birth. After all, the brain of the newborn, myelinized or not, is a very complex material system. But the possibility of retrieving memories of entire scenes from times preceding conception, often by centuries, seemed simply too preposterous.

If we subscribe to the materialistic worldview of Western science, ancestral and racial memories would have to be transmitted by the sperm and the ovum, the only material connection we have to events preceding our conception. The carrier of this information would have to be the chromosomes and, more specifically, the DNA. And in the case of past-life memories even this faint material bridge to the past is missing because they cross not only ancestral, but often even racial, hereditary lines. For example, it is not uncommon for Caucasians to have past-life experiences as black Africans, native Americans, or Asians, and vice versa.

It took some powerful personal experiences for me to change my attitude toward past-life memories. This area opened up for me experientially in an LSD session that I had shortly after my arrival in the United States. What happened in this session and around it convinced me that past-life experiences represented authentic phenomena and could not be dismissed as derivatives of events in our everyday life. This extraordinary experience was associated, among others, with remarkable synchronicities that involved other people, who were not present in my session and were not aware that I was having one.

My immigration to the United States, in March 1967, brought about radical changes in my personal, professional, political, and cultural environment. I arrived in Baltimore with some fifty pounds of my personal belongings. Over half of the total content of my luggage was the documentation of my psychedelic research in Prague, and the rest was clothing and some other personal items. This was all that was left of my old life in Europe. It was the end of one large chapter of my life and a new beginning on many different levels. While I thoroughly enjoyed the dedicated and enthusiastic team of my professional colleagues at Spring Grove, the undreamed-of freedom of expression, and all the novel things I was discovering in the world around me, I did not have much success in creating a satisfactory personal life.

All the women in my social environment who were of appropriate age for me and shared my interests seemed to be married or otherwise committed. It was a frustrating situation for me because I was in a stage of my life when I was experiencing a strong need for partnership and felt ready for commitment. My friends and colleagues at Spring Grove seemed to be even more concerned about this situation than I was myself and exerted great effort to remedy it. They searched for potential partners for me and kept inviting them for various social occasions. This resulted in a few frustrating and somewhat awkward situations, but did not bear any fruit. And then this situation suddenly took an unexpected and very radical turn.

A difficult relationship of a fellow therapist, Seymour, had abruptly ended, and my friends invited his ex-girlfriend, Monica, and me for dinner. When Monica and I first met, I immediately felt a strong attraction to her and had a sense of instant deep connection. It did not take very long, and I was deeply in love with her. She was of European origin like me, single, beautiful, and bright. Her unusual charm, wit, and facility with words made her quickly the center of attention at every party she attended. I felt rapidly drawn into the relationship and was unable to be objective and realistic about it.

I did not see any problem in the fact that Monica was considerably younger than I. I also chose to ignore the stories about her extremely traumatic childhood and tumultuous interpersonal history, which I would have normally seen as serious warning signs. I was somehow able to reassure myself that all these were insignificant details, nothing that we would not be able to work through and overcome. Had I been able to be more objective and analytic under the circumstances, I would have recognized that I had met what C. G. Jung called an *anima figure*. Monica and I started dating and had a passionate and unusually stormy relationship.

Monica's moods and behavior seemed to change from one day to another, or even from hour to hour. Waves of intense affection toward me alternated with episodes of aloofness, evasiveness, and withdrawal. The situation seemed to be further complicated by two unusual circumstances. Since my arrival in Baltimore, I lived in a small studio apartment that had been previously rented by Monica's ex-boyfriend, Seymour. When I moved in, I even bought all of Seymour's old furniture and his TV set. Monica used to visit him in this apartment when they were dating and was now coming to exactly the same setting to see a different man. In addition, Monica's brother Wolfgang hated me from the very first time we had met. He and Monica had an unusually intense relationship that seemed to have distinct incestuous features. Wolfgang was violently opposed to my relationship with Monica and treated me like a rival.

I was very committed and determined to make the relationship work, but nothing I was able to do had any influence on the crazy-making roller-coaster ride we seemed to be taking together. I felt like I was alternately exposed to hot and cold showers. I found it very frustrating but, at the same time, my attraction to Monica had a strange magnetic quality, and I was unable to terminate this confusing and unfulfilling relationship.

I desperately needed some insight into the baffling dynamic in which I was caught. As I mentioned earlier, Maryland Psychiatric Research Center, where I worked at the time, had a program offering mental health professionals the opportunity to have up to three high-dose psychedelic sessions for training purposes, and the members of our therapeutic team were eligible for this program. As the difficulties in my relationship with Monica were reaching their peak, I decided to apply for an LSD session to reach some clarity in this confusing situation.

In the middle of my session I suddenly had a vision of a dark rock of irregular shape that looked like a giant meteorite and seemed extremely ancient. The sky opened up, and a lightning bolt of immense intensity hit its surface and started to burn into it some mysterious, arcane symbols. Once these strange hieroglyphs were carved into the surface of the rock, they continued to burn and emit blinding incandescent light. Although I was unable to decipher the hieroglyphs and read them, I sensed that they were sacred, and I could somehow understand the message they were conveying. They revealed to me that I had had a long series of lives preceding this one and that, according to the law of karma, I was responsible for my actions in these lives, although I could not remember them.

At first, I tried to refuse responsibility for things of which I did not have any memory, but was not able to resist the enormous psychological pressure forcing me to surrender and comply. Finally, I had to accept what clearly was an ancient universal law against which there was no recourse. Once I yielded, I found myself holding Monica in my arms, just as I remembered holding her on the previous weekend. We were floating in air in an archetypal pit of immense size, slowly descending in an extended spiral. I felt instinctively that this was the Abyss of Ages and that we were traveling back in time.

The descent took an eternity, and it seemed it would never end. Finally, we reached the bottom of the pit. Monica disappeared from my arms, and I found myself walking in a hall of an ancient Egyptian palace, dressed in ornate clothes. All around me on the walls were beautiful bas-reliefs accompanied by carved hieroglyphs. I could understand their meaning as clearly as I would understand the message of the posters pasted on a Baltimore billboard. On the other side of the large hall, I saw a figure who was slowly approaching me. I understood intuitively that I was the son of an aristocratic Egyptian family and that the man approaching me was my brother in that lifetime.

As the figure came closer, I recognized that it was Wolfgang. He stopped about ten feet from me and looked at me with immense hatred. I realized that in this Egyptian incarnation Wolfgang, Monica, and I were siblings. I was the firstborn and, as such, I had married Monica and received many other privileges that came with that status. Wolfgang felt cheated and experienced agonizing jealousy and strong hatred toward me. I saw clearly that this was the basis of a destructive karmic pattern that then repeated itself in many variations throughout ages.

I stood in the hall facing Wolfgang and feeling his deep hatred toward me. In an attempt to resolve this painful situation, I tried to send him a telepathic message. It was something like this: "I don't know in what form I am here or how I got here. I am a time traveler from the twentieth century, where I took a powerful mind-altering drug. I am very unhappy about the tension that exists between us, and I want to do anything to resolve it." I stretched my arms into a very open position and communicated to him in the same way: "Here I am, this is all I have! Please, do anything you need to do to liberate us from this bondage, to set both of us free!"

Wolfgang seemed very excited about my offer and accepted it. His hatred seemed to take the form of two intense rays of energy resembling powerful laser beams that burned my body and caused me extreme pain. After what seemed an extremely long time of excruciating torture, the beams gradually lost their power and eventually completely faded. Wolfgang and the hall disappeared, and I found myself holding Monica again in my arms, feeling that a great weight had been lifted from my shoulders.

We ascended through the same Abyss of Ages, this time moving forward in time. The walls of this archetypal pit were opening into scenes from different historical periods showing Monica, Wolfgang, and me in many previous lifetimes. All of them depicted difficult and destructive triangular situations in which we seriously hurt each other. It seemed that a strong wind, a "karmic hurricane," was blowing through centuries, dissipating the suffering involved in these situations and releasing the three of us from a fatal, painful bondage. When this sequence ended and I returned fully into the present, I was in a state of indescribable bliss and ecstatic rapture. I felt that, even if I would not achieve anything else for the rest of my days, my life had been productive and successful. In the state I was in, resolution and release from one powerful karmic pattern seemed a sufficient accomplishment for one lifetime!

Monica's presence in my experience was so intense that I was convinced she had to feel the impact of what was happening with me. When we saw each other the following week, I decided to find out what she had experienced on the afternoon when I had the session. At first, I deliberately did not tell her anything about my session, trying to avoid any possibility of suggestion. I simply asked her what she did between 4:00 and 4:30 on the day I was experiencing the Egyptian karmic sequence in my LSD session.

"Strange that you should ask," she answered. "It was probably the worst time of my entire life!" She then proceeded to describe a dramatic showdown she had had with her superior that ended by her storming out of the office. She was sure she had lost her job, felt desperate, and ended up in a nearby bar drinking heavily. At one point, the door of the bar opened up, and a man walked in. Monica recognized Robert, a man with whom she had had a sexual relationship at the time she met me. Robert was very rich and gave her many expensive gifts, including a new car and a horse.

Unbeknownst to me, Monica had continued the relationship with Robert after we started dating, not being able to make a choice between the two of us. When she now saw Robert entering the bar, she walked to him and wanted to give him a hug and a kiss. Robert made an evasive maneuver and shook her hand instead. Monica noticed that he was accompanied by an elegant woman. Clearly uncomfortable, Robert introduced her to Monica; it happened to be his wife. For Monica this was a shock because during their entire relationship Robert had claimed that he was single.

At this point, Monica felt that the ground disappeared from under her feet. She left the bar and ran to the parking lot to her Mustang, the car that Robert had given her. She got in and, drunk and in heavy rain, she raced down the beltway, reaching speeds of over ninety miles an hour. Too much had happened that day, and nothing seemed to matter any more; she was determined to end it all. It turned out that exactly at the time when I reached the resolution of the karmic pattern in my LSD session, an image of me emerged in Monica's mind. She started thinking about me and about our relationship. Realizing that she still had somebody in her life she could rely on, she calmed down. She slowed down the car, drove it off the beltway, and parked it at the curbside. When she sobered up to the point that she could drive safely, she returned home and went to bed.

The day after this discussion with Monica, I received a phone call from Wolfgang, who asked for an appointment with me. This was an absolutely unexpected and surprising development because Wolfgang had never called me before, let alone asked for a meeting. When he arrived, he told me that he came to see me about a very intimate and embarrassing matter. It was a problem that is called in psychoanalysis the prostitute-Madonna complex. He had had a number of casual and superficial sexual relationships in his life, including many one-night stands, and never had had any problems developing and maintaining erection. Now he felt that he had found the woman of his dreams and, for the first time in his life, was deeply in love. However, he was unable to have sex with her and experienced repeated, painful failures.

Wolfgang was desperate and afraid that he would lose this relationship unless he did something about his impotence. He told me that he was too embarrassed to talk about his problem with a stranger. He thought about discussing the issue with me, but had rejected the idea because of his strong negative feelings toward me. But then his attitude toward me suddenly changed radically. His hatred dissolved as if by magic, and he decided to call me and seek help. When I asked him when this had happened, I found out that it exactly coincided with the time when I had completed the reliving of the Egyptian sequence.

A few weeks later, I retrieved the missing piece of the Egyptian story. I did a hypnotic session with my friend Pauline McCririck, a psychoanalyst from London. As soon as I entered the trance, I found myself lying in the sand of a hot, sun-scorched desert. I felt agonizing pain in my belly, and my entire body was in spasms. I knew I had been poisoned and was going to die. I realized from the context that the only people who could have poisoned me had to be my sister and her lover. According to the Egyptian law, she had to marry me as her oldest brother, but her affection belonged to another man.

He was a very handsome, athletic man, by profession a caretaker of wild animals in the royal palace. He thus belonged to a different social class, and his relationship with my sister was illicit according to the ancient Egyptian law. I had found out about their affair and had attempted to interfere with their relationship. This did not leave them any other alternative than to assassinate me. At one point, I had a vision of my sister's Egyptian lover and recognized that he was in the present lifetime Seymour, Monica's ex-lover. It seemed to make a lot of sense because Seymour was extremely athletic and spent several hours a day weight-lifting and bench-pressing. With his enormous hypertrophic muscles, he looked more like a professional body builder than a psychologist.

As I was dying in extreme pain, the realization that I had been betrayed and poisoned brought with it blind, consuming anger. I died alone in the desert with my entire being filled with hatred. The reliving of this situation brought a very interesting insight. I seemed to remember that in my Egyptian lifetime, I was actively involved in the mysteries of Isis and Osiris and knew their secrets. I felt that the poison and the hatred toward my sister and her lover intoxicated my mind and obscured everything else, including my esoteric knowledge. This made it impossible for me to take advantage of the secret teachings at the time of my death. For the same reason, my connection with this arcane knowledge was brutally severed.

I suddenly saw that much of my present life had been dedicated to an unrelenting search for these lost teachings. I remembered how excited I had been every time I had come across some information that was directly or indirectly related to this area—any information about Egyptian culture and history, any reference to ancient mysteries, and any allusion to mystical experiences and esoteric knowledge. This quest culminated when I discovered LSD and had my first experience of cosmic consciousness. In the light of this insight, my work with psychedelics revolving around psychospiritual death and rebirth seemed to be a rediscovery and modern reformulation of the processes involved in the ancient mysteries.

In a subsequent meditation, I was unexpectedly flooded with a fugue of images representing highlights of my experiences with Monica and Wolfgang, some of them from real life, others from my sessions. The intensity and speed of this review rapidly increased until it reached an explosive climax. It felt as if a giant bubble had burst and my head was suddenly clear. In an instant, I felt a deep sense of resolution and peace. I knew that the karmic pattern was now fully resolved. Monica and I remained friends for the rest of my stay in Baltimore. The tension and chaos disappeared from our interactions, and neither of us felt any compulsion to continue an intimate relationship. We both understood that we were not meant to be partners in our present lifetime.

IN THE CATACOMBS OF
PECHORSKAYA LAVRA

Past Life in Czarist Russia

Since my early childhood, as far as my memory goes, I have been fascinated by foreign countries, their geography, people, and culture. A deep craving to travel abroad and explore the world has always been an essential part of my personality. But in my young years, it seemed that I was born at the wrong time and in the wrong place to harbor such a passion. The German occupation of Czechoslovakia from 1939 to 1945 and the specter of Nazism that it brought along rendered a severe blow to my childhood dreams of worldwide travel. After the defeat of Germany by the Allies, our country enjoyed a short period of liberty, including the freedom of movement for its citizens. In the summer of 1947, my brother and I were able to spend five weeks in the small fishing village of Trpanj, on the Peljesac Peninsula in Yugoslavia.

The beauty of the Adriatic coast and the adjacent mountain range made a deep impression on me and whetted my appetite for more extensive travels in the future. However, my enthusiasm and my hope were short-lived. The Communist takeover in February 1948, which put Czechoslovakia under political control of the Soviet Union, once again sealed the borders of our country. In the following decade, the Eastern European satellites of the Soviet Union were gradually opened for travel but, for many years, the Soviet Union itself remained closed for Czech tourists.

In 1959, I had the opportunity to spend my summer vacation in Romania, most of this time in Mamaia. This international resort, the largest one on the

Black Sea, was famous for its wide beaches of extremely fine sand extending over more than five miles, low precipitation, cloudless sky, and pleasant temperature of the ocean water. Taking advantage of these ideal conditions, I was spending many hours every day on the beach. Here I met a Russian epidemiologist, docent at the University of Kiev, who was vacationing in Mamaia with his family. They drove from Kiev to Mamaia in their new Moskvitch, the reward for many years of waiting and even more years of a Spartan lifestyle and painstaking saving.

In our discussions, it soon became clear that my new friends hated the Soviet regime as much as I did. Our daily contact on the beach was for me an opportunity to practice my Russian and to get some inside information about life in the Soviet Union. We covered a very broad range of topics, but one of them made a particularly profound impression on me. Talking about Kiev's historical sites, my Russian friends mentioned Pechorskaya Lavra, a Russian Orthodox monastery situated inside a large mountain. This monastery consisted of an intricate system of catacombs and grottoes that turned the mountain's interior into a complex underground labyrinth resembling a giant Swiss cheese. The corridors were lined with open coffins containing the bodies of all the monks who had lived there over the centuries. Constant draft and favorable climactic condition preserved them for posterity by causing dry mummification.

Pechorskaya Lavra was originally part of a large religious complex that also included Uspensky Sobor, a magnificent Russian Orthodox temple, a candle-producing factory, an enterprise for large-scale production of icons, and other constituents. My friends told me that the Russian Bolsheviks, carrying a determined crusade against religion, considered by the Marxists "opium of the masses," were well aware of the significance this spiritual center had for the Ukrainian people. However, they refrained from brutal interventions against the monks and nuns and reluctantly opted for tolerance because they were afraid of a popular uprising.

The relationship between the Ukrainian people and the Soviet government was extremely tense from the very beginning. Since 1922, when Ukraine was annexed by the Soviet Union, the rebellion against Russian dominion left over from the Czarist times was further fueled by Soviet atrocities, including two manmade famines, the second instigated by Joseph Stalin and his henchman Lazar Kaganovich. The main goal of these artificial famines, resulting in the deaths of many millions of people, was to break the spirit of the Ukrainian farmers and to force them into collectivization, as well as to stifle the renaissance of Ukrainian culture.

The story of Pechorskaya Lavra fascinated me. As I was listening to my friends talking about it, I sensed waves of chill running up my spine, and my heart was beating faster. My reaction surprised me and baffled me; it was very unusual and atypical for me. It was clear to me that there had to be some deep, unconscious reason for the intensity of my emotions, and I started feeling a strong desire to visit Pechorskaya Lavra to find out what was behind it. Two years later, when the Soviet Union opened up for Czech visitors, I took part in one of the first tourist tours to Russia that included Kiev, Leningrad, and Moscow. In all the places that we visited, we were rigorously supervised by official Soviet Intourist guides and were ordered to stay in the group under all circumstances. Independent, individual sightseeing was strictly prohibited, and violations of the rules would have had serious political consequences.

The most important reason I had chosen this trip was to visit Kiev and see Pechorskaya Lavra. I was very disappointed to find out that this important historical site was not included in the itinerary of our Soviet trip. When I asked about it, the official answer was that Uspensky Sobor was destroyed by the Germans during World War II and there was nothing interesting to see there. I had heard a different story from my Russian friends in Mamaia. They claimed that the Uspensky Temple was filled with explosives by the Soviets before they withdrew from Kiev and that these were detonated by them after the Germans took over Kiev. The Soviets thus killed two birds with one stone: they destroyed the spiritual symbol of the Ukraine and turned the anger of the Ukrainians against the Germans.

But what happened to Uspensky Sobor was not very relevant for me and my personal quest. My primary interest was in Pechorskaya Lavra and its catacombs. And from what I knew, Pechorskaya Lavra was still there; it had survived unscathed the Soviet rule, as well as the German invasion. Soon after our train arrived in Kiev, I started feeling very restless. My passionate desire to visit the mysterious underground cemetery turned into an irresistible obsession. This was again something very exceptional and uncharacteristic for me. I was known as a rational person who steered through life with a relatively even keel and without significant emotional upheavals.

Taking considerable political risk, I finally decided to split from the group and visit Pechorskaya Lavra on my own. Because I spoke at that time fluent Russian, I was able to get a cab and direct it to the monastery. I got inside and walked through the maze of catacombs lined by the mummies of all the monks who had lived and died there in all the centuries of the monastery's existence. Their skinny hands covered with brown parchment skin were joined as if in the last prayer. At times, the corridors would open into little caves decorated with powerful icons and lit with candles. Through clouds of heavy smoke of fragrant incense, I could see groups of monks with long beards involved in monotonous singing; they all seemed to be in deep trance and their chant sounded otherworldly and haunting.

I realized I was in a very unusual state of consciousness myself. I felt that I knew the place intimately, and walking through the complex dark catacombs, I could anticipate what was coming next. The sense of déjà vu and déjà vecu was overwhelming. At one point I saw one of the mummies whose hands were in a strange position and were not joined in prayer. I felt a wave of emotions that seemed to be coming from the depth of my being; I had never experienced anything even remotely similar. I ended my excursion and, very moved, I left the place in a hurry. There was no doubt in my mind that I was running away from the risk of an even more profound and disorganizing reaction. It was clear to me that my illicit visit to Pechorskaya Lavra and the adverse circumstances did not provide the ideal set and setting for deep psychological processing of my experience.

I returned to my hotel strangely dissatisfied and with a distinct sense that my visit was an incomplete Gestalt. On the other hand, I was very pleasantly surprised to find out that the Intourist guides had not noticed my absence, which was a small miracle in itself. I spent the New Year in Moscow enjoy-ing the cultural treasures of this city, and following the old advice "when in Rome, do as the Romans do," I imbibed impressive doses of excellent Starka, vodka made according to an old Czarist recipe. I had no more extraordinary experiences comparable to those in Pechorskaya Lavra. My most remarkable adventure in consciousness during the rest of my stay was a visit to Moscow's famous attraction—a complex of open-air swimming pools where one could swim in hot water and dive into it from the top of towers enveloped in freezing cold reaching 30 degrees below zero Celsius.

After my return from Russia, I kept replaying and reviewing the Kiev epi-sode in my memory, trying to understand the strange emotions that it evoked in me. However, my preoccupation with this peculiar intermezzo in my life did not last very long. I became deeply immersed in my LSD research at the Psychiatric Research Institute in Prague, running two psychedelic sessions a day and trying to make sense of what I was finding. I was encountering so many challenging and paradigm-breaking experiences and observations every day that it was easy to forget my Russian adventure. However, the story had an unexpected continuation many years later, after I had left Czechoslovakia and was working at the Maryland Psychiatric Research Center in Baltimore.

The director of the center, Dr. Albert Kurland, invited for a four-week visit Joan Grant and Dennys Kelsey, a European couple known for their interesting use of hypnotic therapy. Joan was a French woman who had an extraordi-nary ability to put herself into an autohypnotic trance and experience episodes from other times and countries that had the quality of past-life memories. She had published a number of books based on her reconstructions of entire lifetimes, such as *The Winged Pharaoh*, *Life As Carola*, and *So Moses Was Born*. Dennys was a British psychiatrist, trained as a hypnotist. In their work togeth-er, Dennys asked hypnotized clients to go as far as they had to go to find the source of the problems they brought into therapy. Joan had an extraordinary ability to tune into the experiences of the clients and help them to resolve their problems. Frequently, the source of the clients' emotional and psychosomatic symptoms appeared to be in past-life episodes. The Kelseys therefore chose for their joint publication, in which they described their work, the title *Many Lifetimes* (Grant and Kelsey 1967).

During the time the Kelseys stayed at the center, all the staff members had the opportunity to experience their work in personal sessions. The problem I wanted to work on was a conflict between sensuality and spirituality I experienced at that time. Generally, I was excited about life and was able to enjoy with great zest the various pleasures that human existence has to offer. However, occasionally, I had a strong impulse to withdraw from the world, find a remote ashram, and dedicate my life entirely to spiritual practice. Dennys hypnotized me and asked me to go back in time to find where this problem started.

As soon as I entered the hypnotic trance, I experienced myself as a young Russian boy standing in a large garden and looking at a palatial house. I knew that I was in Russia and was the son of an aristocratic family. I heard Joan's voice coming as if from a great distance. In a gentle but assertive tone of voice, she kept repeating the sentence: "Look at the balcony!" I did what she was asking me to do, without wondering how she knew that I was looking at a house and that this house had a balcony. I took a close look at the balcony and noticed an old woman with crippled and contorted fingers sitting in a rocking chair. I knew instinctively that it was my grandmother and felt a strong wave of love and compassion for her.

Then the scene changed, and I found myself walking on a road in a nearby village. I remembered that I had come here on numerous occasions. The simple but colorful peasant world of the muzhiks represented for me an exciting escape from the rigid and boring life of my family. The roads of the village were covered with mud and puddles, and the smell of dung permeated the air. The houses were covered with ruffled thatched roofs, and people walked around dressed in dirty rags, but the place was pulsing with life.

I walked into a dark and primitive workshop of a blacksmith. He stood there in front of a glowing furnace, a giant and muscular man, half-naked and covered with curly black hair. With powerful blows of a heavy hammer, he was molding a red-hot piece of iron lying on the anvil. I suddenly remembered the scene from the first act of Wagner's *Siegfried*, where Siegfried forges Nothung, the broken sword given by Wotan to his father, Sigmund. Watching this scene and listening to the powerful music, in which Wagner masterfully imitated all the sounds associated with forging, had always had a strong impact on me. It made my right eye burn, twitch uncontrollably, and overflow with tears. All of a sudden, the same thing happened to me, only incomparably stronger. I felt a sharp pain in my right eye, the right side of my face went into a spasm, and a stream of tears poured down my cheek.

Unlike on previous occasions, this time I understood where my reaction was coming from. As I stared at the blacksmith, transfixed with fascination, a piece of hot iron hit my face and eye and caused severe burns. Some emotionally very painful scenes followed. I relived my mother's horror when she saw my face, burnt beyond recognition, and her subsequent withdrawal and avoidance. I felt again the agony I had experienced as a ghastly, disfigured youngster during the years of puberty, tortured by unfulfilled sexual longing and hurt by repeated rejections. I saw that after realizing there was no place for me in the secular world, I escaped in utter despair and despondence into monastic life. Replacing the shame and humiliation of forced celibacy with the false pride of renunciation, I was ordained as a monk in Pechorskaya Lavra.

As I was consciously connecting with the memory of my life in this monastery, my hands went into a severe spasm. I realized that, during the decades spent in the darkness of the catacombs, my fingers on both hands had become severely disfigured. Was it arthritis caused by unfavorable living conditions or a hysterical reaction of a neurotic, reflecting profound dissatisfaction with life? Is it possible that I used as a model for this psychosomatic symptom the organic disease afflicting the hands of my beloved grandmother?

The last scene of my hypnotic regression involved my death. It ended a life that was full of misery and could have been experienced as liberation, as release from the prison of an irreparably damaged body. But an unexpected complication interfered with my capacity to find peace and reconciliation in my final hour. In Pechorskaya Lavra, it was customary to place the bodies of the deceased in open coffins lining the walls of the catacombs and join their hands in a praying position. It was a symbolic expression of a successful closure of a well-lived life dedicated to God.

But my crippled hands, transformed by some pathological process into ugly deformed claws, could not be linked together in a symbolic blessing gesture indicating successful closure of my monastic life. I started to cry, overwhelmed by a mixture of anger, grief, and self-pity. I hated the life in the monastery and envied the fortunate people with intact, beautiful bodies enjoying the world outside. My stay there was not the result of free choice; I withdrew from the world, running away from shame, rejection, and humiliation. And the inability to find a formal closure on what already was a life of indescribable misery was more than I could take. I was sobbing uncontrollably, my entire body was shaking, and tears were pouring from my eyes.

At this point, Joan intervened with incredible intuition. She started to massage my spastic and contorted hands with great gentleness and tenderness. When they finally relaxed, she brought them together in a praying gesture and held them in this position with her own cupped hands. I felt that I was rapidly reaching closure and reconciliation on my unhappy life spent in Pechorskaya Lavra. Enormous amounts of negative emotions that had accumulated in my psyche and body during many decades of existence as an involuntary monk were now on their way out. They were gradually replaced by feelings of deep relaxation, inner peace, bliss, and love. There was no doubt in my mind that what I just had experienced was profoundly healing. My subsequent life has confirmed this intuition. Since the session with the Kelseys, I have never felt any conflict between spirituality and the ability to enjoy what life has to offer—nature, work, food, sex, and many other things that "flesh is heir to."

I ended the session with a convincing feeling that I had reached a closure in this matter. However, several years later certain elements of this story surprisingly resurfaced in my life in the middle of a monthlong workshop Christina and I were conducting at the Esalen Institute in Big Sur, California. Dick Price, the co founder of Esalen and one of the early students of Fritz Perls, was invited to our workshop as guest faculty and was conducting a Gestalt session with Caroline, a young woman participating in the workshop. Before the onset of the session, Caroline described the unexplainable attraction she felt to Russia, her people and culture. She was learning Russian and liked to sing Russian songs.

The problem she brought into the session was the deleterious effect that the eleven years she had spent in a Catholic monastery had had on her sexual life, her vitality, and joie de vivre. As she was expressing with increasing intensity the enormous anger and grief she was feeling about the wasted years of her youth, I sensed more and more emotional resonance with her story. I immediately realized that this had something to do with the similarity between the story of her life and my past life experience in Russia. But the intensity of my response surprised me. My right eye started to burn, my right eyelid was uncontrollably twitching, and streams of tears were pouring down my face.

As I was watching Caroline through the veil of my tears, her face kept changing, until she looked like my mother from the Russian incarnation. I suddenly found myself back in the situation when I was brought home after the injury in the workshop of the blacksmith, and my mother was confronted with my disfiguration. Caroline was clearly processing emotions from her own current life, but in my perception she was part of my past life. She was my mother, heartbroken by what happened to me. The session ended, and I got up, deeply emotionally touched by what just had happened. Still a little shaken and puzzled, I walked to the door on the way to lunch; I opened it and froze in astonishment.

I was looking at an incredibly disfigured face of a young woman who was trying to enter the room just as I was leaving it. I was still so identified with my Russian past life that, for a moment, I felt I was looking into a mirror. It turned out that the visitor, who arrived at the scene with such astonishing timing, was Caroline's friend Victoria. She had read about the Maryland program of psychedelic therapy for cancer patients and had come to explore the possibility of having an LSD session. I sat down with her, and she shared with me her incredible story.

She was born as an identical twin, but her twin sister died shortly after delivery. Her parents later found to their great dismay that the hospital switched by mistake the labels and that the surviving girl carried the name of her dead sister. When she was four years old, Victoria fell out of the rear window of a moving car and came close to death. Shortly after recovery from this injury, she started showing symptoms of a very rare form of skin cancer. During the years that followed, the disease kept progressing, and she had multiple plastic surgeries, which transformed her complexion into a motley of deep scars and patches of skin grafts.

Victoria had a very strange theory concerning the nature of her mysterious affliction. She believed that in her near-death experience she connected with the beyond and assumed the identity of her dead twin sister, whose name she carried. This then found its expression in the progressive deterioration and decomposition of her body. She identified strongly with the ostracized Phantom of the Opera, suffered from deep depression, and was seriously considering suicide as a way out of her misery. None of the approaches she had tried so far had any favorable effect on her emotional condition. When she read about the power of psychedelic therapy, she decided to give it a try.

Christina and I agreed to be her guides in a high-dose LSD session. It was a very profound and meaningful experience for all of us. Victoria's experience covered a very broad range; she dealt with the pain and grief of her tragic predicament, revisited her childhood accident, and connected with the trauma of her birth and death of her twin sister. But she did not dwell very long on any of these themes and spent a large part of her session in a state of bliss and cosmic unity. This experience was so profound and extraordinary that she felt reconciled with the tragic course of her present life and with God.

During the time when she experienced this ecstatic rapture, she seemed to be surrounded by a halo of radiant energy. Although Christina and I were sitting close to her, we were unable to see her scars. Her face appeared to be absolutely smooth and beautiful. This was clearly on our part what we used to call "contact high" and, several hours later, our perception returned to normal. However, Victoria retained much of the new emotional attitude to life she had achieved in the session. For me, seeing Victoria's face healed and beautiful was the final closure on my Russian past-life adventure.

Although more than quarter of a century has elapsed since our session with Victoria, I have not encountered anything that would add another piece to this karmic jigsaw puzzle. On and off, I have returned in my mind to this extraordinary adventure, trying to understand the exact relationships between the past and present protagonists of this story. While the connection between my present identity and the unhappy monk seems pretty straightforward, the relationship between Victoria and the disfigured monk, Caroline and my Russian mother, the present me and Victoria, Victoria and Caroline, as well as the role of Christina in the story are more obscure and enigmatic.

Although my experiences described in this story, interwoven with extraordinary synchronicities, revealed the intricate invisible fabric underlying our everyday reality, enough of the deep dynamic remained hidden to protect the mysterious nature of the laws operating in the world of karma.

WHEN SPIRITUAL EXPERIENCES CAN BE DANGEROUS

Revisiting the Salem Witch-Hunt

In 1976, Christina and I lived for several months in the Round House at the Esalen Institute in Big Sur, California. It was a small, charming structure located by the creek dividing the Esalen property into two parts. The creek's busy waters rushed down from the mountain ridge and formed a large waterfall just before joining the Pacific Ocean. In front of this house was an opening in the ground spewing hot mineral waters into a little private pool. According to the local lore, the Esalen hot springs had their origin in an interconnected system of volcanic underground caverns that spread under much of California.

The rushing of the creek and the roaring of the waterfall represented a very powerful sensory input. However, even more impressive was the psychic power of this place. Over the years, we had invited to our Esalen workshops as guest faculty many people with extraordinary psychic abilities—clairvoyants, shamans from various parts of the world, members of the Spiritist Church, Indian yogis, and Tibetan masters. They all seemed to concur that the area around the Round House was a "power spot," a place endowed with extraordinary spiritual energy. Those trying to find some scientific explanation for the impact it had on people attributed it to a high concentration of negative ions due to the proximity to the ocean, the crashing waters of the waterfall, and to the presence of giant redwoods lining the creek on both sides.

In any case, whatever the reason for it, living in the Round House had a very powerful psychological impact on both of us. It was unusually easy to go into a meditative state; I found myself often slipping into a trance in which I forgot our geographic and historical coordinates and felt that our little eyrie was situated somewhere in an archetypal domain beyond time and space. Christina, who was at that time undergoing her spiritual emergency, experienced there an extraordinary intensification of her inner process. One weekend, her experiences reached such intensity that they resembled a psychedelic session.

After a period of intense anxiety and uncomfortable physical feelings, she had a powerful experience of what she felt was a memory from one of her past lives. She became an adolescent girl living in New England's Salem who had episodes of non-ordinary states of consciousness. Her fundamentalist Christian neighbors interpreted these episodes in their bigoted craze as possession by the devil. This brought an accusation of witchcraft; she was tried by two judges, dressed in ceremonial robes, and sentenced to death by drowning.

The past-life memory culminated in an experience of execution by drowning. Christina found herself being carried to a pond, tied to a board, and submerged, head first, under water. She managed to notice that the pond was surrounded by birch trees. As she was reliving her death by drowning, she was screaming, choking, and bringing out a lot of mucus, both from her mouth and nose. The amount of nasal secretions that she produced was extraordinary. That day, I was wearing a flannel shirt, and when Christina's experience ended, its front was completely impregnated by dried mucus.

While living in Hawaii, Christina had suffered from severe allergies and sinusitis. She had many medical examinations, tests, and treatments, including a series of injections for desensitization. Her doctors, frustrated by the failure of all therapeutic efforts, finally suggested a surgical procedure, involving scraping and cleaning the sinus cavities. Christina decided to refuse such a radical procedure and accepted her predicament. She discovered to her great surprise that, following the episode in which she relived the Salem trial and death, her sinus problems disappeared.

Fortunately, by this time, my belief in what I once had held as a "scientific worldview" that had been rigorously proven beyond any reasonable doubt was already seriously undermined by many similar observations. Without it, this episode would have left me in a serious intellectual crisis. There was certainly an element of cosmic humor in the fact that Christina's difficulties, which had resisted the concerted efforts of scientific experts, were resolved by reliving a karmic episode involving ignorance, religious fanaticism, and false accusation of witchcraft.

This episode had a very interesting sequel many years later, when Christina and I visited Boston to conduct a Holotropic Breathwork workshop. The workshop ended in the evening, and our flight back to San Francisco was not until late afternoon the next day. We thus had a good part of a day for sightseeing. We decided to call Marilyn Hershenson, a psychologist and dear friend of ours, who had been a member of Swami Muktananda's inner circle. We became very close in the early 1980s, when she coordinated with us a large international transpersonal conference in Bombay. Marilyn was very excited and offered that she would spend the day with us and drive us around.

When we discussed what would be a good place for lunch, Marilyn suggested her favorite restaurant, situated on the ocean near Salem. As we approached it, we found out that its name was Hawthorne Inn. This immediately brought to mind Nathaniel Hawthorne, his *Scarlet Letter*, and the topic of witchcraft. As we were having lunch, Christina recounted for Marilyn the story of her past-life memory involving Salem witch trials. Marilyn was astounded because she had relived a similar episode of her own in one of her meditations in the Siddha Yoga ashram.

Because we were only several miles from Salem, it suddenly seemed very appropriate to visit this town between lunch and our departure for California. As we were entering Salem, Christina asked Marilyn if there was a pond in Salem. Marilyn, who had spent her entire childhood in Salem, decisively denied it. But then she suddenly took a wrong turn, which was surprising because she knew the town well. This unplanned detour unexpectedly brought us to a pond on the shore of the ocean. It seemed like it was originally a bay that was separated from the body of water by an old stone dam.

Christina got out of the car, as if in a haze. She was looking around and seemed disappointed. "I don't see any birch trees," she said and started walking around the pond. "Where are you going?" we asked her. "There have to be some here," she said and continued walking. We parked the car and followed her. Finally, on the other side of the pond, Christina discovered a birch tree; its trunk was broken, and its crown was submerged in water. "You see, they were here," she said. "This must be the last one."

We returned to the car and decided to visit the courthouse where the trials had been held. On the way there, Christina told Marilyn that she recognized in the two judges in her past-life experience her ex-husband and father in her present life. "But there was only one judge at the trial," Marilyn object-ed. "There were *two judges!*" Christina said assertively. When we came to the courthouse, we found out it was closed. But by the front door was a large tab-let, describing the trials. It confirmed Christina's experience that there were two judges involved in the Salem trials.

Before we returned to the car, I bought in a gift shop a little illustrated booklet on Salem that included the story of the witchcraft trials. As Marilyn was driving us to the airport, I was reading aloud selected passages from this booklet. We found out that the girls who were accused of witchcraft had spent much time with the slave servant Tituba, who was accused of being the link to the devil. Tituba was an Indian from an Arawak village in South America, where she was captured as a child, taken to Barbados as a captive, and sold into slavery. We concluded that Tituba was probably teaching them some shamanic techniques that were misun-derstood and misinterpreted by ignorant neighbors as work of the devil.

The most interesting information I found in the guidebook was that Old Salem, where many of the historical events had happened, was currently called Danvers. That came as a shock to us. Danvers was the place where in 1978 we held a large conference of the International Transpersonal Association (ITA). It was a conference in which we presented for the first time our concept of "spiritual emergency," implying that many episodes of non-ordinary states of consciousness that mainstream psychiatrists diagnose as psychoses and often treat with drastic methods, such as insulin coma and electroshock, are actually psychospiritual crises.

In our lecture in Danvers, we suggested that properly understood and sup-ported, these crises of spiritual opening can actually be healing, transformative, and even evolutionary. We gave the talk in a hall from which one could see, on the other side of the valley, an old-time psychiatric hospital that had one of the worst reputations in the country. They were still using shock methods, which bore great similarity to the practices of the Inquisition and similar witch hunts. We were stunned by this incredible synchronicity. Of all the possible locations, we presented our modern plea for a radical change of attitude toward non-ordinary states of consciousness in a place that, unbeknownst to Christina, was the site of her past-life memory. And her suffering and death in this karmic episode were caused by misunderstanding and misinterpretation of non-ordinary states of consciousness.

Immersed in this drama, we arrived at the airport at the last minute. We ran to the gate, and the door of the airplane closed behind us as soon as we were inside. We sank into our seats, fastened the seatbelts, and started to discuss and process the extraordinary events of the day. As soon as we were in the air, the stewardess from the first class appeared in the economy class, carrying a tray with glasses of white and red wine.

I could not believe my eyes. She had very dark skin, and all around her head was a large corona of long unkempt dreadlocks sticking in all directions. I could not believe that she had passed the scrutiny of her superiors, who are usually meticulous about their personnel's appearance. "Here is Tituba, your Barbados maid," I jokingly said to Christina. The hostess approached us and gave Christina a very long and meaningful look. "We have some wine left over from the first class," she said. "Would you like some?" And pausing a little, she added with a very serious tone in her voice, as if her question was one of great importance: "Would you like *white* or *red*?"

We each took a glass of wine and were pondering on yet another strange synchronicity. The stewardess appeared again, this time carrying a tray with carnations. She smiled at us and asked: "We have also some flowers left. Would you like some?" And, presenting the tray to Christina, she asked with the same serious tone of voice: "Would you like a *red* one, or a *white* one?" Christina hesitated for a while and then she chose the white one. Later, she told me that, in the context of everything that had happened that day, this simple choice seemed to be loaded with great karmic significance. Choosing the white carnation seemed like a successful closure of this dramatic episode of her life.

The existence of past-life experiences with all their remarkable characteristics is an unquestionable fact that can be verified by any serious researcher who is sufficiently open-minded and interested to check the evidence. It is also clear that there is no plausible explanation for these phenomena within the conceptual framework of mainstream psychiatry and psychology. While all these impressive facts do not necessarily constitute a definitive "proof" that we survive death and reincarnate as the same separate unit of consciousness, or the same individual soul, they represent a formidable conceptual challenge for traditional science, and they have a paradigm-breaking potential. Having observed hundreds of past-life experiences and experienced many of them myself, I have to agree with Chris Bache that "the evidence in this area is so rich and extraordinary that scientists who do not think the problem of reincarnation deserves serious study are either uninformed or boneheaded" (Bache 1988). ·

PART 5

ESP AND BEYOND

Exploring the World of the Paranormal

The stories in this section of the book describe events and experiences that involve phenomena known as paranormal, psychic, or psi. Systematic scientific research of psychic phenomena has been conducted primarily by parapsychologists, although various forms of such research have also been described in the literature of other disciplines, such as anthropology and comparative religion. Throughout the twentieth century, parapsychology was the subject of heated controversy because it specializes in the research of extrasensory perception (ESP) and other abilities, events, and processes that cannot be explained by existing scientific theories.

Traditional scientists consider psychic phenomena impossible because they imply transfer of information or even influence on material processes without the mediation of known channels and energies. The common denominator of the experiences and events that belong to this category is that they transcend the usual limitations of space and time. Psychic phenomena can manifest under ordinary circumstances and do not necessarily require a change in consciousness. However, holotropic states greatly increase their incidence.

To create a context for the narratives of this section, I will briefly describe and define psychic occurrences that have in the past attracted the interest and received the attention of parapsychologists. *Telepathy* is direct access to the thought processes of another person without using words, nonverbal clues, signs, or other conventional means of communication. *Out-of-body experiences* are episodes during which disembodied consciousness is capable of moving in space and accurately perceiving the environment. When such perception involves remote locations, it is referred to as *astral projection.*

Precognition is accurate anticipation of future events without any objective clues. *Clairvoyance* is the capacity to access information about the past, present, and future without using the ordinary channels; it involves transcendence of spatial barriers, temporal barriers, or both. *Psychometry* is a process of obtaining information about the history of an object or facts and impressions about a person to whom this object belonged by extended tactile contact with that object. The term *psychokinesis* refers to situations in which material objects or processes are influenced by psychological means.

Another problem that has fascinated parapsychologists since 1882, when two Cambridge dons founded the Society for Psychic Research and parapsychology became an independent discipline, is the possibility of *survival of consciousness after death*. The belief in continuation of existence beyond the point of biological demise had been shared by all the ancient cultures, preindustrial societies, and spiritual traditions of the world. In the past, the efforts of parapsychologists to amass supportive evidence for survival were pooh-poohed and ridiculed by the scientific community and academic circles. However, in the second half of the twentieth century, consciousness research amassed a large body of observations suggesting that this idea is not as preposterous as it might appear to somebody brought up in the intellectual climate shaped by materialistic science. While these new data cannot be considered a "proof" of survival of individual consciousness after death, they certainly represent a major conceptual challenge for traditional science. They also help us understand why this belief is so universal and persistent.

The idea that consciousness can survive death is not really a belief, a completely unfounded wishful fantasy of ignorant people who cannot accept impermanence and their own death. It is based on a variety of extraordinary experiences and observations that resist the rational explanation of materialistic science. We have already explored earlier in this book the observations and scientific research related to past-life memories and to the question of reincarnation. Another important source of scientific information relevant for the question of survival of consciousness after death is thanatological research of near-death experiences (NDEs). These fascinating experiences occur in about one-third of the people who encounter various forms of life-threatening situations, such as car accidents, near-drowning, heart attacks, or cardiac arrests during operations.

Raymond Moody, Kenneth Ring, Michael Sabom, Bruce Greyson, and many others (Moody 1975, Ring 1982, Sabom 1982, Greyson and Bush 1992) have done extensive research of this phenomenon and described a characteristic experiential pattern of NDEs. In its full form, it includes an out-of-body experience (OOBE), life-review, and passage through a dark tunnel. It culminates in an encounter with a radiant Being of Light, divine judgment with ethical evaluation of one's life, and visits to various transcendental realms. Less frequent are painful, anxiety-provoking, and infernal types of NDEs. In the late 1990s, the research conducted by Ken Ring added an interesting dimension to these observations. Ring has been able to show that people who are congenitally blind for organic reasons can, during near-death experiences, experience visions, including those the veracity of which can be confirmed by consensual validation ("veridical out-of-body experiences") (Ring and Cooper 1999).

Veridical OOBEs are not limited to near-death situations and episodes of clinical death. They can also emerge during spiritual practice and in sessions of powerful experiential psychotherapy, such as primal therapy, rebirthing, or Holotropic Breathwork. Administration of psychedelic substances—particularly the dissociative anaesthetic ketamine—can greatly facilitate their occurrence. OOBEs can also emerge spontaneously, in the middle of everyday life, either as isolated episodes, or repeatedly as part of a crisis of psychic opening or some other type of spiritual emergency.

Veridical OOBEs are of special importance for the question of survival of consciousness after death because they demonstrate that consciousness is capable of operating independently of the body. They are of special interest for thanatologists and other consciousness researchers, because they represent a phenomenon that lends itself to scientific study and objective verification. The usual objection against seeing this research as supportive evidence for survival of consciousness after death is that people who have had OOBEs came close to death, but they did not really die. However, it seems reasonable to infer that if consciousness can function independently of the body when we are alive, it could be able to do the same after death.

Another area of interest for parapsychologists that is closely related to the question of survival of consciousness after death involves encounter and communication with deceased people. Apparitions of dead people, usually relatives and friends, appear frequently in connection with NDEs and as part of deathbed visions. The deceased seem to welcome the individual approaching death and try to ease his or her transition to the next world (the "welcoming committee"). The supportive evidence in this regard must be evaluated particularly carefully and critically. The vision of a dead person or persons does not really amount to very much. It can easily be dismissed as a wishful fantasy or hallucination that the brain constructs from memories. Some important additional factors must be present before such experiences constitute interesting research material.

For this reason, psychic researchers have paid much attention to the fact that the "welcoming committee" always consists exclusively of deceased people, including those about whose death the dying individual does not know. Such instances have been referred to as "peak in Darien" cases (Cobbe 1877). Specific communications that can be objectively verified also represent important research material. Of special interest is the quasi-experimental evidence suggestive of survival of consciousness after death that comes from the highly charged and controversial area of spiritistic seances and mental or trance mediumship. The best mediums have been able to accurately reproduce in their performance voice, speech patterns, gestures, mannerisms, and other characteristic features of the deceased previously unknown to them.

More recently, a worldwide network of researchers, including Ernest Senkowski, George Meek, Mark Macy, Scott Rogo, and others (Senkowski 1994, Fuller 1951, Macy 2001 and 2005, Rogo and Bayless 1979), have been involved in a group effort to establish "interdimensional transcommunication." They claim to have received many paranormal verbal communications and pictures from the deceased through electronic media, including tape recorders, telephones, FAX machines, computers, and TV screens. Another interesting innovation in the area of connecting with the deceased is the procedure described in Raymond Moody's book *Reunions: Visionary Encounters with Departed Loved Ones* (Moody 1993). In the preparatory phase of his research, Moody conducted a systematic review of literature on crystal-gazing, scrying (remote observation through psychic abilities), and similar processes. Using a large mirror and black velvet drapes, he then created a special environment (psychomanteum) that, according to him, can facilitate visionary encounters with the deceased loved ones.

One more phenomenon that should be mentioned in this context is *channeling*. It is a contemporary term for a situation in which an individual transmits through automatic writing, speech, or action messages from a source external to his or her everyday personality. The source often identifies itself as a being from a nonphysical reality; the hierarchical rank of this entity varies from an archetypal figure (deity or angel) or spiritually advanced superhuman being to a discarnate or even living human. The quality of the transmission also varies widely from trivial chatter to profound and remarkable psychological or spiritual communications.

The rich material amassed by modern consciousness research has strangely ambiguous implications for parapsychology. On the one hand, it brings strong supportive evidence for many of the phenomena traditionally studied by parapsychologists. On the other hand, it threatens the existence of parapsychology as an independent discipline. Once we accept the existence of transpersonal experiences, we realize that all or most of them can mediate access to new information through channels unknown to present science, whether they involve other people, other life forms, archetypal figures and realms, or various episodes from human history. Once the ability of the human psyche to access new information without the mediation of senses is generally accepted, there will be no need for a discipline specializing in the study of a relatively narrow selection of specific psychic phenomena. What in the past was considered "paranormal" will be seen as a normal capacity of the human psyche.

SEEING WITHOUT THE EYES (MINDSIGHT)

The Story of Ted

An interesting example of a veridical out-of-body experience in a near-death situation involves Ted, a twenty-six-year-old African American teacher suffering from inoperable cancer. In the course of his disease, Ted had three high-dose LSD sessions that he found very useful in helping him to cope with his cancer and his fear of death. Later, his condition deteriorated, and one of the metastatic tumors obstructed his ureter. This caused dangerous stagnation of urine in the calyx of his kidney, resulting in accumulation of toxic metabolic products in his blood.

After Ted had spent eight days in progressively worsening uremia, we received an urgent telephone call from his wife, Lilly. Ted asked to see me and Joan, who was my wife and cotherapist at the time, to discuss an issue that he considered to be of utmost importance. By the time we arrived at the intensive care unit of Sinai Hospital, Ted's condition had deteriorated considerably, and he appeared to be in a coma. He was surrounded by several of his relatives, who tried to communicate with him. Ted did not respond, except for occasional quite incomprehensible mumbling. It was apparent that his death was imminent.

While I was comforting Lilly and the other family members, trying to help them accept the situation, Joan sat down by Ted's side and talked to him gently, using her own Westernized version of the instructions from the *Bardo Thödol*. In essence, she was suggesting that he move toward light and merge with it, unafraid of its brilliance. At the time when everybody in the room seemed to have accepted Ted's imminent death, a very unexpected thing happened. In the last moment, the surgical team decided to operate after all. Without forewarning, two male attendants suddenly entered the room, transferred Ted to a gurney, and took him to the operating room. All the people in the room were shocked by what appeared to be a brutal intrusion into an intimate and special situation. We later found out that, during the operation, Ted had two cardiac arrests resulting in clinical death and was resuscitated on both occasions.

We went home to take a shower and change our clothes because we had plans to go out that evening. On the way to the downtown area, we decided to stop by the hospital once more to see how Ted was doing. When we arrived, he was in the intensive care unit recovering from anesthesia. This time, he was conscious and able to talk. "Hi. Thank you for stopping by twice in a single day," he greeted us. He looked at Joan and surprised her with an unexpected, yet accurate, comment: "You changed your clothes; are you going somewhere tonight?" He then proceeded to tell us that he saw us come earlier that day, but was unable to communicate with us because his consciousness was high up at the ceiling, and he could not connect with his body.

This was several years before thanatological research established veridical out-of-body experiences as a clinical fact. Unwilling to believe that somebody who was in a coma could have correctly observed the environment and remembered such a subtlety, we started inquiring about the nature of Ted's experiences earlier that day. He proceeded to describe in great detail what we were wearing during our earlier visit. It became obvious that he had correctly perceived the people present in the room, although his eyes were closed all the time. At one point, he had even noticed that tears rolled down Joan's cheeks. While fully aware of his environment, he also had had a number of unusual experiences.

While he was aware of what was happening in the room and able to listen to Joan's voice, his inner experience seemed to follow her suggestions. The initial darkness was replaced by brilliant light, and Ted was able to approach it and fuse with it. The feelings that accompanied his merging with the light were a sense of sacredness and deep inner peace. Yet, at the same time, he saw a movie on the ceiling, a vivid reenactment of all the bad things he had done in his life. He saw the faces of all the people whom he had killed in the war and all the youngsters he had beaten up as an adolescent hoodlum. He had to suffer the pain and agony of all the people whom he had hurt during his lifetime. While this was happening, he was aware of the presence of God, who was watching and judging this review of his life.

"I am glad I had the LSD trips with you guys," he told us before we left. "What happened to me today took me to the same place as those trips. Thanks to you, I knew that territory. I would have been scared by what was happening, but knowing these states, I was not afraid at all."

MESSAGES FROM THE ASTRAL REALM

The Story of Richard

One of the most interesting observations related to the problem of survival of consciousness after death that I remember comes from the LSD therapy of Richard, a young, severely depressed, and suicidal homosexual patient. He was the same individual whose "prenatal visit" to the annual village mart appears earlier in this book. In one of his LSD sessions, Richard had a very unusual experience involving a strange and uncanny astral realm. He suddenly found himself in a space that had an eerie luminescence and was filled with discarnate beings who were trying to communicate with him in a very urgent and demanding manner. He could not see or hear them, but he sensed their almost tangible presence and was receiving telepathic messages from them.

I wrote down one of these messages, which was very specific and could be subjected to subsequent verification. One of the discarnate beings implored Richard to connect with the being's parents in Kroměříž, a city in Moravia, and let them know that their son Ladislav was doing all right and was well taken care of. The message included the couple's name and telephone number; this was information that was unknown to both Richard and me and had no relevance to either of us. This experience seemed to be an alien enclave in Richard's experience, totally unrelated to his problems and the rest of his treatment. The whole thing was very puzzling and mysterious.

After the session, I decided to do what certainly would have made me the target of my colleagues' jokes had they found out. I went to the telephone, dialed the number in Kroměříž, and asked if I could speak with Ladislav. To my astonishment, the woman on the other side of the line started to cry. When she calmed down, she told me with a broken voice: "Our son is not with us anymore; he passed away; we lost him three weeks ago." One might argue that this was not really a proof that their deceased son had sent them a message from the Beyond, but the improbability that this was a meaningless coincidence is certainly staggering.

PROOF FOR THE EXISTENCE OF THE BEYOND?

The Story of Walter

Another equally extraordinary observation of this kind involved a close friend and colleague of mine, psychiatrist Walter N. Pahnke, who was a member of our psychedelic research team at the Maryland Psychiatric Research Center in Baltimore. He was the initiator and principal moving force behind the LSD program for patients dying of cancer at the Maryland Psychiatric Research Center in Catonsville. Walter had a deep interest in parapsychology, particularly in the problem of consciousness after death, and worked with many famous mediums and psychics, including our joint friend Eileen Garrett, founder of the Parapsychology Foundation

In summer 1971, Walter went with his wife, Eva, and three children to Maine for a vacation in their cabin on the shore of the Atlantic. Before leaving Baltimore, he had bought from a friend of his some scuba-diving gear and got some lessons in diving. One day, he went scuba diving all by himself and without a marker and did not return. An extensive and well-organized search failed to find his body or any part of his diving gear. Under these circumstances, Eva found it very difficult to accept and integrate his death. Her last memory was of Walter leaving the cabin, full of energy and in perfect health. It was hard for her to accept that he was not part of her life anymore, and she did not feel free to start a new chapter of her existence without a sense of closure of the preceding one.

Being a psychologist herself, she qualified for an LSD training session for mental health professionals offered through the program in our institute. She decided to have a psychedelic experience, hoping to get some more insight into her situation, and she asked me to be her sitter. Eva was a close and dear friend, and I accepted with pleasure. In the second half of the session, she had a very powerful vision of Walter and carried on a long and meaningful telepathic dialogue with him. He gave her specific instructions concerning each of their three children and released her to start a new life of her own, unencumbered and unrestricted by a sense of commitment to his memory. It was a profound and liberating experience.

Just as Eva was questioning whether the entire episode was a wishful fabrication of her own mind, Walter appeared once more for a brief period of time and asked Eva to return a book that he had borrowed from a friend of his. He then proceeded to give her the name of the friend, the name of the book, the room where it was, the shelf, and the sequential order of the book on this shelf. Curious and eager to verify this extraordinary message, we went to Eva's house as soon as her session ended. Following the instructions, Eva was actually able to find and return the book, the existence of which she had had no previous knowledge.

Giving Eva this kind of specific confirmation of the authenticity of their communication was very much in Walter's style. During his life, he had had extensive contact with psychics from different parts of the world and had been fascinated by the attempt of the famous magician Harry Houdini to prove the existence of the Beyond. I was personally present in a situation in which Walter was trying to arrange a similar experiment with Eileen Garrett, after she had told us that she was soon going to die.

"Eileen," demanded Walter, "you have to promise me that, if you can, you will give me some clear sign that the Beyond really exists." Eileen, known for her exquisite sense of humor, did not seem to take Walter's request seriously. "Rest assured, Walter," she responded, "you're gonna get your proof. I'll show up in your next LSD session and grab your dick with my cold, clammy hand!" Considering Walter's preoccupation with proof, it seemed plausible that he would use this strategy to give more weight to his own posthumous communication.

CUT ROSES IN AUNT ANNE'S ROSE GARDEN

The Story of Kurt

The next example involves Kurt, one of the psychologists participating in our three-year professional training program in transpersonal psychology and Holotropic Breathwork. When Kurt enrolled in the training, he was by far the most scientifically minded and skeptical member of our training group. What he observed and experienced in the training had profound influence on the belief system he had inherited from his academic teachers. I described earlier Kurt's birth experience associated with the scent of fresh leather. This episode undermined his conviction that consciousness and psychological life begins after we are born.

At the time he had the following experience, Kurt was facing another conceptual challenge, one that forced him to vastly expand his professional horizons. The problem he was struggling with was the nature of transpersonal experiences. Were they ontologically real phenomena, indicating the existence of normally invisible transcendental realms, or products of human imagination? In the course of the training, he had witnessed a wide variety of transpersonal experiences of his colleagues, but had not experienced any himself. He kept insisting that such experiences had to be products of the brain, as he had been taught in medical school.

Then, in one of his holotropic sessions, Kurt had an intense experience, followed by an unusual synchronicity, which convinced him that he needed to be more open-minded as far as the farther reaches of human consciousness were concerned. Toward the end of this session, he had a vivid experience of encountering his grandmother, who had been dead for many years. Kurt had been very close to her in his childhood and was deeply moved by the possibility that he might be really communicating with her again. In spite of his deep emotional involvement in the experience, he continued to maintain an attitude of professional skepticism about this encounter.

As he later explained to the group, he suspected that his mind might have easily created an imaginary encounter from his old memories because he had had many real interactions with his grandmother while she was still alive. But meeting his dead grandmother was so emotionally profound, heart-opening, and convincing that he simply could not dismiss it as a wishful fantasy. Toward the end of this encounter, he decided to ask his grandmother for proof that the experience was real and not just his imagination.

No sooner had he raised this telepathic question than he received the following message: "Go to Aunt Anne and look for cut roses." Still skeptical, he decided on the following weekend, "just for the fun of it," to visit his Aunt Anne's home and see what would happen. To his astonishment, Kurt found upon his arrival his old aunt working in the garden. She was in her gardener's outfit, holding pruning scissors in one hand and a rose in the other. The lawns and paths in the garden were covered with cut roses. The day of Kurt's unplanned visit happened to be, unbeknownst to him, the one day of the entire year when his aunt decided to do some radical pruning of her roses.

Materialistic scientists reject and often ridicule the possibility of survival of consciousness after death simply because of the incompatibility of such a belief with their basic metaphysical assumptions about existence. Their position is not based on a scientific "proof" that continuation of existence after death in any form is impossible. As a matter of fact, their conclusions are made at the expense of ignoring a vast amount of observations, such as the above, for which the current paradigm lacks adequate explanation.

LUIZ GASPARETTO
Painters and Paintings from the Beyond

Although we had heard much about Brazil from our friends, nothing had prepared us for the cultural shock we experienced during our first visit to this extraordinary country. Because of our involvement in psychedelic research and transpersonal psychology, we were in daily contact with many people who, as individuals, were very open-minded and for whom spirituality was an important part of everyday life. However, it was clear that, in the larger context of Western industrial civilization, they certainly represented exceptions, islands in the ocean of a largely pragmatic culture.

Encounters with Brazilian people and discussions with them made us feel that we were on a different planet. The majority of Brazilians, including members of the upper class and the educated elite, seemed to accept the existence of realities that in Euro-American culture were relegated to the realm of infantile nonsense, fantasy, primitive superstition, or mental illness—discarnate entities, possession by spirits and benevolent or malevolent deities, spiritual healing, successful intervention by psychic surgeons, visitations by UFOs, and many others. All these phenomena appeared to be normal and integral parts of their worldview, in many instances based on personal experiences, rather than unfounded beliefs and superstitions or sensational topics for cheap tabloids.

This seemed to be closely related to the fact that Brazilians had easy access to holotropic states of consciousness and thus many opportunities for direct experiences of the transpersonal domain. For many of them, this was made possible by ritual use of ayahuasca, a psychedelic brew that had been used for centuries as a sacrament and powerful medicine in the Amazonian region. It had been sanctioned by the Brazilian government and practiced by indigenous healers (ayahuasqueros) and by the members of the Santo Daime Church and by another major group called União do Vegetal.

A significant part of the population was also involved in Afro-Brazilian syncretistic cults, such as umbanda, candomble, and macumba, combining elements from African tribal religions with Brazilian indigenous belief systems and Christianity. We became particularly interested in spiritism, a fascinating spiritual movement based on the work of nineteenth-century French educator and philosopher Allan Kardec. Spiritism is based on a belief that spirits of deceased people are able to communicate with humans and intervene in the material world through individuals with mediumistic abilities. The Spiritist Church had become well-known, particularly for the fact that it produced famous psychic surgeons, such as the Philippine Tony Agpaoa and Brazilian Ze Arrigó, the "Surgeon of the Rusty Knife."

During our stay in São Paulo, we heard about Luiz Antonio Gasparetto, a psychologist and member of the Spiritist Church, who was using his mediumistic abilities in a very unique way. He was known for channeling the spirits of a wide range of famous dead painters and producing extraordinary paintings in a variety of styles. With the help of our Brazilian friends, we were able to get an appointment and visit Luiz in his house in the suburbs of São Paulo.

Luiz was a tall, handsome man with dark hair and expressive eyes. He was dressed in casual slacks and a white shirt and was polite, warm, and amiable. Luiz looked more like a run-of-the-mill academician than an eccentric psychic with a wild reputation. Nothing in his appearance or in the interior of his house seemed to foreshadow what was coming, except a large number of shelves carrying giant stacks of paper. As we were about to find out, these shelves had been specially crafted to store his "paintings from the Beyond," more than five thousand of them.

After offering us some tea, Luiz started sharing with us the extraordinary collection of his paintings. We were treated to an astonishing display of paintings in the style of great masters of all times and countries. They were not copies of the existing paintings, but new motifs rendered in easily recognizable styles of individual artists. There were Monet's rich bouquets of flowers, Modigliani's slim figures of young women, Toulouse-Lautrec's dancers and other characters from Moulin Rouge, Henri Rousseau's naïve jungle scenes with wild animals, Rembrandt's chiaroscuro portraits, Leonardo da Vinci's androgynous faces, Picasso's still life and figurative paintings, Georgia O'Keeffe's flowers, Frida Kahlo's expressive compositions, and many others.

Occasionally, these paintings did not reflect the fully developed mature style of these deceased masters, for which they were well known, but various earlier periods of their artistic evolution. Later, when we got to know Luiz well and had many opportunities to witness his work, we had to consult in some instances specific monographs featuring collected works of the painters whom Luiz claimed to channel to verify that he actually captured accurately their early styles.

As we were treated to this astonishing array of remarkable creations, Luiz shared with us some stories about his life and work. He had been gifted with psychic abilities since he was a child. The Gasparetto lineage was famous in Brazil for paranormal abilities, which apparently ran in the family. Luiz's mother was also a psychic, expressing her talent through automatic drawing. She taught him a lot and helped him to develop his own talent. Luiz's experiences with discarnate artists started when he was thirteen years old. They kept appearing to him on a regular basis, teaching him about the existence of the astral realm and about the meaning of life. Some of them were very famous, and he knew them and their art. Others were completely unknown to him, and he had to verify their authenticity by searching in art history books.

The spirits of dead masters told him that they wanted to show their work all over again and convey the message that they still existed. Another reason for their contact with Luiz was to give people a tangible proof of the existence of the Beyond. They revealed to him that they had planned this since before he was born. Luiz never knew who was going to come and what they were going to do. He could not simply choose to paint on his own; without the assistance of discarnate painters, he was not able to perform at all. When the spirits were present, he could feel all they felt and could see the world through their eyes. He compared the experience to an orgasm. His experience with the masters had changed his own way of seeing the world; it had opened his eyes to its magic beauty.

We were very impressed by Luiz and his art and decided to invite him as guest faculty in our forthcoming monthlong seminar. It was part of a series of experimental educational programs that we conducted twice a year at the Esalen Institute in Big Sur, California, where we lived. These events gave us the opportunity to choose a topic that we were interested in and invite as guest faculty individuals who were prominent representatives of their field and had a special relation to the theme of the workshop.

The invited guests covered a wide range from scientists, such as Fritjof Capra, Karl Pribram, and Gregory Bateson, to Tibetan lamas, Indian spiritual teachers, Native American and Mexican shamans, and Christian mystics. The spectrum of topics was equally broad. The monthlongs focused on such themes as Buddhism and Western Psychology, Schizophrenia and the Visionary Mind, Maps of Consciousness, Aboriginal Healing and Modern Medicine, Ancient Wisdom and Modern Science, Higher Creativity, and Frontiers of Science.

The topic of the forthcoming seminar was Energy: Physical, Emotional, and Spiritual. In the brief description of it that had appeared in the Esalen catalog, we promised to explore theoretically and experientially these different forms of energy and how to work with them. Luiz was clearly an ideal guest teacher for this program. Our budget allowed us to offer him a honorarium that would just about cover his traveling expense, and he was excited about this prospect of a visit to California.

Our monthlong seminars took place in the Big House, on a beautiful cypress-covered cliff overlooking the Pacific Ocean and separated by a creek from the rest of the property. Esalen Institute took its name from an Indian tribe that lived in Big Sur before the arrival of European colonizers. The Indians considered the land around the hot springs to be sacred healing and burial grounds. When the foundations for the Big House were being laid, the workers found many skeletons of the Esalen Indians lying in fetal position and facing west. Two additional burial sites were discovered on the property at different times, arranged in a triangle with this one.

Our first direct encounter with Luiz's psychic abilities occurred immediately after his arrival at the Big House. He moved around the house and its immediate environment as if he were looking for something. We did not know what was happening and asked him what he was doing. "Do you know that many Indians lived and died here?" he said. "This place is full of Indian spirits; I can feel them all around me." This was quite remarkable because Luiz did not have any previous knowledge of the history of Esalen.

During the month that he spent with us, he conducted healing sessions with participants of the workshop that brought much additional evidence for his unusual paranormal talents. However, our most extraordinary experience with Luiz was a performance that he did at Huxley, which is the large meeting room adjacent to the Esalen lodge on the main part of the property. Although it was part of our seminar, we opened it for the Esalen community. We placed a table and two chairs in the middle of the room, one for Luiz and the other for Christina, whose task it was to hand Luiz sheets of paper. During the performance, all lights were turned off, except a lamp with a red bulb on the table that Luiz was using.

On his way to Big Sur, Luiz had stopped in Los Angeles in the house of a good friend of mine, psychologist and parapsychological researcher Thelma Moss. During Luiz's performance for a close circle of her friends, lights went off for some time in the entire block. To their astonishment, the guests (and Luiz himself) discovered that this had in no way interfered with his performance. He continued to paint, correctly choosing the colors, and produced during the dark period several beautiful paintings.

Performance in total darkness would have been a very impressive experiment, but it would have prevented the viewers from observing the process. We decided to choose red light as a compromise because it allowed people to observe Luiz, but effectively blocked his ability to distinguish colors. Luiz requested that we play Vivaldi's *Four Seasons* throughout the entire session because he found this music particularly inspiring for his work. Within a few minutes after the music had begun, Luiz's head and body went through a few jolts; he seemed to have entered a trance. At the same time, Christina, who sat close to him, started to feel enormous heat radiating from his hands; this then continued during the entire session.

Luiz started to paint and, with astonishing speed, he kept producing one remarkable painting after another, each in the style of a different famous painter—van Gogh, Picasso, Gauguin, Rembrandt, Monet, and many others. He was using both of his hands, at times painting two pictures simultaneously, one with each hand. Much of the time, he was not looking at the paper at all; he kept closing his eyes and bending his head backwards or to the side. He actually painted a Manet portrait upside down, under the table, and with his right foot, without looking at all. Luiz's stunning performance lasted a little over an hour. When he stopped painting, the floor around him was covered with large paintings, twenty-six of them altogether. In spite of the red light in the room, all the paintings were painted in appropriate colors.

People in the room started to move, eager to come closer and inspect the paintings. However, it was obvious that for Luiz the process was not yet completed. He sat for a while in quiet meditation and then he announced: "There is a spirit here who calls himself Fritz Perls; he wants to have his portrait painted by Toulouse-Lautrec." He then produced a painting of the legendary South African therapist and founder of Gestalt practice, who had spent the last years of his life at Esalen. It was not only a very accurate portrait of Fritz, but it bore all the unmistakable characteristics of Toulouse-Lautrec's style.

Luiz finished the painting, but gave no indication that the performance was over. After a brief moment of reflection, he said: "There is another spirit here; her name is Ida Rolf. She would also like to have her portrait made, not the way she looked before she died, but when she was forty years old." Ida Rolf was another Esalen legend and idol. A German physicist, she had developed a famous technique of bodywork that carried her name. She had lived for many years in an Esalen house, about one-and-a-half miles from the main premises, which became our residence after Ida had left Esalen.

The portrait of Fritz showed him as people remembered him or knew him from his photographs. The portrait of Ida that Luiz painted was artistically very interesting and showed a middle-aged female figure, but there was no way of assessing the accuracy of the portrait. Nobody in the Esalen community had any idea what Ida Rolf had looked like at the age of forty because by the time she had arrived at Esalen from Germany, she was already old. Dick Price, the cofounder of Esalen, was fascinated by Luiz's performance, but particularly by his portraits of the two people from the Esalen history Luiz did not know. Subsequently, Dick spent much time and effort to obtain from Germany Ida's photograph from the time she was forty. When the photograph finally arrived, the extraordinary resemblance between her "portrait from the Beyond" and her actual middle-age appearance became very convincing evidence of Luiz's extraordinary psychic gifts.

A PARTY FOR EXU

Interview with the Orixás

The next story describes another extraordinary experience that Christina and I had during our first visit to Brazil. During the years when we lived at the Esalen Institute in Big Sur, California, our financial means were very limited. It was due partly to significant losses both of us had suffered during our respective divorces, partly to the fact that we had deliberately chosen what Duane Elgin called "voluntary simplicity." We had opted for simple life in the beautiful setting of the Big Sur coast rather than a more lucrative lifestyle that would have required moving to the city.

In exchange for a certain number of workshops, Esalen provided for us a house situated on a steep cliff on the Pacific coast, with a spectacular 200-degree view of the ocean. We were thus able to live in close contact with spectacular wildlife, watching the play of sea otters, sea lions, and dolphins. We could see seagulls, cormorants, pelicans, and other sea birds flying through the air and floating in the ocean in the fields of giant kelp. Twice a year, for several weeks, gray whales were passing by on their way between Alaska and Baja California, and, on rare occasions, the appearance of killer whales further enriched this already extraordinary zoological display. Big Sur was also an important stop on the route of another group of indefatigable migrants—the beautiful Monarch butterflies.

The shadow side of this life in paradise was that it did not offer much opportunity to earn money. Esalen Institute provided food and lodging for us, but the income from workshops that we conducted in addition to those that paid for our house was meager. The workshop leaders received twenty percent of the fees Esalen collected from the participants in their workshops, which was by far the worst deal we have encountered anywhere in the world. There were many reasons why the guest teachers were willing to come and work under these conditions.

The Big Sur coast is without any doubt one of the most beautiful scenic areas in the world. The strip of land on which the Esalen Institute is built was considered sacred by the Esalen Indians, whose name it carries, and is undeniably a "power spot." In addition, Esalen is the legendary "Mecca of the human potential movement," world-known as an exciting human laboratory and a place of cutting-edge thinking, associated with the names of such pioneers as Aldous Huxley, Alan Watts, Abraham Maslow, Gregory Bateson, Fritz Perls, Moshe Feldenkreis, and Ida Rolf.

For the reasons mentioned, we had to seek additional sources of income outside of Esalen, in other parts of the United States and abroad. We tried to arrange our trips in such a way that we would at least cover our expenses and come out even. This was also the situation during our first visit to Brazil, where we traveled to attend the Fourth International Transpersonal Conference in Belo Horizonte. We had arranged several lectures and a couple of workshops in different parts of Brazil expecting to make enough money to pay for our trip.

But we ran into an unexpected complication. Unbeknownst to us, our workshop in Rio coincided with a soccer match between Brazil and Peru that was part of the World Cup competition. And, as we found out, trying to compete with a soccer match in South America would mean having the chance of a snowball in hell. We ended up with five participants for a Holotropic Breathwork weekend, which was a small miracle considering the circumstances, but was not enough to go ahead with the workshop. We had to apologize to the small group of people gathered for the event and cancel the workshop with the painful awareness that it meant incurring significant financial loss.

We suddenly had a lot of time for sightseeing in Rio or some other alternative program. One of the people who came for the workshop was Sergio, a young Brazilian psychologist. We started talking, and he told us that he was conducting research on the Brazilian umbanda, a very popular syncretistic Afro-Brazilian cult that combines elements of traditional African tribal religions, Roman Catholicism, and indigenous Indian cultures of Brazil. He was using in his study a Jungian perspective, trying to describe the archetypal dynamics manifesting in the rituals. When he saw our interest in this subject, he invited us to accompany him to an evening umbanda ceremony.

Umbanda originated in Rio de Janeiro in the 1920s and since then has spread vigorously throughout Brazil. The umbanda communities are guided by *Pais de Santos* ("fathers of the saints") or *Mães de Santos* ("mothers of the saints"), who oversee *Filhos and Filhas de Santos* ("sons and daughters of the saints"). These are mediums consecrated to specific deities of West African origin, or *orixás*, such as Xango, Oxum, and Iemanja. Rituals are performed in special centers, called *terreiros* or *tendas*. They involve singing and chanting in Yoruba, accompanied with beating of drums, or *atabaques*, in different rhythms for each orixá. The mediums fall into trance and embody their respective deities.

We had some previous intellectual knowledge about umbanda from the lectures of Stanley Krippner, a famous American parapsychologist with strong anthropological interests, who had come several times as guest faculty to our monthlong seminars at Esalen. We also had had a chance to experience the umbanda ritual personally for the first time during our visit to Belo Horizonte about ten days earlier. That experience had given us an interesting insight into the complexity of the Brazilian academic world.

When we expressed at the ITA conference our interest to attend an umbanda ritual, our Brazilian host, a psychologist who taught at the department of psychology of the university in Belo Horizonte, at first tried to dissuade us from participating. He took a very professional stance and told us that umbanda was based on superstition of simpleminded people and that there was nothing of interest there for educated professionals. When we insisted, it turned out that his cousin was in charge of the local umbanda group and that it was very easy for us to obtain the permission to attend.

The house in which the ritual took place had two stories and a cellar. The second floor represented heaven; it was all painted in bright white and pink colors and was adorned with large roses and garlands of flowers made of plaster and heavily gilded. The basement portrayed hell and was aesthetically the polar opposite of the former. Its walls were painted black and dark red, and the floor was covered with offerings for the dark deities, consisting of cigarette butts and bottles of aquavit, a very strong alcoholic beverage. The ground floor, which was the setting for the ritual, was richly decorated with potted trees and bushes and ponds of water.

The impression that this somewhat corny interior decoration made on us dissipated when the ritual started. The chanting and drumming was very powerful, and many people soon started falling into trance. We could see many emotional and physical abreactions and had no doubts that this process was authentic and had strong healing potential. As a matter of fact, much of what we saw reminded us of the processes we had seen over the years in psychedelic sessions and in Holotropic Breathwork.

The next day, we told our host how impressed we were by our experience in the umbanda ceremony. When he heard it, the truth slowly started to come out. He shared with us that, on the basis of his personal experience, he was personally convinced about the value of the umbanda rituals and their healing potential. If somebody in his family had emotional or psychosomatic problems, he would not recommend a Freudian analyst or a behaviorist, but send them to an umbanda cabildo to be treated. He even mentioned a situation when his family secretly smuggled an umbanda healer into the hospital room to conduct a private ritual with one of its members.

Our experience in Belo Horizonte had whetted our appetites, and we accepted with pleasure Sergio's invitation to attend another umbanda ritual. Late in the afternoon, we got into his car and drove from the downtown area to the suburbs. The place was on the outskirts of the city, and it took us a long time to reach our destination. When we arrived at the site where the ritual took place, we were surprised by what we found. While the ritual in Belo Horizonte was conducted in an upper-class setting, the scene here was on the other side of the spectrum.

We first walked into a dark garage lit by colorful Christmas lights, suspended on long lines crisscrossing the ceiling. Near one of the walls was a three-tiered altar covered with little plaster figures representing the orixás, matched with their Christian counterparts, effigies of Catholic saints. We recognized Xango, the deity of aggression and sex, paired with St. George, and Iemanja, the goddess of the ocean, sharing space with Virgin Mary. We also knew from the past Caboclo, the dark-skinned man in a loincloth, wearing a feather headdress and wielding bows and arrows, and Preto Velho, the stooped, old black man sitting on a little stool with a pipe in his mouth.

Sergio then showed us two iron figures, red and black, with horns and prominent sexual features, representing a female and a male devil. He also pointed out Pomba Gira, a deity in the form of a sexy woman in a low-cut dress, laughing derisively and looking like a prostitute. He then took us to a large adjacent area, the "embodying room," the site of the ritual, which was just about to begin. We were introduced there to an old witchy-looking woman with one eye and disheveled hair who was in the role of Mãe de Santos, "mother of the saints," and was clearly in charge of the ceremony.

As we witnessed her killing a black chicken and smearing various objects with its blood, Sergio explained to us that this was *ebo* or *despacho*, ceremonial offering. This ceremony would be different from the one we attended in Belo Horizonte because this one was held on Bara's Day, or St. Anthony's Day, and it was a party in honor of Exu. Sergio told us that Exu is an irresponsible, mischievous trickster who causes trouble and thrives on confusion. Some see him as a bridge between humans and orixás, others as a dark force of nature comparable with the Christian devil.

Once the drumming and chanting started, the Filhos and Filhas de Santos began to dance and fall into trance. Several assistants watched the floor, and when they recognized grimaces, gestures, and behaviors characterizing specific orixás, they dressed the people embodying them into appropriate costumes. Two of the women stood out by their provocative, lewd conduct; Sergio told us that they seemed to be impersonating Pomba Gira. Very proper and reserved before the trance, they were now lifting their skirts high exposing their underwear, shouting obscenities, and approaching men with obscene gestures symbolizing intercourse. We watched as each of them downed three large bottles of aquavit, a strong distillate with about 45 percent alcohol, without showing any signs of motor instability.

The scene was wild, and the atmosphere dense and somewhat bizarre. However, Christina and I were able to watch it with the detachment of anthropologists doing fieldwork and with relative equanimity. But this changed when the witchy Mãe de Santos approached us with a meaningful grin and asked us if we wanted a *consulta*. This is a name used in umbanda for an interview with the spirits, during which the medium channels the messages and advice of the orixás to participants. We agreed to "talk to the spirits," seeing it as an opportunity for an interesting experience. It turned out that we were completely unprepared for what was about to happen.

The old crone led us to one of the women who were acting out sexually and had consumed huge quantities of aquavit. She pushed us both from behind until we stood very close to the medium. The woman's face was contorted into a strange grimace, and she was chewing and smoking a large cigar. "So you want to talk with the spirits?" she asked us with a derisive grin. Without waiting for an answer, she reached unabashedly under Christina's waist, touching and squeezing her underbelly. "Female problems, heh?" she cackled. "Pains and bleeding. And a lot of energy!" Sergio translated for us her comments, given in Portuguese.

"You are sad, very sad and upset," she continued with a voice that sounded like croaking. "It's hard to be separated from your two children, isn't it? To have them so far, on an island?" We were astounded; Christina was at the height of her Kundalini awakening, characterized by strong energies. The process was at this point focusing on her belly and was causing a lot of gynecological problems for which there was no medical basis. She had also recently lost in a lawsuit with her ex-husband the custody of her children, who were now living in Hawaii with their father. This was for Christina a cause of constant irritation and depression.

The woman's eyes then turned to me, and she looked at me with an expression and gesture that was somewhere between mocking and teasing: "Having a good time in Brazil, aren't you? Loving Brazilian food and all those great spices, heh? Just don't worry about finances; that would spoil the fun for you! Don't be afraid; you will not lose money on this trip!" That was another direct hit. My love for food is one of my great weaknesses, as Christina and all my friends know. When I come to a country I do not know, I cannot wait to explore its cuisine. We had just been to Bahia, where I had fallen in love with the extraordinary mixture of African and Brazilian spices. And after the cancellation of our workshop in Rio, thoughts about our financial situation certainly had been in the back of my mind much of the time.

This was astonishing because our only link with this umbanda community was Sergio, and he did not possess any of the information that the woman in trance was channeling. The discovery that the mediums had such extraordinary clairvoyant or telepathic abilities and how transparent we were to them certainly changed our feelings about the ritual and our attitude toward it. We suddenly had much more respect for what was happening there, and the situation started looking much more authentic and serious. Being in an unfamiliar suburban part of Rio, in the grotesque setting of the party for Exu, and surrounded by people who had such paranormal abilities, triggered in us even a few waves of paranoia.

The reassurance concerning the financial outcome of our trip to Brazil, which I received from the woman channeling Pomba Gira, turned out to be correct. In spite of the setback with the canceled workshop in Rio de Janeiro, we managed to come out even. At the end of our journey, we found out that our expenses and earnings were almost exactly the same.

THE TABOO AGAINST KNOWING THAT WE ARE CLAIRVOYANT

Sessions with Ann Armstrong

During the years I worked at the Maryland Psychiatric Research Center, my friendship with Walter Pahnke brought into my life many great psychics of our time, among them Eileen Garrett, Hugh and Charles Cayce, Joan Grant, and others. During our fourteen-year stay at the Esalen Institute in Big Sur, California, Christina and I had many additional opportunities to meet individuals with extraordinary psychic abilities, such as Luiz Gasparetto, Uri Geller, Helen Palmer, Keith Harrary, and Jack Schwartz.

However, it was our long-standing friendship with Anne Armstrong that provided for us the most convincing and consistent evidence about the possibility of paranormal access to information about other people and the world. Anne's extraordinary psychic gifts opened up in the course of her "spiritual emergency," which lasted twenty years. The process of her inner development started when she and her husband, Jim, started experimenting with hypnosis in an attempt to cure Anne's agonizing migraine headaches.

Their therapeutic experiment succeeded when they were able to trace Anne's headaches to a past-life memory of being an athlete associated with the Roman Colosseum who had been subjected to severe torture because his captors wanted to extort from him some important secret information. To the great surprise of both of them, the perpetrator in this karmic memory turned out to be Jim himself. The marriage of the Armstrongs survived this revelation, and the two of them embarked on a journey of shared spiritual discovery. After years of inner struggle, Anne developed into a remarkably reliable and well-grounded practicing psychic.

Anne and Jim came regularly as guest faculty to our monthlong workshops, usually during the last week. Before they joined the group, the members of the group had spent together on average ten hours a day, during which they shared a variety of in-depth explorations, including regular sessions of Holotropic Breathwork. Anne appeared in the group without knowing anybody except Christina and me. And yet, she instantly gained access to all kinds of intimate information about the group members that was new to all of us. Her specialty was exploration and elucidation of interpersonal relationships. All she needed to know for her readings were the names of the people involved. She could even give very accurate and reliable readings on the telephone.

Besides giving surprisingly revealing and accurate individual readings for different members of the group, she also took participants, with Jim's assistance, through a series of exercises, teaching them to discover, own, and cultivate their own psychic abilities. The Armstrongs' favorite exercise was the "group scan," which combined both of these processes. Little pieces of paper with the names of the participants were folded and deposited into a hat. A designated group member then blindly drew out of the hat the name of the person who would receive the group reading. That person would then present the problem about which he or she needed psychic information.

The instruction for the group members was to suspend any doubts about their own psychic abilities and write down everything that came to their mind, without the slightest reservation and without any censorship. After the participants shared their insights into the presented problem, Anne did her own psychic reading, so that we all could compare our insights with hers. The last stage of the process was the feedback of the target people concerning what they considered hits and misses of the reading.

Anne's readings were consistently correct and often truly remarkable. But it was extraordinary how accurate were many of the images and insights of various group members who had never thought of themselves as having any psychic abilities. One of the major difficulties was to clearly interpret the emerging images and associations, something that Anne was doing with incredible ease. I will illustrate this problem by one of my own attempts at psychometry under Anne and Jim's guidance.

In this particular exercise, half of the group sat down along one wall of the room and the other along the opposite wall. We were instructed to secretly bring into this session an object that, unbeknownst to other people in the group, had emotional significance for us. Jim then gave each half of the group a large shopping bag and asked us to furtively deposit our objects into it. He then switched the bags, and each of us had to pull out an object belonging to somebody from the opposite side. The instruction was to hold this object in one's hand and do a psychometric reading—to write down all associations and images that would emerge in this process.

The object I drew out of the bag was a metal pendant, a little more than an inch in diameter. It had the shape of a circle that contained a stylized human figure with outstretched arms and legs, like the famous drawing of the Vitruvian Man by Leonardo da Vinci. Following Anne's instructions, I held it in my left hand, focused my attention on it, and let my mind wander the way I used to do in my Freudian training analysis. I then wrote down with my right hand all my free associations to it, as they were emerging. I was surprised by the ease with which they came and by their richness.

First, I remembered several of my trips to Europe during which I visited quaint little German towns with cobblestone streets and picturesque houses decorated with paintings, woodcarvings, and flower boxes. From there, my chain of thoughts took me to my medical studies, to the various institutes that I had visited as a student for lectures or practice. It started as a general overview, but then it very quickly focused with extraordinary intensity on my memories related to anatomy and physiology of malignant tumors. Following this, my association shifted to my work with terminal cancer patients at the Maryland Psychiatric Research Center and stayed there for a while. And then, without any warning or transition, a memory of a joke I had heard recently suddenly popped up in my mind and made me laugh. The joke went like this:

An adventurous tourist visiting North Africa called on an Arab merchant to buy a camel. His intention was to cross the Sahara desert, and he made it clear to the merchant that he needed a really good camel, one that would last a long time without water. The Arab brought what he claimed was his toughest and most reliable camel, and the man paid for the animal the requested handsome sum of money. He then embarked without delay on his desert adventure. To his unpleasant surprise, after a few days, the camel became increasingly weak and started to slow down. Although he had used all the water planned for the trip, he seemed to be completely dehydrated and was panting, his dry tongue stretched out of his mouth. A couple of days later, he refused to continue and collapsed in the desert.

They would have both died had it not been for a caravan with a sufficient supply of water, traveling in the opposite direction that saved their lives. After returning from his ill-fated desert crossing, the infuriated man went back to the Arab merchant and demanded the return of his money. "What kind of camel did you give me?" he raged. "After a few days in the desert, he collapsed and would not continue; I almost lost my life out there!"

"I don't understand it," the Arab merchant said, shaking his head. "Did you brick him?" "What do you mean, brick him?" asked the unfortunate traveler, completely confused. "I'll show you," said the merchant and led the camel to a well. As the camel started to drink, the Arab approached him with a large brick in each of his hands and patiently waited. Just as the camel finished drinking, he smashed the animal's testicles with the bricks. The camel let out an ungodly scream, sucking in an additional couple of gallons of water.

It is not easy to convey the punch line of this joke in writing. To deliver the story correctly, the narrator has actually to make the sound the camel made when his testicles were being smashed. The stream of air that is forcefully sucked in while making this sound makes it very explicit what volume was added to the camel's water supply by "bricking" him. The camel joke was my last association in the psychometric exercise. It reverberated in my head for a few minutes after the experiment ended.

Under Anne and Jim's guidance, we then identified the owners of our objects and started the group sharing. I could not believe how many of my free associations were direct hits, particularly because I had never thought of myself as being psychic. I approached the psychic game with healthy skepticism, doubting that anything relevant would come out of it. However, I was wrong! It turned out that the owner of the pendant I used in this psychometric exercise was Myra, a woman from Germany, who grew up in a little town that looked just like I had imagined it. She was a medical doctor who recently had become interested in alternative approaches and started attending "new age" workshops and seminars.

The camel joke turned out to be an incredibly accurate psychic hit, although the information came in such a funny disguise. Actually, the situation to which this association alluded was even more outrageous and hilarious than the joke. The pendant was the emblem of the Center for the Whole Person, a group involved in deep self-exploration based on a modified and widely expanded form of primal therapy. Myra had participated in a weekend workshop led by Bill Swartley, one of the group leaders of this organization; this workshop was a nude marathon that took place near Atlantic City, New Jersey.

Nude marathon was a radical form of therapy developed in the 1960s by Californian psychologist Paul Bindrim. It combined nudity, sleep deprivation, and fasting with experiential group work in a swimming pool that was body temperature. The pool was about five feet deep, of the same depth in all its parts. At the beginning of this marathon, Bill Swartley showed the participants the pendant symbolizing his center and told them that it would be awarded at the end of the workshop to the person who during that weekend did the most outrageous thing. Not knowing how adventurous and daring Myra could be, Bill had no idea what he was setting himself up for.

One of the exercises used in the nude marathon to evoke powerful emotional reactions was exposing floating nude bodies of participants to close-up inspection by their peers. The group members, standing in the pool, created two lines facing each other. Then, beginning at one end, one body after another was floated belly-up through this challenging gauntlet. Those who completed the journey extended the line on the other end. In this situation, the genitals of both sexes and the breasts of the women were exposed to the eyes of all the other group members. For many people, this ruthless invasion of privacy was an emotional trigger of extraordinary power.

It was quite common that some of the participants could not stand this situation and emotionally fell apart, or "went into process," as it was called. At this point, the rest of the group surrounded this person and supported him or her in working through whatever came up for them. When the process was finished, the lines were recreated and the floating of the nude bodies continued. The egalitarian role of the leader was reflected not only by his sharing the nudity, but also by his participating in this exercise. When the group floated Bill Swartley, Myra saw her opportunity to win the prize of the weekend. She threw herself toward Bill Swartley and attacked with her teeth his scrotum and his testicles. Naturally, she became the uncontested winner of the pendant.

During the group scan, many of us came up with associations that were clearly related to the personalities and the lives of the owners of the objects. The main difference between us and Anne in this regard was not only that her imagination was richer than ours, she was also able to decipher her own images and associations and translate them into clear and cohesive readings, which we were not able to do.

Although most of my associations turned out to be astonishing hits once the owner of the pendant was identified and I received her feedback, I would not have been able to decipher my imagery by myself and come up with a concrete, specific, and unambiguous reading. Surprisingly, my psychometric reading had one important part, the relevance of which was not immediately obvious. The memories of my medical studies and my later professional work focusing strongly on situations involving cancer were more than just allusions to Myra's medical profession. Several months after our Esalen monthlong, Myra was diagnosed with cancer, and eventually succumbed to this disease.

ANTS OF THE GREAT
MOTHER GODDESS

A Visit to Palenque

The next story shows that transpersonal experiences in holotropic states of consciousness can provide "paranormal" access to new information about archetypal and historical spheres of the collective unconscious. In many instances, it is possible to verify the accuracy of the information about deities and mythological domains of other cultures, as well as various periods of human history, obtained in this way. It does not seem to matter whether or not these mythologies, cultures, or historical facts were previously known to the subject. These observations parallel and confirm C. G. Jung's discovery that, besides the Freudian individual unconscious, the psyche of each of us also has access to the collective unconscious, which harbors the records of the history and mythological heritage of humanity.

The events described here happened at the end of November 1971, when my brother, Paul, and I attended the Fifth World Congress of Psychiatry in Mexico City. Paul, a psychiatrist like myself, worked at the time at the Psychiatric Hospital of McMasters University in Hamilton, Ontario, and I lived and worked in Baltimore. The congress offered us a welcome opportunity for a reunion. We decided to use the time after the conference for a joint trip to the Yucatán Peninsula to explore the ruins of the ancient Mayan cities.

When the Congress ended, we rented a car and after a long drive reached Mérida, the capital of Yucatán. Using our hotel in Mérida as a base, we explored the surrounding ruins—Chichen Itza, Dzibilchaltún, Uxmal, and

Tulum. In the middle of intense sightseeing, I developed flu symptoms and a very sore throat. I could not give up seeing the monuments of the ancient Mayans, a culture that since my adolescent years had been for me a subject of very intense interest. The high fever and large quantities of daiquiri I drank to combat my pharyngitis and laryngitis added a very interesting dimension to my experience. I got in touch with a few past-life memories and had some very interesting intuitive insights about the places we visited.

In spite of the fact that I was able to rest only at nighttime, I managed to reach a reasonable degree of recovery before our return to Mexico City. On the way back, we decided to stop in Villa Hermosa and visit Palenque, one of the most remarkable Mayan ruins. Although my physical condition was not quite back to normal, I decided against my better judgment to take some methyl-enedioxyamphetamine (MDA), a psychedelic, or entheogen, closely related to Ecstasy. My original plan was to take the substance in Chichen Itza, but I was not able to because I felt too sick. Doing a session in this extraordinary location was part of my exploration of the cultural effect of psychedelics. I knew from my previous experiences that these substances were able to provide extraordinarily deep insights into the archetypal dynamics of sacred places.

Although I was aware of the importance of safe set and setting for psychedelic experiences, this was an opportunity I did not want to miss. On the basis of my previous sessions with MDA, I felt confident that I could handle its effects in a public place without attracting too much attention. I covered my eyes with dark glasses so that the other visitors could not see my dilated pupils and took 125 milligrams of the substance. Whether it was my incomplete convalescence, the power of the place, or particularly powerful astrological transits, the effects of the MDA were incomparably more powerful than at any time in the past.

The onset of the experience was extraordinarily sudden and dramatic. I found it increasingly difficult to relate to the ruins surrounding me simply as an admiring visitor. I felt waves of deep anxiety permeating my whole being and an almost metaphysical sense of oppression. My perceptual field was becoming darker and darker, and I started noticing that the objects around me were endowed with awesome energy and had begun to undulate in a most ominous fashion.

I realized that Palenque was a place where thousands of human sacrifices had taken place and felt that all the suffering of ages somehow still hung around as a heavy cloud. I sensed the presence of wrathful Mayan deities and their thirst for blood. They obviously craved more sacrifice and seemed to assume that I would be their next sacrificial victim. As convincing as this feeling was, I had enough critical insight to realize that this was an inner symbolic experience and that my life was not really in danger.

I closed my eyes to find out what was happening inside my psyche. All of a sudden, it seemed that history came alive; I saw Palenque not as ruins, but as a thriving sacred city at the height of its glory. I witnessed a sacrificial ritual in incredible detail; however, I was not simply an observer, but also the sacrificial victims. This was immediately followed by another similar scene, and yet another. As I was getting extraordinary insights into pre-Columbian religion and the role that sacrifice played in this system, my individual boundaries seemed to have completely disappeared, and I felt increasingly connected to all those who had died in Palenque over the centuries to such an extent that I became them.

I experienced myself as an immense pool of emotions they had felt; it contained a whole spectrum of feelings—regret over the loss of young life, anxious anticipation, and strange ambivalence toward their executioners, but also peculiar surrender to their fate and even excitement and curious expectation about what was going to come. I had a strong sense that the preparation for the ritual involved the administration of some mind-altering drugs that raised the experience to another level.

I was fascinated by the dimensions of the experience and by the richness of insights that it entailed. I climbed the hill and lay down by the Temple of the Sun to be able to concentrate better on what was happening. The scenes of the past kept bombarding my consciousness with extraordinary force. My fascination was rapidly being replaced by deep metaphysical fear. A message seemed to come loud and clear: "You are not here as a tourist eavesdropping on history, but as a sacrificial victim, like all the others who were sacrificed in the past. You will not leave here alive." I felt the overpowering presence of the deities demanding sacrifice, and even the walls of the buildings seemed to be thirsting for more blood—my own.

I had experienced altered states of consciousness before in my psychedelic sessions and knew that the worst fears in these experiences do not reflect objectively existing danger and usually dissipate as soon as consciousness returns to normal. As convincing as the experience was, I wanted to believe that it was "just another one of those." But the feelings of impending doom became increasingly real. I opened my eyes and a feeling of bloodcurdling panic took over my entire being. My body was covered with giant ants, and my skin was erupting into hundreds of red bumps. This was not just in my mind; this was really happening.

I realized that this unexpected complication provided an element that was previously missing to make my fears absolutely convincing. Earlier I had doubted that MDA alone could kill me, but now I was not sure what large amounts of the toxin of hundreds of giant Mexican ants could do to someone whose sympathetic nervous system was strongly activated by MDA, an amphetamine derivative. The ants brought an unknown into the equation—the chemical ingredients of their toxin and its interaction with the substance I had taken. I decided to run, to escape from the ruins, remove myself from the influence of the deities. However, time seemed to have slowed down almost to the point of stopping, and my whole body felt enormously heavy, as if it were made of lead.

I desperately tried to run as fast as I could, but it seemed that I was progressing as if in a slow-motion movie. I felt as if I were caught in a tractor beam; the deities and the walls of the ruins had a firm grip on me and were holding me under their spell. As this was happening, images of the entire history of Palenque were still flashing through my mind. I could see the parking lot full of cars separated from the ruins by a heavy chain. There was the predictable rational world of my everyday reality. I set my mind on the task of getting there, feeling that this would somehow save my life. At the time, I saw the chain as a boundary where the influence of the magic world of ancient gods ended. Has not our modern world conquered and discredited the empires based on beliefs in such mythical realities?

My expectation turned out to be correct. After what seemed like eternity and with enormous effort, I reached the parking lot. At that moment, it was as if a heavy weight—physical, psychological, and spiritual—was lifted off my being. I felt light, ecstatic, reborn and pulsing with exuberant life energy. My senses felt cleansed and wide open; the glorious sunset during my return trip from Palenque, the dinner in a small restaurant in Villa Hermosa, watching the pulse of life in the streets, and tasting of fruit juices in the local *jugerías* were truly ecstatic experiences.

However, I spent much of the night taking cold showers to alleviate the pain and burning sensations from all the ant bites. As the effects of MDA withered away, hundreds of itching bumps covering my entire body became my dominant reality. Several years later, a German friend of mine, Christian Raetsch, a famous anthropologist and ethnobotanist, who had studied extensively Meso-American cultures and actually lived for a long time with the Lacandon Mayas, told me during his visit to Esalen that ants played an important role in Mayan mythology and were deeply connected with the Earth goddess and with the death-rebirth process.

ULURU AND ALCHERINGA
An Adventure in Dreamtime

This story describes some extraordinary adventures in non-ordinary realities that Christina and I had during our visit to Australia, more specifically to central Australia and its spectacular Ayers Rock, or Uluru. What makes this experience particularly interesting is that we were able to find independent verification for the new information about the archetypal and ritual world of the Aborigines that we obtained in our respective holotropic states—me in a psychedelic session and Christina in her spontaneous experiences, which were part of her spiritual emergency.

Australia has many features that make it unique and remarkable—its isolated location in the Southern Hemisphere, the vastness of its central desert, the picturesque giant Ayers rock in the middle of the continent, and, particularly, its fauna, which has no parallels in the world—the marsupial kangaroo, wombat, and Tasmanian devil, and the monotreme duck-billed platypus and echidna. But for anthropologists, psychologists, and consciousness researchers, the most intriguing aspect of this continent is its original inhabitants, the Australian Aborigines.

This remarkable group of hunters and gatherers has been in Australia for at least fifty thousand years and has essentially coevolved with the changing continent. The Aborigines adapted to the harsh Australian environment by living in seminomadic groups in conditions externally not very different from the Stone Age. And yet, their inner life has been extraordinarily rich. They have a fascinating ritual and spiritual life and complex mythology closely related to the land in which they live. Researchers who have lived with the Aborigines and studied them report that these people spend much time in a remarkable state of consciousness called *alcheringa* (Dreamtime).

We have read and heard many stories about the remarkable psychic abilities of the Aborigines. These accounts described that they were able to communicate with each other without the aid of any physical means, such as messengers, sounds, or smoke signals; they could accurately transmit thoughts, feelings, and ideas to friends and relatives who were hundreds of miles away. The intuitive connection the Aborigines had with nature was equally remarkable. They knew, for example, that a small local rain, a rare and precious occurrence in the desert, would fall several miles away, and would run there with impeccable timing to intercept it. According to some other stories, they have been able to reconstruct crimes, identify and track down criminals, and locate strayed cattle and lost valuables. They also had incredible ability to see and identify small objects at great distances.

These reports together with our knowledge of the mythology, paintings, and music of this extraordinary group of people generated in us great interest in getting to know them better. Our first opportunity came when we were invited by our friends Alf and Muriel Foote to conduct a Holotropic Breathwork workshop in their center in Blackwood, near Melbourne. Another reason for our meeting was to prepare ground for a conference of the International Transpersonal Association (ITA) in Phillip Island, near the Australian coast.

During our stay in Blackwood, we started exploring with our friends the possibility of spending some time with the Aborigines and meeting their elders. This turned out to be a much more difficult problem than we expected. We found out that they were not a homogeneous group; several hundred thousand surviving Aborigines spoke among them more than two hundred languages. In addition, they were divided into a number of so called "skin groups," each with its own mythology, rituals, and strict rules for intermarriage. It was generally not easy to find "cultural brokers," who mediate the contact with the various Aboriginal groups, and the few that we found out about were very protective of them, because of some bad experience in the past, and very cautious about foreigners whom they did not know.

While still in California, we had decided to include central Australia in our trip and visit Ayer's Rock, a unique geological formation in the middle of the continent that the Aborigenes call Uluru and consider their "Cosmic Mountain." Because all our attempts to find useful contacts had failed, we had to undertake this trip on our own. As it turned out, our encounter with the Aboriginal culture took a different form than we expected. It happened through powerful inner experiences rather than external contacts.

We flew from Melbourne to Alice Springs, and instead of using a small plane for a flight to Ayers Rock, we decided to rent a car. We wanted to get an intimate feeling for the awesome red desert covering most of Australia. The distance between Alice Springs and Uluru was almost three hundred miles, and the drive in scorching heat lasted many hours. The Aborigines are able to perceive many interesting nuances in the desert territory and have various mythological stories attached to them. In addition, they believe that every meaningful activity or process that occurs at a particular place leaves behind a vibrational residue in the earth, in the same way that plants leave an image of themselves as seeds. The shape of the landscape thus carries and reflects vibrations, which echo the events that created them, as well as footprints of the mythological beings that were instrumental in this process. This energy pattern, *guruwari,* or seed power, is an integral part of the terrain and lends it profound metaphysical meaning.

To us, as Western observers, the scenery seemed beautiful and awesome, but monotonous. On occasion, we noticed along the road bleached skeletons of dingoes, camels, and other animals. A welcome distraction on our long journey was an encounter with a perentie, a giant monitor lizard (*Varanus giganteus*) basking in the sun a few yards from the road. We later discovered that the meat of this animal was considered a delicacy by the Aborigines.

Ayers Rock, or Uluru, is the world's largest monolith, roughly oval in shape. It is a spectacular sandstone formation with the circumference of almost six miles, towering a thousand feet above hundreds of miles of red desert. It is thought to be the tip of a mountain that extends miles below the surface. When we finally arrived there exhausted after many hours of driving through the desert, we discovered to our delight a small motel, located only about 200 yards from the majestic monolith. We checked in and decided to go for a walk and get the first impression of the environment.

The sun was setting, and we walked far into the desert to get a good view of the rock. When we reached a sufficient distance from the motel, the panorama of Uluru with its reddish-orange sharply contrasting with the dark blue sky was absolutely magnificent. This wonder of nature was known to shine with its full breathtaking beauty at sunrise and sunset. The motel, located in such an auspicious place, seemed like a perfect setting for a psychedelic experience. I had with me some LSD, a leftover from my research in Czechoslovakia, where I had been principal investigator in a program of psychedelic therapy and had unlimited access to the substance.

Although I felt somewhat tired after the long drive through the desert, I decided to use this unique opportunity and embark on an inner journey. Christina, who at that time was wide open and had had many spontaneous experiences as a result of her Kundalini awakening, decided not to join me in this adventure. She offered that I wake her up if I needed somebody to "hold my kite string," as we called it. I took 400 micrograms of LSD and made myself comfortable on my motel bed.

After I engaged in about forty-five minutes of quiet meditation, the substance started to take effect, and my state of consciousness underwent very rapid and profound changes. I felt that my experience had transported me rapidly to Dreamtime and to the beginning of the world. I had some passing knowledge of Australian mythology, but what I witnessed by far surpassed anything I have ever read or heard about. And yet, I somehow did not have any doubt that my experience of this mythic domain of the Aborigines was absolutely authentic.

I saw the surface of the Earth, flat, nondescript, and featureless, and witnessed the arrival of mythic figures of many different forms. They chanted some mysterious songs, and as they were doing that, they seemed to give shapes to the landscape, bringing into existence rocks, mountains, canyons, and waterholes. Some of them had human forms, others the shape of snakes or other animals. Among them were several giant anthropomorphic figures that particularly attracted my attention. I had never heard before that giants were part of the mythology of the Aborigines.

Initially, I just played the role of an observer witnessing this fantastic display of Dreamtime scenes. Suddenly, this situation changed; the inhabitants of the Dreamtime world now turned against me as an unwelcome intruder, threatening to destroy me and demanding that I reveal the motivation of my daring trespassing. I tried to explain that I was coming with much respect and humility, that my intentions were friendly, and that my only motive was search for knowledge. I underwent what seemed to be rigorous psychological and spiritual scrutiny by these mythic beings and was finally granted permission to visit their domain. The condition was to fully submit to its rules.

Having overcome this difficult impasse, I was able to continue unimpeded my journey through the Great Dreaming (or Dreamtime). In front of my eyes, the majestic mass of Uluru emerged out of the primordial abyss existing somewhere beyond space and time as we know it. It was not an inorganic geological mass, as it appears to be in our world, but a giant crouching creature, a terrifying monstrous reptile. I heard deafening thunder as it opened its massive jaws and could see the inside of its maw. It was filled with what seemed like whirling volcanic magma, which occasionally spewed out in monumental discharges.

But describing the inside of the creature's maw as volcanic magma captured only the surface appearance of this mysterious substance. Like hot lava it seemed to have the potential to destroy or create, but on a much deeper level and a much larger scale. It seemed to be the archetypal essence that underlies volcanic activity. Like the Greek primordial matter, *hyle*, or the *prima materia* of the alchemists, it seemed to be the universal principle of creation and destruction. It was the essence of existence, from which forms emerge and into which they return. I watched this awesome spectacle and felt that I was witnessing the ultimate mystery of the cosmos.

Before I could fully recover from this shattering encounter with the primordial Uluru reptile of creation and destruction, I was confronted with another giant figure. It was the Great Mother Goddess in the form of a female kangaroo. Suddenly, I realized that I had become a tiny kangaroo fetus in her womb, undergoing the process of birth. The passage through the birth canal was easy as compared with my human birth, which I had experienced in my previous psychedelic sessions.

What was an exceedingly challenging ordeal, a true rite of passage, was the following climb to her pouch and the struggle to reach her nourishing teats. This journey was so demanding that I felt several times I would not be able to finish it and would die on the way. But, finally, I was able to reach my goal, and the nourishing milk pouring generously from the nipple of the Great Mother Kangaroo tasted like ambrosia; it made me forget the hardships of the tedious journey. The ecstatic union with the Kangaroo Goddess was the last major experience of my session.

The dawn was breaking, and Christina woke up, curious about my adventures on the night journey. I briefly shared with her some of the highlights of my experience, and we decided to climb Ayers Rock to watch the sunrise and enjoy the view of the surrounding desert from the top. The ascent was rather steep, and in many places we needed to use the chains provided for the visitors. As we were about one-third of the way to the top, the weather changed rapidly, and we were repeatedly hit by powerful gusts of wind.

Christina suddenly sensed that she had encountered an impenetrable force field that prevented her from continuing her climb. It was as if invisible hands were pushing her off the rock. She decided to yield to this pressure, return to the base, and wait for me there. I had not yet completely returned to my ordinary state of consciousness and felt a strong determination to continue to climb and reach the summit. As I was fighting the onslaughts of the wind, I was receiving inner messages from an unknown source telling me that among the Aborigines climbing the rock was a special privilege, but that I had gained the right to do it by undergoing the rite of passage the preceding night.

The view of the vast desert painted red-orange by the rising sun was spectacular. Several tourists reached the top after me; they took pictures of each other, involved in a loud conversation. Among them was a woman in a T-shirt that carried a proud inscription: "I climbed Ayers Rock." I did not stay very long and started my descent, seeking reunion with Christina and quiet time for reflection. I found her in a small cave, deeply immersed in meditation.

She told me that being in a very open and receptive state of mind she was having powerful experiences of her own, hearing ritual music and chanting. Wondering if what she was hearing was a *corroboree*, a ceremony of Aboriginal people, she tried to go where the sound seemed to be coming from to check it out. But there were no Aboriginal people around. She showed me specific places that she was convinced were ceremonial grounds. Later we found out in the motel that since Uluru had become a tourist place, no Aboriginal ceremonies were taking place there. This situation lasted until October 1985, when the title to the land around Uluru was passed to the Aborigines.

It turned out that when Christina was waiting for me, she had also had some interesting insights concerning her experience during the climb. "I understand why I could not climb the rock," she explained. "For the Aborigines, this was a place of male initiation, where women were not allowed. At one point, I got a very clear message: 'You are a woman; you should not be here.'" We decided to spend the rest of the day driving around the rock and exploring its environment, with the help of a guidebook that we purchased in the motel. We embarked on our journey, making frequent stops to admire the exquisite work of nature.

It was easy to understand why Uluru had engaged so powerfully and deeply the imagination of the Aborigines. The surface of the giant rock was heavily weathered and broken into a rich array of bizarre cliffs and deep caves. The whimsy of weather had shaped the surface layer of the malleable sandstone into myriad fantastic formations. Our guidebook provided a detailed description of the most important patterns in the rock's surface and the Aboriginal myths associated with them. In these stories, each of the distinct combinations of forms was accounted for and explained by an event in Dreamtime that had created it. We were astonished, because the little booklet confirmed much of the information that we obtained through our inner experiences during the preceding night and in the early morning.

We found out that tribal people of the area, the Pitjantjatjara and Yankunyt-jatjara, also known as Anangu, pictured Uluru as a gigantic primordial reptile, which was the principle of creation and destruction. Among the figures featured in the Dreaming were giants over nine feet tall, just as I saw them in my session. Climbing Uluru was an annual ritual event allowed only to two selected members of the tribe and represented special honor. One of the caves we saw during our circling around the rock was an initiation cave for rites of passage and carried the name Kangaroo Pouch. The booklet also confirmed all of Christina's insights. The places where she heard music and chanting were ceremonial grounds, where sacred rituals used to be conducted. She also correctly identified the ceremonial sites where male initiations took place and women were not allowed.

I thought about the visiting buses full of tourists, who see Uluru as nothing more than a sightseeing attraction and see climbing to its top as a physical exercise. And particularly about the young woman with the triumphant inscription on her T-shirt, whom I met at the top of Uluru. For her, it did not seem particularly difficult to accomplish what Christina found impossible to do. She could move around with utter insensitivity for the ancient taboos. It was not the wind or lack of physical stamina or prowess that prevented Christina, with her body seasoned by years of hatha yoga, from continuing the climb, but something else, much more mysterious and profound.

Apparently, the non-ordinary state of consciousness Christina was in, which enhanced her psychic abilities and gave her access to remarkable insights about the sacred sites, also made her susceptible to the taboos that were mandatory for native people. It was obvious that the industrial civilization had dulled the intuitive faculties of its members, made them oblivious of the hidden dimensions of reality, and immunized them against the numinous aspects of existence. Entering non-ordinary states spontaneously or with the use of some form of mind-altering technology lifts this veil and opens us up to ordinarily invisible and inaudible realities.

For our return to Alice Springs, we decided to use a different route and spend the night in one of the ranches in the desert. When we were leaving Uluru, Christina was still deeply immersed in her experience. We expected that the influence this powerful place had on her would subside as our distance from it grew. But that is not what happened. The image of the orange rock in the rear window of our car was getting smaller and smaller and finally disappeared. But that did not seem to have any noticeable effect on Christina's condition.

The spell Uluru had on Christina was finally broken when we arrived at Collin Springs, a small oasis in the desert, where we stopped to buy some cold drinks and snacks. Walking around the grounds, we discovered that the owner of the place had a small collection of birds. Most of them were confined to a large cage, but several peacocks were allowed to move freely on the premises. Christina was astonished and excited to see them. Not only was it extremely unlikely to find peacocks in the middle of the Australian desert, but peacocks had a great symbolic significance for her spiritual journey.

In the past, visions of peacocks had formed an important part of the most profound and meaningful experiences she had had in her inner process, and peacock symbolism repeatedly appeared in her paintings. In addition, the peacock was a very important symbol in Siddha Yoga, Christina's primary spiritual discipline. Her teacher, Swami Muktananda, had often used a wand of peacock feathers scented with sandalwood oil to give shaktipat, to awaken the spiritual energy in his disciples.

She decided to buy some bread and feed it to the peacocks. As she was offering the bread to the birds in a conscious and meditative way, she felt that she was connecting in a powerful way to her own spiritual tradition: to her teacher, to Siddha Yoga, to India, and to everything that this represented for her. At the same time, this process seemed to have brought her into her ordinary state of consciousness and completed her experiential journey into the world of the Aborigines.

We spent the night in a hospitable ranch in the desert that offered its guests a warm swimming pool and a barbeque dinner. I discovered to my great delight that among the items offered for dinner were grilled witchetty grubs, a delicacy of the Australian Aborigines that I had been very curious and eager to try. This was the finale of my journey into Dreamtime, much less dramatic and spiritual than Christina's closure with the peacock ritual. The next day, we returned to Alice Springs and reconnected with the "Big World," as we jokingly referred to modern technological society at the time of our inner explorations.

TEMPTATIONS OF A NON-LOCAL UNIVERSE

Failed Experiment in Astral Projection

O ne of the most extraordinary adventures in consciousness that I have personally encountered during the fifty years of my inner exploration was a powerful experience of what the spiritual literature refers to as astral projection. It occurred in a high-dose psychedelic session that I had in 1967 in the Research Unit of Spring Grove State Hospital, which later moved to the new Maryland Psychiatric Research Center built on the same premises in Baltimore. As I have mentioned, one of the research programs conducted there allowed psychiatrists, psychologists, and other mental health professionals to have up to three high-dose psychedelic sessions for training purposes. Shortly after I arrived in the United States and joined the staff, I decided to take advantage of this unique opportunity.

The studies conducted at Spring Grove were using an approach called psychedelic therapy. It involved administration of large doses of LSD (400 to 600 micrograms), and the sessions were strictly internalized by the use of eyeshades and headphones. An alternative method called psycholytic, used primarily by European therapists, involved an entire series of sessions with lower dosages of psychedelics. The experimental subjects were during their sessions under the constant supervision of a male-female dyad of therapist and nurse. Several hours of preparation allowed, among other things, to create a strong bond and a good working relationship between the client and the guides. My guides for the session were psychologist Sandy Unger, the person who conceived and designed the Spring Grove studies, and Nancy Jewell, a middle-aged nurse with a Southern Baptist background and a warm, maternal presence.

The LSD used in this session came from Sandoz pharmaceutical company in Switzerland, and the dose was 400 micrograms. It was a very powerful experience, as I expected; the dose of 400 micrograms was in the range for which psychedelic therapists very appropriately used the term "single overwhelming dose." However, nothing that happened during the first few hours was significantly different from what I had experienced in my previous sessions in Prague. And then, sometime in the second half of my session, I found myself in a very strange and unusual state of mind. It was a feeling of serenity, bliss, and naïve simplicity, mixed with awe in regard to the mystery of existence. I sensed that what I was experiencing was similar to what the early Christians must have experienced.

It was a world where miracles were possible, acceptable, and even plausible. In this state of mind, I started to think about the nature and origin of time and space and the enigmas and paradoxes associated with them, such as the mysteries of eternity and infinity. I had to laugh that I had ever believed that linear time and three-dimensional space were absolute and mandatory dimensions of reality. It appeared to me rather obvious that there were no limits whatsoever in the realm of spirit and that time and space were arbitrary constructs of the psyche.

I suddenly realized that I did not have to be bound by the limitations of time and space and could travel in the space-time continuum quite freely and without any restrictions. This feeling was so convincing and overwhelming that I wanted to test it by an experiment. I decided to see if I could travel to my parents' apartment in Prague, which was many thousand miles away. After determining the direction and considering the distance, I imagined myself flying through space to the place of my destination. I had the experience of moving through space at an enormous speed, but, to my disappointment, I was not getting anywhere.

I could not understand why the experiment did not work because my feeling that such space travel should be possible was very convincing. All of a sudden, I realized that I was still under the influence of my old concepts of time and space. I continued to think in terms of directions and distances and approached the task accordingly. It occurred to me that the proper approach would be to make myself believe that the place of my session was actually identical with the place of my destination. I said to myself: "This is not Baltimore; this is Prague. Right here and now, I am in my parents' apartment in Prague."

When I approached the task in this way, I experienced peculiar and bizarre sensations. I found myself in a strange, rather congested place full of electric circuits, tubes, wires, resistors, and condensers. After a short period of confusion, I realized that my consciousness was trapped in a television set located in the corner of the room in my parents' apartment. I was trying, somehow, to use the speakers for hearing and the tube for seeing. After a while, I had to laugh because I realized that this experience was a symbolic spoof ridiculing the fact that I was still imprisoned by my previous beliefs concerning space, time, and matter.

The only way of experiencing what was happening in distant locations that I could conceive of and intellectually accept was by means of television technology. Such a transmission, of course, would be restricted by the velocity of the electromagnetic waves involved. But human thought and consciousness were not limited even by the speed of light. At the moment when I realized and firmly believed that my consciousness could transcend any limitations whatsoever, the experience changed dramatically. The television set turned inside out like a three-dimensional Möbius strip, and I found myself walking in my parents' Prague apartment.

At this point, I did not feel any drug effect, and the experience was as real as any other situation in my life. The door of my parents' bedroom was half-open. I looked in, saw their bodies on the bed, and heard them breathing. I walked to the window in the living room and looked out. The clock on the street corner showed a six-hour difference from the time in Baltimore, where the experiment took place. In spite of the fact that this number of hours reflected the actual time difference between the two zones, I did not find it to be convincing evidence of the veracity of my experience. Because I intellectually knew the time difference, my mind could have easily fabricated this particular detail.

I lay down on the couch in the corner of the living room to reflect on my experience. I realized that it was the same couch on which I had spent my last psychedelic session before my departure to the United States. Shortly before that session, my request for permission to travel to the United States on a fellowship had been turned down by Czech authorities. My last session in Prague had happened at a time when I was waiting for the response to my appeal. Thinking about it, I suddenly felt a wave of overwhelming anxiety.

An alarming idea emerged in my mind with unusual force and persuasiveness: maybe I had never left Czechoslovakia and was now coming back from the psychedelic session in Prague. Maybe the positive response to my appeal, my journey to the United States, joining the team in Baltimore, and having a psychedelic session there was just a visionary journey, an illusory product of strong wishful thinking. I was trapped in an insidious loop, a spatiotemporal vicious circle, unable to determine my real historical and geographic coordinates.

For a long time, I felt suspended between two realities, both of which were equally convincing. I could not tell whether I was experiencing an astral projection to Prague from my session in Baltimore or coming down from a session in Prague in which I had experienced a trip to the United States. I had to think about the Chinese philosopher Chuang Tzu, who awoke from a dream in which he was a butterfly. For some time, he was unable to decide whether he was a human who just had a dream of being a butterfly, or a butterfly dreaming that he was a human.

I felt that I needed much more convincing proof of whether what I was experiencing was "objectively real" in the usual sense. I finally decided to perform a test—to take a picture from the wall and later check in the correspondence with my parents if something unusual had happened at that time in their apartment. I reached for the picture, but before I was able to touch the frame, I was overcome by an increasingly alarming feeling that it was an extremely risky and dangerous undertaking. I suddenly felt under the attack of evil forces and perilous black magic. It seemed to me that what I was about to do was a hazardous gamble in which the price was my soul.

I paused and made a desperate effort to understand what was happening. Images of the world's most famous casinos were flashing in front of my eyes— Monte Carlo, Lido in Venice, Las Vegas, Reno. I saw roulette balls spiraling at intoxicating speeds, the levers of the slot machines frantically moving up and down, and dice rolling on the green surface of the tables during a game of craps. Groups of gamblers were feverishly passing around cards, playing baccarat, and watching the flickering lights of the keno panels. I felt the tempting lure of riches, luxury, and unlimited possibilities that money can provide.

This was followed by visions portraying meetings of secret organizations that run human history from behind the scenes, international summits of heads of states, encounters of powerful politicians with representatives of multinational companies, interiors of military headquarters, and think tanks of topnotch scientists. This time it was the lure of power, rather than riches, but equally seductive and intoxicating. The story of Faust, the seeker who traded his soul for unlimited possibilities, came to my mind and began haunting me.

I was desperately trying to understand why the possibility of transcending the limitations of time and space appeared to me to be so abysmally dangerous. Suddenly, I could see my predicament with unusual clarity. The images were showing me that I had not yet overcome my egocentrism and was not able to resist the temptation of money and power. The danger of the situation was associated with my temptation to use paranormal faculties for personal goals, to abuse the potential that I was discovering.

If I could conquer the limitations imposed on us by time and space, I would gain an unlimited supply of money, together with everything that money can buy. All I would have to do was to go to the nearest casino, stock market, or lottery office. Unlimited means would become available to me, and my world would turn into a cornucopia. If I could have mastery over time and space, no secrets would exist for me. I would be able to eavesdrop on summit meetings of political leaders and have access to top-secret discoveries. This would open undreamed-of possibilities for directing the course of events in the world.

I remembered passages from different spiritual books warning against toying with supernatural powers before we overcome the limitations of our egos and reach spiritual maturity. They suddenly appeared eminently clear and understandable. But my fear of ethical repercussions for my spiritual impurity was just part of the picture. I realized that I was also extremely ambivalent in regard to the outcome of my test. On the one hand, it seemed extremely enticing to be able to liberate myself from the slavery of time and space. On the other hand, it was obvious that a positive outcome of this experiment would have far-reaching and serious consequences. It clearly was much more than an isolated experiment revealing the arbitrary nature of space and time.

If I could get confirmation that it was possible to manipulate the physical environment at a distance of several thousand miles, my entire universe would collapse as a result of this one experiment. The world as I had known it would not exist any more. I would lose all the maps I relied on and with which I felt comfortable. I would find myself in a state of utter metaphysical confusion. I would not know who, where, and when I was and would be lost in a totally new, frightening reality, the laws of which would be alien and unfamiliar to me. If I had these powers, there would likely be many others who would have them, too. I would have no privacy anywhere, and doors and walls would not protect me anymore. My new world would be full of potential dangers of unforeseeable kind and unimaginable proportions.

I was not able to carry through with the experiment and decided to leave the question of the objectivity and reality of the experience unresolved. This made it possible for me to toy with the idea that I had actually been able to transcend time and space. At the same time, it left open the possibility of seeing the entire episode as a fantasy journey caused by a powerful psychedelic substance. Objective verification of the fact that reality as I knew it was an illusion was more terrifying than I could tolerate under the circumstances.

The moment I gave up on the experiment, I found myself back in the room in Baltimore where I took the substance. Within a few hours, I gradually returned into ordinary consciousness and the familiar "objective reality" of the material world. I had no more doubts that my journey to the United States had actually happened and that I was in Baltimore. I never forgave myself for having wasted such a unique and fantastic opportunity of subjecting the phenomenon of astral projection to experimental scrutiny. However, the memory of the metaphysical terror involved in this test makes me doubt that I would be more courageous if I were given a similar chance in the future.

Ancient Indian teachings see the experience of the phenomenal worlds as *lila*, or divine play, created by Absolute Consciousness, or Brahman. They see our perception of the material world as a cosmic illusion, or *maya*. In the twentieth century, quantum-relativistic physics brought important supportive evidence for this view of reality. My experience of astral projection to Prague taught me how deeply we are imbedded in our belief in an objectively existing and predictable material world and how strong the emotional investment and commitment we have in maintaining this illusion. A sudden collapse of our understanding of the nature of reality and violation of Alan Watts's "taboo against knowing who we are" can be associated with indescribable metaphysical terror and panic.

CHANNELING THE AVATAR

My Mother, Sai Baba, and Holotropic Breathwork

I n the late 1960s, Czechoslovakia was experiencing a wave of liberal- ization that culminated in 1968 in the famous "Prague Spring." This movement preceded by two decades Mikhail Gorbachev's "perestroika" and "glasnost," similar developments in Russia that eventually led to the dissolution of the Soviet Union. Czech political leaders were involved in an unprecedented experiment aimed at creating what they called "socialism with a human face." In 1967, my brother, Paul, and I were able to leave Czechoslovakia and find new lives on the North American continent, Paul in Canada and I in the United States.

On August 21 of the following year, the hopes of Czech and Slovak people for freedom and democracy were brutally squashed by the Soviet military in- vasion. What had begun for us as a legal visit changed into emigration that was considered illegal by Czech authorities. As a result, Paul and I could not travel freely between Czechoslovakia and the United States or Canada. However, we stayed in regular contact with our parents by frequent correspondence and occasional meetings outside of Czechoslovakia.

Both our parents were retired and as such were allowed to travel abroad. The Communist regime was not interested in keeping in the country people who were not productive and contributing members of the society. As a mat- ter of fact, they encouraged emigration for this category of its citizens because this would have meant confiscation of their apartments, a rare commodity in the Communist world, and discontinuation of their pensions and other social benefits. Our parents were thus able to visit Paul and me in America and meet with us during our visits to Western Europe.

While my parents were able to get the permission to travel, it was impossible for them to buy any hard currency. During their stay abroad, they were thus entirely dependent on our financial support. This was very easy for Paul and me, but presented an emotional conflict for my mother. She was an extremely generous person who found it much easier to give to others than to receive. As a result, she always felt great need to reciprocate by contributing in some significant way to our lives. This character trait of my mother plays an important role in the story I am about to tell.

In 1973, when I moved to Big Sur, California, the Esalen Institute provided for me a charming house on a cliff overlooking the Pacific Ocean in exchange for leading a certain number of workshops. When Christina began living and working with me, we were able to turn a patch of land separating our house from the ocean into a lovely vegetable garden. It took a lot of hard labor because the land was overgrown with wild chaparral, thistles, gorse, plants with prickly burs, and the infamous poison oak. Our gardening represented a constant battle, with nature trying to invade and reclaim this land.

When my mother arrived in Big Sur for her first solo visit after the death of my father, she quickly discovered that some serious gardening work had to be done in our little plantation on the Pacific. Without consulting us, she threw herself into the project, determined to free our garden and its immediate environment from everything that appeared to be useless weeds. All of us living in Big Sur were well acquainted with poison oak, a botanical menace that has the potential to turn life in paradise into living hell. Many of us learned about the ravages of poison oak the hard way—by painful exposure at the time of our ignorance. My mother was a newcomer and lacked the necessary knowledge.

After exposure to the resin on the leaves and branches of poison oak, most people develop extensive skin eruptions and leaking blisters that cause agonizing itching. It takes usually three to four weeks for the condition to subside. In more serious cases, the reaction is very severe and systemic, rather than local; inhalation of smoke from burning branches of poison oaks has the potential to cause pulmonary edema. Old-timers keeping alive the oral tradition of Big Sur lore pass on a horror story about two naïve and unsuspecting East Coast tourists, a father and his son, who during their California tour ran out of toilet paper and made an attempt to replace it with leaves of poison oak.

My mother suffered from various allergies, and her response to the exposure to poison oak was horrendous. Her entire body was covered with red eruptions and leaking blisters; the itching caused her unimaginable torment. Several days after the exposure, her physical condition seemed to be critical and resulted in an intense visionary state. In the middle of the night, she experienced the visit of her dead relatives—her parents and her brother. She also envisioned my dead father, who had arrived in an old-fashioned *cocher de fiacre*, a carriage drawn by two horses, which was popular as a means of transportation in European cities before the advent of taxis. He wore a tuxedo and a cylinder hat and tried to persuade her to join him on the other side.

I sat at my mother's bedside for many hours and became increasingly concerned. Having done extensive work with terminal cancer patients and being familiar with thanatological literature, I recognized the similarity between my mother's visions and the experiences of the "welcoming committee" known from bedside observations of dying people. I happened to have several ampoules of cortisone, an effective remedy for poison oak, and decided to give it to her intramuscularly as a last resort before undertaking the fifty-mile trip to Carmel Hospital, the nearest medical facility.

Within an hour, my mother's condition improved as if by magic. She regained physical strength and her mind cleared. As the day was breaking, she decided to step out of the house on our large deck to watch the sunrise over the Ventana wilderness and observe the Pacific Ocean. She was ecstatic, and her eyes were radiant. "Stan, you live in an incredible place!" she said enthusiastically. "The air is so clear here, and all the colors are radiant! Have you ever noticed the sparkles in the branches of these pine trees? And look at the reflections of light on the waves!" There was no doubt she was experiencing what I had witnessed many hundreds of times in my work with psychedelics and, more recently, with Holotropic Breath-work—a profound psychospiritual rebirth!

The following day, my mother described in some detail the experiences she had had during the night when her condition reached a critical point and those following the injection of cortisone. Shortly after I gave her the shot, she had a powerful vision of an Indian saint, appearing in blinding radiant light. His rich, bushy hair and long red robe helped her to identify him as Satya Sai Baba. He reached inside her body and performed miraculous healing. There was no doubt in her mind that his intervention was a critical turning point in her physical and emotional condition; she was convinced that it was Sai Baba rather than the cortisone that brought her back from the threshold of death.

In India, Satya Sai Baba is considered the new incarnation of Sai Baba from Shirdi in Maharashtra, a famous Indian saint. He is known all over the world for his siddhis, supernatural feats that reflect the power of his mind over the material world. Among these is the capacity to material-ize various objects, from gold rings and small effigies of deities to large quantities of sacred ashes called *vibuddhi*. He also has the reputation of appearing in several places at once. Many people believe that he is the avatar of the modern age, one of the rare instances in the history of humanity when the Divine decides to incarnate in a human form to influence the course of events in the world.

During our 1980 visit to India, Christina and I met Sai Baba personally in Puttaparthi, where he resides in his palatial abode. Our weeklong visit coincided with Christmas holidays, the time when Sai Baba pays special attention to Westerners. We had the opportunity to witness at close range what appeared to be siddhis at work. With swift movements of his arm, he produced large quantities of candy, which he distributed to children, and handfuls of vibuddhi, which he smeared on the forehead of his devotees. All that with short sleeves that would have made any magic tricks very difficult, particularly as the appearance of the ashes is concerned.

My mother's knowledge of Sai Baba came from Al Drucker, who at the time was a rolfer, acupuncturist, and workshop leader at Esalen. Al was originally a mathematician and physicist working for the U.S. government as an expert computing the trajectory of missiles. After a powerful spiritual experience that made it morally impossible for him to continue working for the military, he left his job and came to Esalen. He heard about Sai Baba and decided to go to Puttaparthi and check out the claims about this man's ability to materialize objects, a phenomenon that fascinated Al as a physicist.

Among several extraordinary feats that Al personally witnessed during his visit to Puttaparthi was Sai Baba's materialization of a silver ring, which he subsequently transformed into a gold one. As a result, Al returned to California as an ardent devotee, determined to spread Sai Baba's message. My mother, who was very interested in Eastern spiritual philosophies, met Al at Esalen, and they became friends. He told her many stories about Sai Baba and lent her several books about him. His own connection with Sai Baba was so strong that he later actually moved to India, obtained Indian citizenship, and became Sai Baba's "right-hand man."

I have already mentioned my mother's longtime interest in Eastern religions and philosophies. She belonged to a group of Czech followers of Paul Brunton, a British philosopher and writer who had popularized Indian philosophy. She also read Sri Ramana Maharshi, Sri Aurobindo, Rabindranath Tagore, and other spiritual teachers. In the late 1960s, I had guided her at her request in three high-dose LSD sessions, which turned out to be very profound spiritual experiences for her. They also generated in her an interest in depth psychology, a broad range of psychological approaches using techniques for exploring unconscious motives of human behavior and for treating emotional disorders. During her stay at Esalen, she participated in our monthlong workshops, which featured as guest faculty spiritual teachers, new paradigm scientists, and transpersonal psychologists.

She enjoyed very much the theoretical lectures presented at the monthlong, but became particularly fascinated by the Holotropic Breathwork sessions, which were a standard and important part of the program. She had several additional opportunities to experience the breathwork, both personally and as a "sitter" for others, when I invited her to the workshops that I conducted in Scandinavia and in Switzerland. I knew that she loved this work but, at the time, I did not have the slightest idea where this interest would take her.

When my mother was back in Prague, we regularly exchanged letters. After my father's death, her letters became increasingly sad and pessimistic. She wrote about the relentlessly shrinking circle of her friends, something that is bound to happen to a person who approaches eighty years of age. There were reports about diseases and operations of relatives and acquaintances—strokes, heart attacks, cancer, arthritis, and back surgeries. Once in a while, my mother's letters included an obituary announcing the death of yet another neighbor.

But then the tone of the letters suddenly changed. My mother wrote to me that she had decided to try out the Holotropic Breathwork with several friends and acquaintances, including a couple of my former patients. Encouraged by the results of her pioneering venture, she decided to continue. The news about the Holotropic Breathwork sessions spread by word of mouth, and the growing circle of my mother's clients soon included young psychiatrists and psychologists eager to experience and learn the new technique.

The references to aging, diseases, and death all but disappeared from my mother's letters and were replaced by reports about experiences she had witnessed in holotropic sessions. She kept asking me for new selections of music for the sessions because it was too monotonous and boring to play the same pieces all the time. She also used her letters as a means for technical consultation about specific situations that came up during Holotropic Breathwork. At one point, she shared with me proudly that the number of (mostly young) people attending her group had reached forty. It was clear that her way of being in the world was radically transformed, as if she had a new lease on life. She suddenly had a new strong sense of *raison d'être, élan vital*, and extraordinary zest for life.

By the time of my mother's eighty-fifth birthday, the situation in Czechoslovakia had changed to such an extent that I was able to go to Prague and participate in the celebration of this auspicious anniversary. On this occasion,

I was invited to give a lecture and conduct a Holotropic Breathwork seminar at the Psychiatric Department of the Charles University School of Medicine, my old alma mater. Two of the psychiatrists participating in the seminars came all the way from Slovakia. They told me that they had attended several weeks earlier a similar event in Slovakia led by my mother. It was a Holotropic Breathwork seminar for Slovak psychiatrists and psychologists followed by a theoretical discussion.

I could not believe what I was hearing. Before she had met my father and gotten married, my mother was an accomplished and successful concert pianist. But in spite of her great talent and technical skill, public performances made her uncomfortable, and she suffered from stage fright. The idea that she would lead a seminar for psychiatrists and psychologists in an area in which she had no training was too fantastic to be true. But my Slovak colleagues assured me that the experiential workshop was a great success and that during the discussion my mother answered all the theoretical and technical questions to everybody's satisfaction.

I was puzzled, and that very same evening I brought up the subject of the Slovak seminar in an after-dinner discussion with my mother. "I understand you recently conducted a breathwork workshop for Slovak psychiatrists and psychologists. How did it go?" I asked as soon as we finished dinner.

"It was fine," my mother answered somewhat sheepishly, probably because she knew that we allowed only fully trained and certified facilitators to conduct public workshops. "They seemed to enjoy it."

"The Slovak colleagues who attended my workshop at the psychiatric clinic told me that there also was a discussion following the breathwork, during which you answered questions. How was that for you? Were some of the questions technical and difficult to answer?" I probed further.

"It was okay," my mother answered and then went into a long silence. It was clear that she wanted to add something and was looking for the right words to do it. I sat in the armchair without saying anything, awaiting patiently what was about to come. "It is not quite true," she said finally with a guilty expression in her face. "Actually, half of the time, I had no idea what they were talking about. But then the answer suddenly came. But, to be honest, I don't think I did it."

"You don't think *you* were giving the answers?" I asked in utter astonishment. "If it wasn't you, who was it?"

"He did," my mother said in a tone of voice that did not leave any space for doubt. "SaI BaBA!"

She then proceeded to tell me that since the time Sai Baba had appeared to her in Big Sur, she often felt his presence in everyday life, particularly in situations related to Holotropic Breathwork. The seminar in Slovakia was just one of many similar occasions. The same happened regularly during the bodywork in the breathwork sessions. When the participants needed some physical intervention to reach a better completion of their experiences, all my mother had to do was to wait several seconds and then guidance came from levels that she ordinarily was not in touch with. She then conducted the bodywork without any hesitation and usually successfully, to the great satisfaction of the group members.

Her interventions were often extraordinary and surprised those who were observing them. My brother, Paul, had an opportunity to witness the efficacy of our mother as facilitator in 1992, when we were conducting a Holotropic Breathwork workshop before the meeting of the International Transpersonal Association (ITA) in Prague. It was one of the largest groups we have ever done, with 330 participants from 36 different countries of the world and 35 facilitators, including Paul and our mother.

At one point Paul, a strong man and trained psychiatrist, had great difficulty containing the process of one of the participants, a young Russian obstetrician, and keeping her safe. She was extremely physically active, spastically arching her body high up from the floor and sending strong kicks in all directions. She did not respond to Paul's suggestions, given in fluent Russian, and he could not control her with the full weight of his body. When mother, who was at the time eighty-five years old, saw the scene, she came to them and quieted the young woman with one hand and a few words in Czech, which the Russian doctor did not understand.

The members of the group that my mother created in Prague all loved her and related to her as a mother figure, or even an archetypal Wise Old Woman.

Eventually, after the fall of the Communist regime, twelve of the members of her group were able to complete full training with us in the United States and in Europe and became certified breathwork facilitators. My mother died suddenly several days after conducting her last breathwork session and about an hour after inviting two of her friends, a physicist and his wife, for coffee and a special dessert that she had herself prepared. She has remained for me a great model of graceful aging and of a life dedicated to service.

WHEN ALL IS ONE, THERE IS NO PROBLEM

Feats of the Korean Sword Master

Our Esalen six-week workshop entitled Buddhism and Western Psychology had a stellar cast and remarkable program. Coleader of the workshop was Jack Kornfield, dear friend, psychologist, Vipassana teacher, and Buddhist monk, who taught participants the principles of insight meditation, gave lectures on Buddhism, offered personal darshans, and lead the nine-day *sesshin*, or period of intense meditation, that was an integral part of the six-week experience. The program featured Tibetan Buddhist spiritual teachers Chögyam Trungpa, Tarthang Tulku, and Sogyal Rinpoche. Lama Govinda was in residence with his wife, Li, for two of the six weeks, and during this time, he gave a one-hour lecture on Tibetan Buddhism every day. Religious scholar and philosopher Huston Smith gave lectures on Buddhism, and Joseph Campbell introduced the group to Buddhist mythology in a series of illustrated presentations.

Zen Buddhism was represented by the abbot of the San Francisco Zen Center, Reb Anderson; Korean Zen master Seung Sahn Nim; and Kobun Chino, who performed Zen archery. Taoist teacher Chungliang Al Huang introduced participants to Tai Chi Chuan and to Chinese calligraphy. However, of all the visiting faculty, it was Kwan Ja Nim, a Korean martial artist and master swordsman, who attracted most of the attention of our group and the rest of the Esalen community. He came to Esalen with Seung Sahn Nim, accompanied by two of his disciples. We had heard about his amazing abilities, and his performance promised to be so extraordinary that we decided not to limit it to our group but to make it public. It took place on the large, oval lawn in front of the Esalen office.

Kwan Ja Nim began his presentation with an exhibition, during which he and his two students staged a combat with swords and then with long poles. Following this performance, one of the students, a lanky young man from Poland, took off his shirt and lay down on the lawn. The other student then brought a large sword beautifully decorated with etchings. Kwan Ja Nim demonstrated to the group the sharpness of his sword by cutting a hair, which he held between the thumb and index finger of his left hand. Then he put an apple on a napkin on his Polish student's belly and cut it with a brisk swing of his sword. The two halves of the apple fell apart and the sword left a little indentation on the napkin.

The crowd cheered, impressed by the degree of control the sword master commanded over his formidable weapon. Kwan Ja Nim calmed the group's enthusiasm: "Just a warm-up … don't get excited … wait!" Now the smaller student brought to the lawn two stools, three large watermelons, and a bag made of thick black velvet. He placed one stool with a watermelon by the head of his Polish colleague and did the same at his feet. Following this, he put the third watermelon on a napkin on the Polish guy's belly.

In the meantime, Kwan Ja Nim walked by the row of people lining the oval lawn, carrying a bag made of black velvet and letting everybody see it and touch it. There was absolutely no doubt that the thick double layer of black velvet effectively blocked any attempt to see through it. Kwan Ja Nim then chopped off the ends of the two watermelons on the stools and stabilized them in a vertical position. After this preparation, he walked about fifteen feet from the spot where his Polish disciple lay on the grass, put the black velvet bag over his own head, and tightened its open end around his neck, using a string sewn into its edge. He then assumed a formal warrior posture, grasping his sword in his right hand and holding it erect in a vertical position.

He stood like this for several minutes motionless and in absolute silence. People in the circle around him watched him intently, barely breathing. Suddenly, at exactly the same time, all the Esalen dogs started to howl. Kwan Ja Nim let out an ungodly warrior scream that merged with the wailing canine choir into an alarming cacophony. Holding the sword in his right hand close to his body, he used his left hand as a pivot and cartwheeled toward his Polish student. He grabbed the hilt of the sword in both of his hands and, still blindfolded, he chopped in two halves each of the watermelons on the stools flanking his student's body. With a powerful swing, he then chopped apart the third watermelon, lying on the belly of his trusting student.

The watermelon fell apart, the two halves landing on each side of the student's body. As earlier, during the apple stunt, the napkin showed just a slight, barely noticeable indentation. The crowd went crazy and cheered. We had all seen earlier what a formidable weapon Kwan Ja Nim's sword was and what it could do. A small error, a miniscule deviation during the fifteen-foot trajectory that Kwan Ja Nim negotiated without any visual control, could have resulted in fatal injury. The extraordinary feat we had just seen seemed to border on a miracle!

Kwan Ja Nim took off his hood and offered to answer any questions people had. Everybody wanted to know how he could have achieved what he did. "Were you able to see the environment without using your eyes, by some form of ESP?" "Was your consciousness out of your body, and was it watching everything from above?" "Did you imprint in your memory a three-dimensional image of the whole scene and keep it vivid the entire time?" People bombarded him with questions. Kwan Ja Nim responded with a healthy belly laugh. "No," he said with a dismissive gesture. "You just meditate and wait, until all is one—the sword master, the sword, the melon, and the disciple—and then, there is no problem."

According to Eastern spiritual literature, advanced yogis, particularly the Siddhas—masters of Tantra—can develop supernatural powers called *siddhis*. The extraordinary feats that these individuals can perform indicate the possibility of hegemony of mind over matter. The precision and certainty with which the blindfolded Kwan Ja Nim wielded his formidable sword in a situation where an extension of the trajectory of two or three inches could have resulted in death or severe injuries of his disciple certainly put his feat into this category. Those of us who witnessed Kwan Ja Nim's performance at Esalen felt strongly that what we had seen could not possibly be achieved by ordinary practice, no matter how long and arduous.

STRANGE LEGACY OF THE ANCIENT MAYA

Mystery of the Crystal Skull

The shamanic lore, religious traditions, anthropological literature, and world mythology contain numerous references to various human-made and natural magic objects endowed with extraordinary powers—fetishes, ritual implements, amulets, rings, weapons, crystals or other kinds of stones, and plants. For example, in the Hindu tradition special properties have been attributed to the *salagrams*, stones or fossils found in nature that have the form of important Tantric symbols or carry their images. Many Muslims believe that the Black Stone used as cornerstone in the Kaaba, Islam's most sacred sanctuary and pilgrimage shrine, has the power to cleanse worshippers of their sins by absorbing them into itself. They say that the Black Stone once had a pure and dazzling white color; it has turned black because of the sins it has absorbed over the years.

In Christianity, the relics of the saints, the weeping or bleeding statues of the Virgin Mary, and the shroud of Turin, a centuries-old linen cloth that bears the image of a crucified man, are seen as objects with miraculous properties. The tombs of the martyrs are said to be places where allegedly "the blind and cripples are restored to health, the dead recalled to life, and devils expelled from the bodies of men." According to legend, the "Spear of Destiny," the weapon that Gaius Cassius Longinus allegedly used to pierce the body of the crucified Jesus, brought its owner the power to conquer the world, but its loss would cause immediate death. Mythological examples of objects with supernatural powers are King Arthur's sword, Excalibur, and the Holy Grail.

The Aztecs and Mayans ascribed great symbolic significance to the human skull, which made it a very popular motif in the pre-Hispanic art of Central America. Archeologists have excavated a number of effigies of human skulls, many of them dating from prehistoric times. They range widely in size and are executed in different materials—silver, gold, bronze, obsidian, onyx, malachite, lapis, turquoise, ruby, sapphire, topaz, and quartz crystal. Among these artifacts, the rare life-size replicas of the human skull made of quartz crystal have attracted special attention. They have become the subject of many books and papers, describing their unparalleled craftsmanship and the extraordinary effects they can have on people.

In the early 1970s, while conducting a workshop at the Esalen Institute, I heard about the Mitchell-Hedges skull, an extraordinary Mayan artifact named after the British lord F.A. Mitchell-Hedges and his adopted daughter Anna. It was a perfectly crafted life-size replica of a human skull, carved from one piece of natural quartz crystal. Many individuals who spent some time in the presence of this mysterious object allegedly experienced as a result of this exposure powerful non-ordinary states of consciousness. Those who observed the skull for a period of time and focused on the opaque veils, slightly clouded areas, and other impurities in the inner structure went into a state of trance and catalepsy or, conversely, agitation.

They saw visions of complex scenes from history or experienced encounters with various mythological beings. This was usually accompanied by powerful emotions that ranged from ecstatic rapture to terror. Among the reported effects were instances of Kundalini awakening associated with kriyas—waves of unmotivated emotions, involuntary sounds, and experiences of powerful energies, vibrations, and contortions. Other effects ranged from mystical raptures, visionary states, and psychic phenomena to psychotic episodes. A few of these individuals actually ended up in a psychiatric hospital.

The skull also had some extraordinary optical properties. The zygomatic arches of the face acted as "light pipes," not unlike modern optic fibers. They channeled light from the base to the excavated eye sockets, where they ended in two miniature lenses. The two protuberances at the base of the skull that rest on the atlas vertebra had the shape of little pyramids, which concentrated light into the interior. With proper lighting, the entire skull glowed in light-green color and its sockets were bright red. On a few occasions, the skull supposedly radiated an incandescent aura, which extended far beyond its surface, and even moved and changed its size. People who were scared by the strange effects associated with this object called it the "Skull of Doom."

The skull was surrounded by an aura of mystery and inspired many speculations as to its origin, age, the way it was created, and its remarkable effects on the human psyche. During the 1970s, it attracted the attention of many scientists, journalists, and other writers. Having heard the rumors about the effects of the Mitchell-Hedges skull, I was very interested in experiencing and studying its effects. I found out that the skull's custodian and curator was Frank Dorland, who lived on Panoramic Highway in Mill Valley, California. I visited him and spent several hours listening to his stories about the skull.

Dorland was obsessed with the crystal skull; he had studied it for about five years, spending every waking hour of his life with it. He concluded that the technical problems associated with the production of this object were so formidable that it should not really exist. Quartz crystal is an extremely hard substance. It rates at a hardness factor of 7 on the 10-point Mohs' scale, only 3 points from the diamond, and it cannot be scratched by a knife. Dorland studied its absolutely smooth surface with a binocular microscope and was not able to detect traces of any tools. Any chiseling would have left scratches on the surface and would have without any doubt cracked the stone, particularly because the skull was carved against the grain of the stone.

The Mayans did not know either the carborundum or the grinding wheel. To do the job manually with sand and water would have taken generations. Dorland toyed with the idea that the Mayans might have employed some kind of paste made according to a secret recipe handed down from ancient times, but nothing of that kind is known at present. He discovered that high temperatures, such as those created by an oxygen acetylene burner, can melt crystal, but it was not very likely that the Mayans had at their disposal this kind of modern technology. But even if they had, this would not be an adequate explanation for the origin of the skull.

Dorland showed me a report that contained a detailed account of the examinations conducted at the Hewlett-Packard crystal laboratories in Santa Clara, California. The experts of the institute came to the conclusion that no known modern technologies could accomplish the task of creating an exact replica of the human skull from one piece of quartz crystal. They even refused Dorland's offer of half a million dollars to replicate the skull. Quartz, with its many impurities and even little pockets of water in its inner structure, was too difficult a material with which to work.

After years of unsuccessful attempts to find the explanation for the skull's origins, Dorland came up with increasingly fantastic theories. He came to the conclusion that it was created by an advanced civilization, by some beings with powerful minds and superior intelligence. He thought that the skull might be a device that made it possible to communicate across space-time or from parallel universes. He even suspected that the creators of the skull might still have the capacity to observe us through the skull's eyes and to exert influence on us. But he was not certain whether these influences were coming from other planets, from other dimensions, or even from other times—the past or perhaps the future.

Over the years, Dorland himself had many strange experiences with the skull and eventually found them too "overpowering" and "uncanny." He told me about the last one, which had occurred just several weeks before our meeting. He woke up in the middle of the night, hearing strange noises coming from the ground floor of his house. He went to check what was happening and was petrified by what he encountered. Looking downstairs from the staircase into the living room, he saw a large body of a jaguar jumping around and wreaking havoc in his house. He ran back to his bedroom, locked himself in, and spent the rest of the night in metaphysical horror. In the morning, he found the living room in disarray, with many pieces of furniture knocked over.

Dorland never figured out what had happened that night. But, in any case, this was the "last straw," as far as he was concerned. After some painful deliberation, he decided to return the artifact to Ms. Mitchell-Hedges. If I wanted to see it, I had to go to Kitchener in Ontario, Canada, where Ms. Mitchell-Hedges had lived since the death of her foster-father. Fascinated by Frank Dorland's story, during my next visit to Canada my brother, Paul, and I decided to call Ms. Mitchell-Hedges and ask if we could see her. To our great surprise, we found her in a motel that she had bought after her adoptive father's death and that she had run ever since.

This was a very unusual thing for her to do, considering the fact that she had inherited fabulous wealth from Lord Mitchell-Hedges, who was a very rich British aristocrat. She explained to us that this was her way to commemorate the death of her "father." When he had adopted her, she was a ten-year-old hungry and homeless orphan, living in that part of Canada. After his death, she wanted to provide shelter and food for other people in the way her father had provided for her.

During our visit, we sat in the motel office, which certainly was quite extraordinary in and of itself. Among the unique art objects decorating it were a large silver pitcher that once belonged to King Ludwig of Bavaria and an ornate beveled mirror that used to be Queen Marie Antoinette's. Ms. Mitchell-Hedges brought out a large collection of newspaper clippings, describing the adventures that she and her adoptive father had experienced in different parts of the world—sailing to different exotic places, hunting sharks and catching other large fish, shooting tigers, living with South American Indians, and excavating pre-Hispanic sites.

The most interesting of these newspaper reports covered the excavations of Lubaantun, the City of the Fallen Stones, which Lord Mitchell-Hedges discovered in the jungles of British Honduras (Belize) during his search for Atlantis. It was there where the crystal skull mysteriously surfaced. On her seventeenth birthday, Anna reportedly found it buried in the ancient ruins. As we were listening, Anna went through the newspaper clippings, one by one, telling us all the fascinating stories that were behind them.

It was clear that these newspaper stories and Anna's memories associated with them were now the main focus of her life. She never married, probably because of her strong Electra complex, because no man could possibly live up to the image of her extraordinary "father," who over the years grew to a mythic figure. Spending the afternoon with Anna Mitchell-Hedges in her Kitchener motel was a fascinating experience but, unfortunately, we did not get to see the skull. It was not in Kitchener any longer.

We found out that, a short time before our visit, Anna had donated the skull to the Museum of the American Indian in New York City. She concluded that the artifact was too powerful to be in the possession of any private individual and that it should have an impersonal owner. When we tried to get a more specific explanation, she brushed us off and did not want to talk about it. Shortly after our visit with Anna, my lecture schedule took me to New York City. One of the first things I did after my arrival was to take a taxi to the Museum of the American Indian, eager to finish my quest.

There I finally was able to see the Mitchell-Hedges skull, the mysterious artifact I had been stalking for so long. It was placed in a vitrine, the glass panels of which reflected light and the surrounding objects, preventing a clear view. In addition, the museum was a popular place, and the scores of visitors milling around represented a serious distraction. All in all, these certainly were not ideal conditions for focused scrying. I decided to visit Dr. Frederick Dockstader, the world's foremost authority on American Indian art and curator of the museum, and ask him for permission to spend a night in the museum, alone and in quiet meditation, with the skull taken out of the vitrine.

Unfortunately, Dr. Dockstader did not have much understanding for my unorthodox quest. He did not respond to my credentials as psychiatrist and consciousness researcher and insisted that I had to abide by the museum rules, like everybody else. Dr. Dockstader's resolute refusal effectively ended my pursuit of the crystal skull. Many years later, I sublimated my frustration by channeling some of my interest in the crystal skull into my fledgling science fiction novel entitled *Call of the Jaguar*.

THE WONDERS
OF SYNESTHESIA
Hugo Zucarelli and the Holophonic Sound

I n the late 1960s and early 1970s, I had the privilege to be part of a small group of people who formulated the basic principles of transpersonal psychology. Abraham Maslow called this new discipline the Fourth Force, because it historically followed behaviorism, Freudian analysis, and humanistic psychology. It was an attempt to create a vastly expanded model of the human psyche by bringing in observations from modern consciousness research and from the great spiritual traditions of the world. By recognizing spirituality as a legitimate and critical dimension of human nature, the new psychology corrected serious omissions and misconceptions perpetuated by academic circles.

Transpersonal psychology was culturally sensitive in that it treated with respect ritual and spiritual traditions of ancient and native cultures, as well as various esoteric systems and mystical schools of thought. The theoretical revisions that it introduced into psychology reflected also the revolutionary observations and paradigmatic challenges from psychedelic research, anthropology, experiential psychotherapies, meditation studies, and other areas of research exploring holotropic states of consciousness.

One of the major challenges in the early stages of the fledgling discipline was the fact that its basic tenets were incompatible with mainstream scientific thinking, which was dominated by the Cartesian-Newtonian paradigm and philosophically anchored in monistic materialism. It thus was very vulnerable to accusations of being unscientific, irrational, and even "flaky." Convinced about the legitimacy of their endeavors, pioneers of transpersonal psychology therefore followed with great interest revolutionary advances in other scientific disciplines, seeking support for their vision and developments that would help them to close this conceptual gap.

None of the developments in new paradigm science attracted more attention for its potential to provide solid scientific basis for transpersonal psychology than the discovery of principles operating in optical holography and their applications in various fields. More specifically, it was Karl Pribram's holographic model of the brain and David Bohm's theory of holomovement. These two systems of thought threw new light on mystical experiences and many transpersonal phenomena by revealing a previously unknown and inconceivable paradoxical relationship between the part and the whole.

At the time of great enthusiasm concerning holographic thinking, Marilyn Ferguson, author of the bestseller *The Aquarian Conspiracy*, published in her *Brain/Mind Bulletin* a report about a sensational addition to the holographic paradigm, the discovery of holophonic sound technology by Argentinean-Italian inventor Hugo Zucarelli. Excited by Hugo's work, Marilyn invited him to the United States, making it possible for those of us who were interested to spend a weekend with him in an estate in Millbrae, near San Francisco. This seminar attracted many prominent representatives of the transpersonal field and turned out to be an extraordinary experience.

Hugo began the seminar by sharing with us an event from his early life that inspired the discovery of holophonic sound. He traced his interest in acoustic perception to an event when, as a little boy, he was almost killed by a truck. At the time of this incident, he was sitting on the side of a road with his back turned to the oncoming vehicle. The driver diverted the truck to the shoulder of the road to avoid collision with another car. Hugo was able to save his life by a last-moment impulsive evasive movement.

Following this event, he often thought about it and wondered how he was able to accurately localize the sound of the approaching truck and respond to it by an appropriate lifesaving maneuver. This led to Hugo's fascination with the mechanism that different species use to localize sound. By careful study and analysis, he came to the conclusion that the existing theories of hearing are not able to account for certain important characteristics of human acoustic perception and the ability to accurately localize sounds.

He noticed that the crocodile, an animal that lacks a flexible, mobile neck, has to turn the upper part of its body to localize where various sounds are coming from. Birds have to rotate their heads to accomplish the same task. Mammals use for this purpose their ability to change the configuration of their ears. But humans can accurately localize the source of incoming sounds without moving their heads or changing the shape of the earlobes (a feat that most of us cannot even do). Moreover, they can accurately localize sound even if they have just monaural hearing.

All this suggested to Hugo that current theories that tried to explain stereophonic hearing and capacity to locate sounds by comparing the input from the right and left ear were inaccurate. He concluded that to account for all the extraordinary characteristics of acoustic perception, it was necessary to assume that the human ear was not only a receiver, but also a transmitter, and that it used holographic principles to localize sounds. According to him, individuals suffering from tinnitus—pathological ringing in the ears—actually hear the sound emitted by their ears. Carefully avoiding any technical details that would give away the secret of his discovery, Hugo explained that he had developed the technology of the holophonic sound by simply replicating this mechanism.

The critical part of Hugo's mysterious technology was a facsimile of a human head, to which the inventor affectionately referred as Ringo. It harbored the recording devices, which were built into it in the areas corresponding to ears. Ringo was permanently cloaked in a bag of thick, dark fabric that protected it from the eyes of curious and frustrated audiences. A cable emerging from Ringo was connected to a box with ten outlets for headphones. After this brief introduction, Hugo proceeded to the actual demonstration. Ten of us at a time were able to put on the headphones and listen to Hugo's experimental tape of holophonic recordings.

We could not believe what we were experiencing. Hugo's recording had an uncanny capacity to reproduce acoustic qualities of a large spectrum of sounds with such vividness, accuracy, and precision of localization that it was virtually impossible without constant visual control to distinguish the perception of recorded phenomena from actual events in the three-dimensional world. A typical example of it was the sound of an oncoming truck, echoing Hugo's childhood experience. When we listened to it with our eyes closed, our bodies instinctively rolled to the side to avoid the impact.

But that was not the whole story. To our surprise, listening to Hugo's holophonic recordings tended to engage other senses and produced a rich panoply of synesthesias. Synesthesia is a condition in which one type of sensory stimulation creates perception in another sense. The most common form of synesthesia is called "colored hearing," in which a person experiences a visual sensation when receiving an auditory signal. However, synesthesias can involve any other sensory area. Hugo's experimental tape not only involved all the senses, but it did it in a way that conveyed information about other aspects of the situation that produced the sound.

Thus the sound of scissors simulating a haircut conveyed a realistic sense of one's hair being cut, the hum of an electric hair dryer produced sensations of the stream of hot air blowing through one's hair, and listening to a sound of a match striking a matchbox transmitted the vision of its flame and a distinct smell of burning sulfur. Similarly, the sensual voice of a woman whispering into one's ear made one feel her warm breath. Needless to say, we were very impressed by what we had experienced.

In the discussion following the demonstration, several people who had had previous experience with holophonic sound shared with other participants an even more interesting example of the potential of this technology, indicating that it was capable of transmitting not only experiences of other senses, but also emotions, including mystical feelings. They described an experiment in which a group of them had taken a psychoactive amphetamine derivative, the entheogen MDMA, known to the young generation as Ecstasy or Adam, gathered in a circle, and collectively chanted the Indian mantra "Om." They claimed that people who listened to the holophonic recording of this event experienced entheogenic effects of this substance, such as visions of numinous light and feelings of cosmic unity.

As the lively discussion continued, the excitement in the group was rapidly growing. Some people pointed out that the extraordinary effects of holophonic technology seemed to throw new light on the important role of sound in various spiritual traditions and esoteric schools. They referred to the mystical and magical properties that the Hebrews and ancient Egyptians ascribed to the sounds of their alphabets, to the relationship between the acoustic frequencies or seed syllables and the chakras in Kundalini yoga or nadayoga, the crucial importance of sound in Tantric science, art, and ritual, and even the cosmogonic power that Indian mythology attributes to the om sound.

Others discussed the important theoretical and practical implications that the discovery of holophonic sound might have for the technology of virtual reality, for physiology and pathology of hearing, for psychiatry, psychology, and psychotherapy, for film, television, and other forms of entertainment. And all of us were excited about it as the latest addition of another piece to the expanding mosaic of the new paradigm in science, providing conceptual support for transpersonal psychology.

However, it soon became obvious that Hugo's rigid ideas about the future of holophonic technology might represent a serious obstacle in its widespread use. He was determined to maintain full control of the way his invention would be used, by whom it would be used, and for what purpose. He wanted to be absolutely sure that no forms of abuse would occur. It was clear that this otherwise admirable position was not very realistic and that it would get in the way of his negotiations with companies interested in bringing holophonic sound to large audiences.

Hugo's concerns were greatly amplified when Marilyn Ferguson took him to the preview of the Metro-Goldwyn-Mayer science fiction movie *Brainstorm*, for which Christina and I served as consultants for special effects sequences. As described earlier in this book, *Brainstorm* is a story about two scientists, a computer wizard and a brilliant brain researcher, who developed a device capable of recording human experiences and allowing other people to share them. The helmet that made this possible could easily be seen as a much more complex and sophisticated version of Hugo's own technology.

In the *Brainstorm* movie, this phenomenal invention was very rapidly expropriated by the wrong people for commercial and military purposes. Watching the movie reinforced the already existing fears that Hugo had concerning the abuse of his revolutionary device. Whether or not Hugo's rigid attitude was the main reason for it, his extraordinary device has not received the enthusiastic reception in the world that those of us who had participated in the Millbrae seminar expected and hoped for.

GATEWAY TO THE ABSOLUTE

The Secret of the Toad of Light

In the minds of most people, the original source of psychedelic substances is the vegetable kingdom. Since time immemorial, native cultures have used plants with powerful mind-altering properties, "flesh of the gods," as the main vehicle for their ritual and spiritual life. Much has been written about soma, the legendary visionary plant of the Vedas, different varieties of cannabis, the pre-Columbian sacraments peyote and magic mushrooms (teo-nanacatl), the sacred shrub eboga used in rituals of African tribes, as well as the South American jungle brew yajé or ayahuasca, and many others.

It is much less known that psychedelic compounds can also be found in the animal kingdom. In 1960, Joe Roberts, a photographer for *National Geographic* magazine, described an intense psychedelic experience with many elements of science fiction, following his ingestion of the meat of *Kyphosus fuscus*. This fish, found off Norfolk Island in the South Pacific, has a reputation among the natives for causing powerful and often nightmarish visions.

The most remarkable contribution of the animal kingdom to the repertory of psychedelic users and spiritual seekers comes from the genus *Bufo*. The toad skin, which contains the psychoactive compound bufotenin, was a regular ingredient of the brews that the witches used in the Middle Ages for inducing the visions of the Sabbath. In the late 1960s, the psychedelic grapevine spread the news about a strange new way of achieving a psychedelic state—by licking the skin secretions of a giant Arizona desert toad, *Bufo alvarius*. This species can be found only in the Sonoran Desert, stretching over the southern half of Arizona and south to Sonora in Mexico.

Being semiaquatic, these toads must remain in the vicinity of dependable water sources in order to survive. For this reason, their principle habitat is within the drainage of permanent rivers and streams of the Sonoran Desert. Their lifestyle is also supported by the fact that more than one thousand years ago, the Hohokam Indians began diverting water from the Gila River and created a complex system of canals to irrigate the arid soil. But even all that would not be sufficient. *Bufo alvarius* features specialized glands, located particularly on the neck and the limbs. They produce a viscous milky-white secretion that protects them against the heat of the Arizona desert, as well as against enemies.

This secretion contains a high concentration of 5-methoxydimethyltryptamine (5-MeO-DMT), a compound with extraordinary psychedelic properties. This substance was first synthetized in the chemical laboratory in 1936, more than twenty years before modern Americans discovered its psychedelic effects. However, Native Americans had known the mind-altering effects of the secretions for centuries and had used them in their shamanic practices. It turned out that the same active principle is also responsible for the effects of psychedelic snuffs of plant origin, such as virola or epená, used by the Tukano, Waika, and Araraibo Indians in Brazil and Venezuela.

The dry material produced by milking and vaporization of the skin secretions of *Bufo alvarius* by heat contains as much as 15 percent of the active principle. Smoking dried secretions induces within seconds a psychedelic state than can be very psychologically challenging because of the rapidity of its onset and the overwhelming intensity. Smoking or snorting of 5 to 15 milligrams of pure 5-MeO-DMT has similar effects. The discovery of the psychedelic effects of the secretions of *Bufo alvarius* by the psychedelic generation was a sensation. It inspired the founding of the Church of the Toad of Light, the members of which smoke this material in their ceremonies as a sacrament.

I followed with great interest the reports on *Bufo alvarius*, as well as another psychedelic species, *Bufo marinus*, which is indigenous in Florida. The latter figures prominently in the novels of Carl Hiassen, in which he describes an ex-governor who goes wild and lives in the Everglades licking these toads. Because of my belief that comparing the effects of various psychedelics is an issue of great theoretical importance, I was looking for an opportunity to try this new addition to the entheogenic pharmacopeia. I had had some previous experiences with related tryptamine derivatives—dimethyltryptamine (DMT) and diethyltryptamine (DET) from our early experiments in Prague, and dipropyltryptamine (DPT) from our studies at the Maryland Psychiatric Research Center.

I discovered to my dismay that I had missed the opportunity to experiment with *Bufo alvarius* during one of my earlier visits to Arizona. In the middle of July, in the desert near Tucson, I had experienced a torrential monsoon rain that temporarily transformed the sun-scorched land at the foothills of the Catalina mountain range near Mt. Lemmon into a river that was more than twenty feet wide and four feet deep. Within minutes, the desert floor was covered with thousands of giant toads, which emerged from their underground hideouts, rapidly paired up, and started copulating. Listening to their sonorous croaking filling the air, I was very impressed by this ecstatic celebration of life. However, not being well-versed in amphibian taxonomy, I was unaware that I was witnessing a group orgy of *Bufo alvarius* and did not get a chance to try their mysterious elixir.

The opportunity to get an insight into the secret of the Toad of Light came when my friend Paul appeared at our door with an impressive supply of 5-MeO-DMT. This substance was not listed in Schedule I—a group of substances considered to have high abuse potential and no therapeutic value—and was readily available for chemists as a starting point for synthesis of other compounds. My friend had already had earlier experiences with 5-MeO-DMT and offered to provide the necessary instructions and expert guidance.

Under Paul's supervision, I put a small amount of the white powder on a glass surface and worked on it for a while with a razor blade to make it as fine as possible. I then shaped the powder into two even piles and put the rest of the powder into a pipe filled with dried parsley. While Paul lit the pipe, I rolled a dollar bill into a narrow tube and snorted the two piles, each with a different nostril. When I finished, I took two or three deep drags from the pipe. Later, I estimated the combined dose of 5-MeO-DMT I had taken and realized that it was very high, probably about 25 milligrams.

The beginning of the experience was very sudden and dramatic. I was hit by a cosmic thunderbolt of immense power that instantly shattered and dissolved my everyday reality. I lost all contact with the surrounding world, which completely disappeared as if by magic. In the past, whenever I had taken a high dose of psychedelics, I liked to lie down and make myself comfortable. This time, any such concerns were irrelevant because I lost awareness of my body, as well as of the environment. After the session, I was told that after taking a couple of drags, I sat there for several minutes like a sculpture, holding the pipe near my mouth. Christina and Paul had to take the pipe from my hand and put my body into a reclining position on the couch.

In all my previous sessions, I had always maintained basic orientation. I knew who I was, where I was, and why I was having unusual experiences. This time all this dissolved in a matter of seconds. The awareness of my everyday existence, my name, my whereabouts, and my life disappeared as if by magic. Stan Grof ... California ... United States ... planet Earth ... these concepts faintly echoed for a few moments like dreamlike images on the far periphery of my consciousness and then faded away altogether. I tried hard to remind myself of the existence of the realities I used to know, but they suddenly did not make any sense.

In all my previous psychedelic sessions there always had been some rich specific content. The experiences were related to my present lifetime—the story of my childhood, infancy, birth, and embryonal life—or to various themes from the transpersonal domain—my past life experiences, images from human history, archetypal visions of deities and demons, or visits to various mythological domains. This time, none of these dimensions even seemed to exist, let alone manifest. My only reality was a mass of radiant swirling energy of immense proportions that seemed to contain all existence in a condensed and entirely abstract form. I became Consciousness facing the Absolute.

It had the brightness of myriad suns, yet it was not on the same continuum with any light I knew from everyday life. It seemed to be pure consciousness, intelligence, and creative energy transcending all polarities. It was infinite and finite, divine and demonic, terrifying and ecstatic, creative and destructive—all that and much more. I had no concept, no categories for what I was witnessing. I could not maintain a sense of separate existence in the face of such a force. My ordinary identity was shattered and dissolved; I became one with the Source. In retrospect, I believe I must have experienced the Dharmakaya, the Primary Clear Light, which according to the *Tibetan Book of the Dead*, the *Bardo Thödol*, appears at the moment of our death. It bore some resemblance to what I encountered in my first LSD session, but it was much more overwhelming and completely extinguished any sense of my separate identity.

My encounter with the Absolute lasted approximately twenty minutes of clock-time, as measured by external observers. As far as I was concerned, during the entire duration of my experience, time ceased to exist and lost any meaning whatsoever. After what seemed like eternity, concrete dreamlike images and concepts began to form in my experiential field. I started intuiting fleeting images of a cosmos with galaxies, stars, and planets. Later, I gradually visualized a solar system and within it the Earth, with large continents.

Initially, these images were very distant and unreal, but as the experience continued, I started to feel that these realities might actually have objective existence. Gradually, this crystallized further into the images of the United States and California. The last to emerge was the sense of my everyday identity and awareness of my present life. At first, the contact with the ordinary reality was extremely faint. I recognized where I was and what the circumstances were. But I was sure that I had taken a dose that was excessive and that I was actually dying. For some time, I believed that I was experiencing the bardo, the intermediate state between my present life and my birth in the next incarnation, as it is described in the Tibetan texts.

As I was regaining more solid contact with ordinary reality, I reached a point where I knew that I was coming down from a psychedelic session and that I would survive this experiment. I was lying there, still experiencing myself as dying, but now without the sense that my present life was threatened. My dying seemed to be related to scenes from my previous incarnations. I found myself in many dramatic situations happening in different parts of the world throughout centuries, all of them dangerous and painful. Various groups of muscles in my body were twitching and shaking, as my body was hurting and dying in these different contexts. However, as my karmic history was being played out in my body, I was in a state of profound bliss, completely detached from these dramas, which persisted even after all the specific content disappeared from my experience.

When I worked at the Maryland Psychiatric Research Center, we used to have a term for the condition that many of our clients experienced for many days and sometimes weeks after a good and well-integrated psychedelic session. We called it "psychedelic afterglow." My afterglow after this experience was unusually intense, profound, and long-lasting. I was able to work on the galleys of my book with extraordinary precision and capacity to concentrate. And yet, when I decided to take a break and closed my eyes, I was within seconds in a state of ecstatic rapture and experienced a sense of oneness with everything. My meditations were unusually deep, and they seemed to be the most natural state I could imagine.

As time went by, everyday sober reality succeeded in regaining some of its ground and made this window to the Absolute more opaque. However, the session left me with deep respect and appreciation for the power of the tools used by shamans. I have often had to laugh at the arrogance of mainstream psychiatrists, who see shamanic techniques as products of primitive superstition and consider their own ploys, such as free associating on the couch or behaviorist deconditioning, to be superior and scientific approaches to the human psyche.

Since this experience I also have new appreciation for the tenet of various esoteric systems that the most noble truth is often found in the most lowly. According to the alchemists, "the Stone is hiding in the filth and dung." For me, it was the toad, an animal that is often seen as a symbol of ugliness, that showed me the shortest and fastest way to the Absolute. I am reminded of it every time I hear or read the famous passage from Shakespeare's *As You Like It*:

Which like the toad, ugly and venomous,
Wears yet a precious jewel in his head;
And this our life exempt from public haunt,
Finds tongues in trees, books in the running brooks,
Sermons in stones, and good in every thing.
I would not change it.

MATTER AND CONSCIOUSNESS

Ketamine and the Reenchantment of the World

In the fall of 1972 I was introduced to the strangest psychoactive substance I have ever experienced in the fifty years of my consciousness research. The effects of this compound are so extraordinary that they stand out even in the group of psychedelics, drugs for which the German pharmacologist Louis Lewin once coined the term *fantastica*. This substance was ketamine, also known by its trade names Ketalar, Ketajet, Ketanest, and Vetalar.

The person who brought the remarkable psychoactive properties of ketamine to the attention of our staff at the Maryland Psychiatric Research Center was Salvador Roquet, a controversial Mexican psychiatrist known for his wild experimentation with psychedelics. Salvador used to conduct sessions with large groups of people, to whom he administered a variety of psychoactive substances (LSD, psilocybin, peyote, datura, and others) while exposing them to movies with shocking aggressive and sexual content. His intention was to induce in his clients profound experiences of ego death followed by psychospiritual rebirth. Salvador had also antagonized his colleagues in Mexico City by serving at a party in his house sandwiches laced (unbeknownst to his guests) with psychedelic mushrooms. The purpose of his visit in Baltimore was to participate in our LSD training program for professionals.

Ketamine is a short-acting anaesthetic related to phencyclidine, an animal tranquilizer known as Sernyl or PCP. Ketamine was discovered by Cal Stevens of Wayne State University in 1961. For many years, it had the reputation of an unusually safe anaesthetic because it has minimal suppressive effects on circulation, breathing, and the cough reflex. It gained great popularity among the medical personnel as an anaesthetic that was heavily used on the battlefields of Vietnam. In later years, its use rapidly decreased, mostly because of bizarre psychological experiences, dubbed "emergency syndrome," which patients reported upon awakening. Nowadays it is still used for short-term surgical procedures in many countries, primarily in children and old people, in whom the "emergency syndrome" seems to be less of a problem.

Those members of our staff who had heard about ketamine before Salvador's visit knew that it was a substance used by surgeons as a general anaesthetic and had heard about the "emergency syndrome" as an untoward complication of ketamine administration routinely treated by administration of tranquilizers. In his presentation for our staff, Salvador Roquet introduced an entirely new perspective; he explained that the "emergency syndrome" was not a side effect of ketamine, but part of its fascinating principal effect. Ketamine was a "dissociative anaesthetic," and its mechanism of action was radically different from the rest of anaesthetics. The administration of this substance did not lead to loss of consciousness, but to separation of consciousness from the body.

The reason the medical personnel could perform surgical interventions on the patients was not that the patients' consciousness was extinguished, as is the case with conventional anaesthetics, but that it had left their bodies. They were experiencing fantastic voyages through a wide range of other realities—extra-terrestrial civilizations and parallel universes, the astrophysical world and the micro-world, the animal, botanical, and mineral kingdoms, other countries and historical periods, and archetypal domains of various cultures. Salvador's clients, who had not taken ketamine as an anaesthetic, but as a therapeutic agent and a vehicle for philosophical and spiritual quest, had profound mystical experiences, and many of them believed that they had encountered God. Some of them were also convinced that they had visited the bardo, the intermediate realm between incarnations, and claimed that they had lost fear of death.

In several members of our staff, including myself, Salvador's lecture generated intense curiosity and a strong desire to have a personal experience with ketamine. Salvador happened to have with him adequate supply of the substance and offered to conduct training sessions with anybody who was interested. Our personal experiences fully confirmed Salvador's report. Ketamine clearly was a fascinating substance that was of great interest to anybody seriously interested in consciousness research. Although its effects were very different from LSD, there was no doubt that it was an important contribution to the armamentarium of psychedelic substances. The astonishing nature of the ketamine experiences seemed to outweigh by far its disadvantages, such as dizziness, impaired coordination, and slurred speech.

Over the years, I continued my personal experimentation with ketamine and did not cease to be astounded by the extraordinary nature of the experiences and the profound insights that they provided concerning the relationship between consciousness, the human psyche, and matter. The effects of ketamine have always been utterly unpredictable, even in the broadest sense. In my experimentation with other psychedelics, I usually had at least a rough idea where I was in my self-exploration and what might come (biographical exploration, reliving of birth, archetypal experiences, and so on). The ketamine experiences were like visits to a Cosmic Disneyland; I never knew what might come, what the "ride" would be about. And the experiences covered a wide range from the most sublime and astonishing to the completely banal and trivial.

I will give at least a few examples to illustrate what I mean. A good point of departure is ketamine's great potential to mediate astral projection. Some of these experiences are fairly straightforward, others have certain features that are bizarre and absurd, as we will see from the following examples. One evening I took ketamine in our house in Big Sur, California, at a time when we were conducting one of our monthlong seminars at Esalen. At one point during this session, I realized that the experience had taken me to the Big House, a part of Esalen about a mile from our house, where all the group activities of the monthlong seminar took place. I saw in great detail several of the group members involved in social interaction. The next day I was able to verify the accuracy of my perception. But at the time when I was witnessing these events,

I experienced myself as a pillow in the corner of the room in the Big House, my body image taking on completely the shape of this object.

On another occasion, I had a similar experience, only even more extraordinary because this time Christina shared it with me. In the middle of a joint ketamine session we were having in the bedroom of our Big Sur house, I found myself suddenly in the Esalen bath and realized that I had become a wet towel hanging over the railing overlooking the ocean. From this perspective, I was able to witness in detail what was happening there and correctly identify the people who were in the bath at that time. Toward the end of the session, I described this bizarre episode to Christina and was astounded to find out that she had had exactly the same experience. The following morning, we were able to verify the accuracy of our joint experience by talking with the people involved.

As the above examples indicate, one of the extraordinary and characteristic aspects of the ketamine experience is the surprising possibility to identify experientially with various material objects and processes that we ordinarily consider unconscious because they are inorganic and we associate consciousness with higher forms of life. And yet, experiences of this kind are very frequent in ketamine sessions, and when they happen, they seem very authentic and convincing. They make it easy to understand the animistic worldview of many native cultures, according to which not only all animals and plants, but the sun and the stars, the oceans, the mountains and rivers, and other parts of inorganic nature are all conscious.

Among my many memorable experiences of this kind were identification with the consciousness of the ocean, of the desert, of granite, of an atomic reactor in a submarine under the arctic ice, of a metal bridge crossed by heavy trucks, of wooden stakes being driven into the earth by hits of giant mallets, of burning candles, of the fire at the end of a torch, of precious stones, and of gold. My list includes even identification with a ski boot on the foot of a cross-country skier, attached to a ski and experiencing all the shifting tensions associated with the movements involved.

Equally frequent are experiences of identification with various other life forms. In one of my ketamine sessions, I became a tadpole undergoing a metamorphosis into a frog, in another one a giant silverback gorilla claiming his territory. On several occasions, this mechanism provided for me extraordinary insights into the world of dolphins and whales. An additional example was what seemed to be absolutely authentic and believable experiential identification with a caterpillar building a cocoon and dissolving into amorphous liquid from which then emerged the form of a butterfly. A particularly impressive experience of this kind was becoming a Venus flytrap, a carnivorous plant in the process of catching and digesting a fly, complete with gustatory perceptions that my human imagination could not possibly have conjured up.

The above examples of fantastic experiences contrast sharply with several of my ketamine sessions that were absolutely trivial and outright boring. I spent them by seeing endless images of brick walls, cement surfaces, and asphalt streets in the suburbs of a large city, or displays of ugly fluorescent colors, questioning why I ever taken this substance. There was a period in my life when I had several consecutive ketamine sessions that were so horrible and disgusting that I was determined never to take the substance again. They revolved around the problem of fossil fuels and the curse they represent for life on our planet. The following is the account of one of these sessions.

The atmosphere was dark, heavy, and ominous. It seemed to be toxic and poisonous in a chemical sense, but also dangerous and evil in the metaphysical sense. Initially, I experienced it on the outside, as part of my environment, but gradually it took over, and I actually became it. It took me a while to realize that I had become petroleum, filling enormously large cavities in the earth. While I was experiencing identification with petroleum as physical material, including its penetrating smell, I realized that I was also an evil metaphysical or archetypal entity of unimaginable proportions. I was flooded with fascinating insights, combining chemistry, geology, biology, psychology, mythology, history, economy, and politics.

I suddenly understood something that I had never thought about before. Petroleum was fat of biological origin that got mineralized; it meant that it had escaped the mandatory cycle of death and rebirth, the recycling that the rest of the living matter is subjected to. However, the element of death was not eliminated in this process, it was only delayed. The destructive Plutonic potential of death continues to exist in petroleum in a latent form as a monstrous time bomb awaiting its opportunity to be released into the world.

While experiencing what I felt was consciousness of petroleum, I saw the death intrinsic to it manifesting as the evil and killing resulting from the greed of those who seek the astronomical profits that it offers. I witnessed countless scenes of political intrigues, economic scams, and diplomatic shenanigans motivated by "petrodollars." I saw countless victims of wars fought for oil laid on the sacrificial altar of this evil entity. It was not difficult to follow the chain of events to a future world war for the dwindling resources of a substance that had become vital for the survival and prosperity of the industrialized countries.

It became clear to me that it was essential for the future of the planet to reorient the economy to solar energy and other renewable resources. The linear policy of plundering the limited deposits of fossil fuels and turning them into toxic waste and industrial pollution was so fundamentally wrong that I could not understand that economists and politicians did not see it. This short-sighted policy was obviously incompatible with the cosmic order and with the nature of life, which is cyclical. While the exploitation of fossil fuels was understandable in the historical context of the Industrial Revolution, its continuation once its fatal trajectory was recognized seemed suicidal, murderous, and criminal.

In a long series of hideous and most-unpleasant experiences, I was taken through states of consciousness related to the chemical industry based on petroleum. Using the name of the famous German chemical industrial complex, I referred to these experiences as "IG Farben consciousness." It was an endless sequence of states of mind that had the quality of aniline dyes, organic solvents, herbicides, pesticides, and toxic gases, all hostile to life.

Besides the experiences related to various industrial poisons per se, I also identified with the states of consciousness associated with the exposure of various life forms to petroleum products. I became every Jew who had died in the Nazi gas chambers, every sprayed ant and cockroach, every fly caught in the sticky goo of the fly-traps, and every plant dying under the influence of the herbicides. And beyond all that lurked the highly possible ominous future of all life on the planet—death by industrial pollution.

It was an incredible lesson. I emerged from the session with deep ecological awareness and a clear sense as to which direction the economic and political development had to take should life on our planet survive.

The series of sessions exploring the pitfalls of the industrial age, like this one, brought me to the point when I decided not to have any more ketamine experiences. But the session that was supposed to be my last attempt at ketamine self-exploration took me to the other side of the spectrum. It was so ecstatic and extraordinary that I decided to keep this door open. Here is a brief account of this experience.

I had a sense of presence of many of my friends with whom I share interest in transpersonal psychology, values, and a certain direction or purpose in life. I did not see them, but was somehow strongly perceiving their presence through some extrasensory channels. We were going through a complex process of identifying areas of agreements and differences among us, trying to eliminate friction points by an almost alchemical process of dissolving and neutralizing. At a certain point, it seemed that we succeeded in creating a completely unified network, one entity with a clear purpose and no inner contradiction.

And then this collective organism became what I called "Spaceship in Consciousness." We initiated a movement that combined the element of spatial flight with an abstract representation of consciousness evolution. The movement was becoming faster and faster, until it reached what seemed to be some absolute limit, something like what speed of light is in the Einsteinian universe. We felt that it was possible to push beyond this limit, but that the result would be completely unpredictable and potentially dangerous. In the highly adventurous spirit that characterizes this group of our friends, we decided to go ahead and face the unknown.

We succeeded to push beyond the limit, and the experience shifted dimensions in a way that is difficult to describe. Instead of moving through space and time, there seemed to be immense extension of consciousness. Time stopped and we entered a state that I identified as consciousness of amber. This seemed to make a lot of sense because amber is a material representation of a situation in which time is frozen. It is a mineralized organic substance (resin), and various life forms, such as plants and insects, are preserved in it unchanged for millions of years.

What followed seemed to be a process of purification, through which any references to organic life were eliminated. The experience became crystal clear and incredibly beautiful. It seemed that we were inside of a giant diamond; countless subtle lattices intersecting in a liquid medium of incredible purity were exploding into all the colors of the spectrum. It seemed that it contained all the information about life and nature in an absolutely pure, abstract, and infinitely condensed form, like the ultimate computer. It seemed relevant that diamond is pure carbon, an element on which all life is based, and that it originates in conditions of extreme temperatures and pressures.

All the other properties of diamond seemed to point to its metaphysical significance—its luster, beauty, transparence, permanence, unchangeability, and the capacity to separate white light into a rich spectrum of colors. I felt that I understood why Tibetan Buddhism is referred to as Vajrayana, the diamond vehicle. The only way I could adequately describe this ecstatic rapture was to call it "diamond consciousness." This state seemed to contain all the creative energy and intelligence of the universe existing as pure consciousness beyond space and time.

I was floating in this energy as a dimensionless point of consciousness, maintaining some sense of individual identity, yet being completely dissolved and one with all of it. I was aware of the presence of my friends who had made the journey with me; they were also completely formless, mere dimensionless points. I felt that we had reached the state of ultimate fulfillment, the source of existence and our final destination, as close to Heaven as I could imagine.

What I have described above were just a few examples of my experiences with the strangest and most extraordinary psychoactive substance I have ever come across. Another property of ketamine deserves notice in this context. Christina and I have taken ketamine on several occasions in foreign countries—in Peru, Brazil, India, and Bali, where this substance was readily available—and discovered that the experiences connected us to the archetypal worlds associated with these cultures, with their mythologies, with the psyche of their people, with their artifacts, and their art.

ON THE INCA TRAIL
Discovering the Secret of Trephination

During our visits to Peru, two facilities helped us to recover from the long flight and the jet lag. The first one was the hospitable hotel Bolivar in Lima, with its comfortable beds, large bathtubs, and its old-world charm. The second was Casa Vasca, a little restaurant located right around the corner and serving excellent Basque dishes. We also discovered that in the Inca Pharmacy, right across the street from the Bolivar, it was possible to get virtually any medicines without prescription. This included Ketajet, which was the South American trademark for ketamine.

We purchased a bottle, excited about the possibility of experimenting with it in Cuzco, the ancient capitol of the Inca Empire. It seemed like a unique opportunity to explore the secrets of the Inca society, the world of its gods, and its glorious artistry. However, the session turned out to be one of the most difficult experiences of my life.

After our arrival in Cuzco, we took ketamine in the evening in our hotel. As soon as the substance started to take effect, I found myself surrounded by four muscular Inca warrior-priests in their ritual attire. They had elaborate headdresses and tunics made of colorful plumage. Their ears and bodies were adorned with heavy gold jewelry. I felt the iron grip of their hands on my wrists and ankles. Then a particularly richly decorated man, who looked like a high priest, approached me with a hammer and chisel and started relentlessly pounding on my skull.

It took a while before I realized what was happening to me. During our stay in Lima, we had visited the anthropological museum and seen a large number of trephinated skulls. The texture of the bone surrounding the wounds indicated that the individual survived the procedure. The captions accompanying them explained that these trephinations showed the medical skills of the ancient Incas. They were most likely surgical interventions removing tumors or some other pathological conditions. I remembered the strange and unexplainable discomfort I had felt looking at these perforated craniums.

Now I was experientially identifying in the most realistic and convincing way with an individual being subjected to this procedure. Although I felt drugged in a way that was different from the effect of ketamine, which was very likely some kind of premedication used in the ritual, the intensity of pain involved was beyond anything I could have even imagined before it actually happened to me. However, in spite of the agony I was in, I was flooded with some extraordinary insights illuminating the nature of the procedure to which I was subjected.

This was not a surgical intervention, but a rite of passage, similar to various indigenous rituals in other cultures involving excruciating pain, such as the Lakota Sioux Sun Dance or the subincision of the Australian Aborigenes. Part of it was clearly an ordeal testing the power of one's mind over the world of matter. The initiate had to demonstrate his capacity to endure extreme physical suffering and remain unperturbed. But the main purpose of the trephination was to remove the obstacle between one's brain and the Sun God, the ultimate deity of the Incas, so that his energy could enter the initiate's inner being.

I had to think about a young man whom I had met during my visit in an Amsterdam antique store. He told me about a Dutch man by the name of Dr. Bart Hughes, who in 1962 started a movement based on the belief that self-trephination can facilitate higher states of consciousness by increasing the blood circulation in the brain, and performed the operation on himself using an electric drill. The young man followed his example and claimed he was very impressed by the results. Several years ago, during our visit in England, Christina and I had a chance to spend some time with Lord James Neidpath and his wife, Lady Amanda Neidpath, both of whom underwent trephination for the same reason. We had a long discussion in which they extolled the positive effects that this procedure had had on their consciousness.

As soon as I understood the nature of the procedure I was subjected to, I tried very hard to assume the stoic state of mind expected from the initiates. But it was a very difficult task because the torture was intolerable. I called on my intellect for help; I realized that the effect of ketamine was approximately fifty minutes to an hour, so that my agony was time-limited. Once in a while, I looked at my watch, checking the time, but the little hand barely seemed to move. Finally, after what seemed like eternity, an hour had elapsed since the administration of ketamine. But to my utter consternation, that did not end my suffering. The pharmacological effect of the drug subsided, but the excruciating pain remained.

Christina had had the usual course of the ketamine experience and after a discussion during which we shared our experiences, she fell asleep. I was lying in my bed in agony, unable to sleep, experiencing every headache that anybody had in the entire history of humanity. For the following day, we had planned a trip to Machu Picchu, the famous ancient fortress city of the Incas. When it was time for our early breakfast, we got dressed and walked down to the dining room. I felt nauseated, and every step down the stairs felt like another blow of the high priest's chisel. I watched Christina eat her breakfast, unable to ingest anything myself.

My agony continued during the train ride to Machu Picchu. The workers who welded the rails had not done a great job, and every time the wheels crossed the place where they were joined, it felt like another blow of the chisel. It seemed that my rite of passage was still going on and that it would never end. Then suddenly, about halfway to Machu Picchu, the pain stopped, and I went into a state of ecstasy. We reached the train station, and a small van took us to the entrance of the ruins after having negotiated the access road with many switchbacks.

It was a beautiful, sunny day, and the sightseeing in the ancient city high in the Andes was an unforgettable experience. I had a strong sense of belonging to the place, as if I had actually once lived there. After lunch, we roamed around in the ruins and then decided to climb Huayna Picchu, which means in Quechua "young mountain," the steep peak overlooking the historical site. The climb was steep and long, but it rewarded us with a fantastic view of the ruins of Machu Picchu, the "old Mountain." Until this day, the visit to this magic place, following my experience of the trephination ritual, remains one of the most powerful memories of my entire life.

UFOs in the Amazon
Alien Encounter of the Third Kind

Shortly after our arrival in Rio de Janeiro on the way to the Fourth International Transpersonal Conference in Belo Horizonte, we found out that in Brazil, like in many other Third World countries, ketamine was not a controlled substance and could be freely purchased over the counter. Because we had earlier discovered that ketamine was an effective means of combating jetlag, we decided to start our first Brazilian trip with a ketamine session in our Rio hotel. For me, most of this experience was a very powerful encounter with what seemed to be extraterrestrial intelligence.

Shortly after the administration of ketamine, I had a very strange sense that the substance had changed my brain in such a way that it was able to communicate with extraterrestrial beings. This feeling culminated in an experience that was reminiscent of teleportation used by the crew of the Enterprise, a spacecraft featured in the American science fiction TV series *Star Trek*. I had a sense of completely disintegrating to a molecular level and reintegrating on an alien spaceship. The environment looked like a futuristic high-tech laboratory full of intricate devices, the nature and function of which were completely mysterious to me.

My head was enclosed in a large helmet connected by color-coded cables to a machine that looked like a giant computer. I had a sense that an enormous amount of information was transmitted from my brain and body to the machine and that I was being examined and studied. Then the process seemed to have reversed itself, and the machine was communicating to me. I started having a series of fantastic experiences, the nature of which is completely beyond description. The best I could understand what was happening to me was that it was a lesson in higher-dimensional seeing and thinking. It was a way of teaching me that the universe has many more dimensions than we think and that without this knowledge any attempt to comprehend existence is futile.

Another series of images portrayed the life on this planet and the detrimental effect industrialization and scientific discoveries have on it. Rapid visual sequences showed me what our planet used to be and what it was becoming as a result of human violence and greed combined with rapid technological progress. I could clearly see the destructive and self-destructive trajectory of this development ending in annihilation of the human species and much of life. Witnessing this apocalyptic show, I was trying to figure out if this was a serious warning of what would come if we do not change or if I was seeing the future. My "alien abduction" differed from the traditional descriptions in that I was communicating exclusively with the world of technology. There were no extraterrestrial beings of any kind, humanoid, insectoid, or otherwise.

When this lesson ended, I experienced again the sense of complete molecular dissolution and materialized on another spacecraft, this time a much smaller one strongly resembling a flying saucer. I was sitting near a window and saw that we were flying by the ocean. I recognized Rio de Janeiro and was able to deduce that we were moving north, following the coast of Brazil. Although we were traveling quite fast, I noticed some characteristic landmarks on the coastline. The spacecraft sped up even more and, in what seemed like a short time, it reached a river delta, an estuary of a large river, and turned inland, flying up the stream.

We flew over enormous stretches of jungle, and I realized that the giant river had to be the Amazon. Then the spacecraft reached what seemed to be its destination and stopped its flight, hovering a few yards over the ground. Looking from the window, I noticed a small village hidden in the jungle—several huts with roofs covered with palm leaves. Amidst the huts was an open space decorated with giant idols bearing superficial resemblance to the Indian sculptures of the American Northwest. Their entire surface was covered with small tiles, which formed intricate mosaic patterns. I vividly remember to this day the colors of the mosaic pieces—combinations of light blue, yellow, and white.

This was where the experience ended. I had again the sense that my body had dissolved and materialized, this time in my hotel in Rio, where I had started my ketamine session. The experience was quite interesting, in and of itself, particularly because it was the only experience involving alien intelligence I had ever had in all my psychedelic sessions. However, it gained special significance because of the synchronicities associated with it. In the morning following the session, Christina and I rented a car and decided to explore the environment of Rio de Janeiro. Without a special intention to validate my session, we decided to drive north, following the ocean. I was astounded when I encountered characteristic landmarks on the coast because of the strong and convincing déjà vu experience that they elicited in me. They were exactly the same landmarks I had observed during my UFO ride the previous night.

After a few days in Rio, we flew to Belo Horizonte to participate in the International Transpersonal Conference organized by French-Brazilian psychologist Pierre Weil. At the conference we reconnected with an old friend of ours, Leo Matos. Originally from Belo Horizonte, where he was born, he now lived in Scandinavia, where he had organized several workshops for us. During a discussion we had with him, he told us to our great surprise about a retired colonel of the Brazilian army living about twenty miles from Brazilia. According to Leo, this colonel had close contact with a tribe in the Amazon that was regularly visited by aliens in flying saucers and he was offering bus rides for guaranteed UFO sightings.

Had it been another country, we would not have paid much attention to such information. However, Brazil seems to be in a category of its own as far as paranormal happenings are concerned. I had heard enough from reliable friends, such as Stanley Krippner and Walter Pahnke, about Brazilian psychic surgeons, miraculous healing, mediums, materializations, and dematerializations to suspend my disbelief. Unfortunately, our schedule was very tight, and there was no way we could have extended our stay and followed this clue. In any case, I found the connection between my ketamine experience, the déjà vu feelings, and Leo's story to be quite unusual and impressive.

PART 6

UNORTHODOX PSYCHIATRY

Surprising Alternatives to Traditional Treatment

The observations from the research of holotropic states of consciousness brought many extraordinary insights concerning the dimensions of the human psyche and the nature and architecture of emotional and psychosomatic disorders. They also opened surprising new perspectives for the treatment of these conditions by revealing therapeutic mechanisms previously unknown to the psychiatric profession.

The model of the psyche currently used in clinical and academic psychiatry is limited to postnatal biography and the Freudian individual unconscious. As suggested by Freud, the newborn is considered a *tabula rasa*, a clean slate, and our personality is shaped by the dynamics in the nuclear family and by emotionally relevant incidents during the first years of life. From this perspective, the events preceding birth, including the birth process itself, are psychologically irrelevant. Disorders for which no organic causes have been found in brain anatomy, physiology, and biochemistry are seen as results of psychotraumatic experiences in infancy, childhood, and later life. It is generally accepted that psychogenic disorders have their beginning at different stages of postnatal history and that their nature and depth reflect the time during which the original psychotraumas occurred.

Conventional therapeutic interventions in psychogenic, emotional, and psychosomatic disorders fall into two broad categories—"covering" and "uncovering" strategies of treatment. *Covering therapy*, currently dominating outpatient practice and institutional treatment, uses a rich array of psycho-pharmacological agents to suppress symptoms. It can bring subjective relief to patients without dealing with the underlying causes of the disorders they suffer from. *Uncovering therapy* uses various psychotherapeutic techniques to get to the roots of the problems. Its goal is not only to alleviate the symptoms, but also to address the factors underlying them and to facilitate positive changes in the personality structure. Unfortunately, the current model of the psyche offers only a limited range of therapeutic mechanisms, such as remembering forgotten and repressed traumatic events or reconstructing them from free associations and dreams, intellectual and emotional insights, analysis of transference, and corrective experience in interpersonal relationships.

As we saw earlier, the study of holotropic states has vastly expanded the cartography of the psyche by adding two new domains—perinatal and transpersonal. It has also shown that psychopathological symptoms and syndromes of psychogenic origin cannot be adequately explained by traumatic events in postnatal biography. Observations from deep experiential psychotherapy have revealed that these conditions have a multilevel dynamic structure, which regularly includes significant elements from the perinatal and transpersonal domains of the psyche.

This discovery explains why verbal, biographically oriented approaches have been generally very disappointing as tools for dealing with serious clinical problems. Because of their conceptual and technical limitations, these methods are unable to reach the deeper roots of the conditions they are attempting to heal. In and of itself, the discovery of the depth of the problems psychiatry and psychotherapy have to deal with would be a very discouraging finding. Fortunately, the work with holotropic states does more than just reveal that emotional and psychosomatic disorders have significant perinatal and transpersonal components. It also provides access to new, highly effective therapeutic mechanisms operating on these deep levels of the psyche that often bring dramatic healing and positive personality transformation.

In this section, I will give a few examples of situations where remarkable therapeutic effects were achieved by mechanisms operating on the perinatal and transpersonal level of the psyche. We will see that sometimes healing might require reliving birth and powerful past-life memories, encounter with an archetypal being from a culture completely unknown to the client, or emergence and full manifestation of an archetypal figure, including a demonic one. It can even involve such highly improbable therapeutic mechanisms as experiential identification with a tree or chanting of a Sephardic prayer. The most interesting and theoretically, as well as practically, important observation from the work with holotropic states is that perinatal and transpersonal experiences have powerful healing potential even if they occur in the context of episodes that contemporary psychiatry sees as manifestations of serious mental diseases—psychoses.

On the basis of our experience with such conditions, Christina and I suggested that many spontaneous episodes of holotropic states, currently diagnosed as psychoses and treated by suppressive medication, are actually psychospiritual crises, or spiritual emergencies. There exists ample evidence that—correctly understood and properly supported—these episodes can result in healing, positive personality transformation, and spiritual opening (Grof and Grof 1989, 1991). Jungian psychologist John Weir Perry described many successfully treated cases of this kind in a series of his books (Perry 1974, 1976).

Included in this section are the stories of two women whose symptoms would be considered by a traditional psychiatrist to be indications of mental disease. And yet, putting such diagnostic labels on them would have been wrong. Another case history incorporated in this part of the book describes a therapeutic approach that is highly unconventional. It shows that using psychedelic therapy to accelerate the psychodynamic processes underlying psychotic symptoms can bring therapeutic results that are far superior to tranquilizing medication. This section of the book closes on a light note with a humorous story showing that, on occasion, a fortuitous synchronicity can bring unexpected therapeutic results.

THE PAIN THAT SURVIVED
THREE CENTURIES

The Story of Norbert

The following story involves Norbert, a fifty-one-year-old psychologist and minister who participated in one of our five-day workshops at the Esalen Institute. His case can be used as a typical example of what I call a system of condensed experiences (COEX system), a multilayer constellation of traumatic memories from different levels of the unconscious—biographical, perinatal, and transpersonal—that underlies emotional and psychosomatic symptoms. Norbert's story also illustrates the therapeutic potential associated with reliving and integration of the trauma of birth and of past-life memories.

During the group introduction preceding the first session of Holotropic Breathwork, Norbert complained about severe chronic pain in his left shoulder and pectoral muscle that caused him great suffering and made his life miserable. Repeated medical examinations, including x-rays, had not detected any organic basis for his problem, and all therapeutic attempts had remained unsuccessful. Serial Prokain injections had brought only brief, transient relief for the duration of the pharmacological effect of the drug.

At the beginning of the session of Holotropic Breathwork, Norbert made an impulsive attempt to leave the room because he could not tolerate the music, which he felt was "killing" him. It took great effort to persuade him to stay with the process and to explore the reasons for his discomfort. He finally agreed, and for almost three hours he experienced severe pains in his breast and shoulder that intensified to the point of becoming unbearable. He struggled violently as if his life were seriously threatened, choked and coughed, and let out a variety of loud screams. Following this stormy episode, he quieted down and was relaxed and peaceful. With great surprise, he realized that the experience had released the tension in his shoulder and muscles, and that he was completely free of pain.

Retrospectively, Norbert reported that there were three different layers in his experience, all of them related to the pain in his shoulder and associated with choking. On the most superficial level he relived a frightening situation from his childhood in which he almost lost his life. When he was about seven years old, he and his friends were digging a tunnel on a sandy ocean beach. When the tunnel was finished, Norbert crawled inside to explore it. As the other children jumped around, the tunnel collapsed and buried him alive. He almost choked to death before he was rescued by the adults who rushed to the scene responding to the children's distress calls.

When the breathwork experience deepened, Norbert relived a violent and frightening episode that took him back to the memory of his biological birth. His delivery was very difficult because his shoulder had been stuck for an extended period of time behind the pubic bone of his mother. This episode shared with the previous one the combination of choking and severe pain in the shoulder.

In the last part of the session, the experience changed dramatically. Norbert started seeing military uniforms and horses and recognized that he was involved in a fierce battle. He was even able to identify it as one of the battles in Cromwell's England. At one point, he felt a sharp pain and realized that his shoulder had been pierced by a lance. He fell off his horse and experienced himself as being trampled by the horses running over his body and crushing his chest. His broken rib cage caused him agonizing pain, and he was choking on blood, which was filling his lungs.

After a period of extreme suffering, Norbert's consciousness separated from his dying body, soared high above the battlefield, and observed the scene from a bird's eye view. Following the death of the severely wounded soldier, whom he recognized as himself in a previous incarnation, his consciousness returned to the present and reconnected with his body, which was now pain-free for the first time after many years of agony. The relief from pain brought about by these experiences turned out to be permanent. Christina and I formed a friendship with Norbert and his wife, and continued seeing them after the workshop ended. It has now been over twenty years since this memorable session, and the symptoms have not returned.

THE MALEKULAN PIG GODDESS
The Story of Otto

Experiences of psychiatric patients labeled as psychotic often involve visions of deities and demonic presences and visits to mythological realms, such as heavens, paradises, and hells. The explanation of mainstream psychiatrists for such experiences is that they are products of these patients' brains afflicted by a pathological process of unknown origin, one which would be identified and fully understood sometime in the future. Although this perspective is frequently presented by the academic circles as a scientific fact that is obvious and beyond any reasonable doubt, it is actually a highly implausible proposition. More than anything else, this view reflects the basic metaphysical assumption of monistic materialism about the priority of matter over consciousness that dominates scientific thinking in the industrial civilization. In reality, it is inconceivable that a pathological process could generate the rich panoply of aesthetically exquisite images and philosophically fascinating ideas that characterize the experiences of these patients.

I have shown in my book *The Cosmic Game* that the insights and revelations imparted by these experiences often strikingly resemble those described in the great spiritual traditions of the East and West, to which Aldous Huxley referred as perennial philosophy. There exists convincing scientific evidence that contradicts the official party line that sees these experiences as pathological artifacts produced by the diseased brain. C. G. Jung and his followers demonstrated that such experiences as a rule accurately portray elements from mythologies of various cultures of the world, including those of which the individuals involved have no intellectual knowledge.

The Jungian observations show unequivocally that these experiences, rather than being pathological products of the brain, have their origin in the collective unconscious that we all share. Psychedelic research and Holotropic Breathwork have generated ample support for the Jungian perspective. Holotropic states of consciousness, regardless of their specific triggers, can provide deep insights into the worldview of the cultures that believe the cosmos is populated by mythological beings and that it is governed by various blissful and wrathful deities. In these states, we can gain direct experiential access to the archetypal world of gods, demons, legendary heroes, suprahuman entities, and spirit guides in the collective unconscious. We can also visit fantastic landscapes and abodes of the Beyond that represent integral parts of this domain of the human psyche.

Deep personal experiences of these realms help us realize that the images of the cosmos found in preindustrial societies are not based on superstition or primitive "magical thinking," but on direct experiences of alternate realities. A particularly convincing proof of the authenticity of these experiences is the fact that, like other transpersonal phenomena, such experiences can bring us new and accurate information about various archetypal beings and realms. The nature, scope, and quality of this information often by far surpass previous intellectual knowledge of the individuals involved concerning the respective mythologies.

One of the most interesting examples of this kind that I have experienced in my clinical practice involved Otto, one of my clients in Prague, whom I treated for depression and pathological fear of death (thanatophobia). In one of his psychedelic sessions, Otto experienced a powerful sequence of psychospiritual death and rebirth. As the experience was culminating, he had a vision of an ominous entrance into the underworld guarded by a terrifying pig goddess. At this point, he suddenly felt an urgent need to draw a specific geometrical design.

Although I generally asked my clients to stay during their sessions in a reclining position with their eyes closed and keep their experiences internalized,

Otto opened his eyes, sat up, and asked me to bring him some sheets of paper and drawing utensils. He drew with great urgency and extraordinary speed an entire series of complex abstract patterns. Showing deep dissatisfaction and despair, he kept impulsively tearing and crumpling these intricate designs as soon as he finished them. He was very disappointed with his drawings and was getting increasingly frustrated, because he was not able to "get it right." When I asked him what he was trying to do, he was not able to explain it to me. He said that he simply felt an irresistible compulsion to draw these geometrical patterns and was convinced that drawing the right kind of design was somehow a necessary condition for a successful completion of his session.

The theme clearly had an extraordinary emotional charge for Otto, and he struggled very hard to understand what it was about. At that time, I was still under a strong influence of my Freudian training, and I tried my best to identify the unconscious motives for this strange behavior by using the method of free association. We spent a considerable amount of time on this task, but without much success. The entire sequence simply did not make any sense in relation to Otto's childhood or his present life. Eventually, the process moved to other areas, and I stopped thinking about this situation. The entire episode had remained for me completely mysterious until many years later, when I moved to the United States.

Shortly after my arrival in Baltimore, I was invited to give a lecture for a conference of the Society for Art, Religion, and Science in New York City, entitled "The Grotesque in Art." My presentation explored the problem of the grotesque, drawing on my observations from psychedelic research, and included a slide show of my clients' paintings. Among the participants was Joseph Campbell, considered by many to be the greatest mythologist of the twentieth century and possibly of all time. He was fascinated by my descriptions of the experiences of patients reliving their birth and by the paintings they had made. At his request, I sent him a manuscript summarizing the findings of my research in Prague. It was a thick volume entitled *Agony and Ecstasy in Psychiatric Treatment* that never got published and later became the source for five books discussing different aspects of my work.

After a few initial encounters, we became good friends, and Joseph played a very important role in my personal and professional life. Christina had developed an independent friendship with him when she was his student at Sarah Lawrence College in Bronxville, New York. Joseph's intellect was remarkable and his knowledge of world mythology truly encyclopedic. He loved the material from psychedelic research, particularly my concept of basic perinatal matrices (BPMs), which helped him understand the ubiquity and universal nature of the motif of death and rebirth in mythology. After I moved to California, I saw Joseph regularly because he was a frequent guest at Esalen, participating as guest faculty in the monthlong seminars that Christina and I organized, and conducting his own workshops.

By the middle of the week, Joseph usually got tired of the Esalen menu, which he called "rabbit food," and was ready for a good steak and Glenlivet whiskey, which he loved. Christina and I invited him regularly to our house for a homemade dinner, catering to his culinary preferences. Over the years, we had many fascinating discussions during which I shared with him observations of various obscure archetypal experiences of participants in our Holotropic Breathwork workshops. In most instances, Joseph had no difficulties identifying various esoteric mythological themes and symbolism that I was not able to recognize and understand.

During one of these discussions, I remembered the above episode from Otto's session and shared it with him. "How fascinating," said Joseph without any hesitation. "It was clearly the Cosmic Mother Night of Death, the Devouring Mother Goddess of the Malekulans in New Guinea." He then continued to tell me that this deity had the form of a frightening female figure with distinct pig features. According to the Malekulan tradition, she sat at the entrance into the underworld and guarded an intricate sacred labyrinthine design. The Malekulans believed they would encounter this deity during the Journey of the Dead.

The Malekulans had an elaborate system of rituals that involved breeding and sacrificing pigs. This complex ritual activity was aimed at overcoming the dependency on their human mothers and eventually on the Devouring Mother Goddess. The Malekulans spent during their lifetime an enormous amount of time practicing the art of labyrinth drawing because its mastery was considered essential for a successful journey to the Beyond. The Pig Goddess would not grant the permission to enter the Beyond to anybody who was not able to perfectly reproduce the requested design. Joseph, with his astonishing lexical knowledge of mythology, was thus able to solve this challenging puzzle, which I had encountered during my research in Prague.

The remaining question, which even Joseph was not able to answer, was why this particular mythological motif was so intimately connected with Otto's tedious emotional symptoms and why Otto had to encounter this Maleku-lan deity as part of his therapy. However, in the most general sense, the task of mastering problems associated with the posthumous journey of the soul certainly made good sense for somebody whose main symptom was thanato-phobia, pathological fear of death.

Interview with the Devil

The Story of Flora

I have already mentioned that experiences of holotropic states of consciousness can mediate access to normally hidden numinous dimensions of reality in the form of archetypal divine beings, celestial realms, and paradisean visions. However, they also frequently reveal the shadow side of the universe, manifesting as dark energies or evil beings of extraordinary power and as frightening chthonic and hellish realms.

Experiences of encounters with various wrathful deities and demonic forces are very common in individuals who have taken psychedelics, participate in sessions of Holotropic Breathwork, or are undergoing spiritual emergency. Careful examination shows that evil entities manifesting in these states are closely connected with extremely difficult and painful traumatic experiences in the present or past life of the individual, such as anoxia at birth or prenatal distress, near drowning, life-threatening events, or physical and sexual abuse. On the collective level, evil archetypal beings and motifs seem to be the moving forces behind wars, bloody revolutions, genocide, and other forms of tragedies and atrocities.

The amount of pain that human beings have inflicted on each other and experienced in the course of their history is truly overwhelming. However, the shadow side of existence is not limited to human society; it is inextricably woven into the fabric of life in general. Antonie van Leeuwenhoek, Dutch microbiologist and the inventor of the microscope, summed it up in one sentence: "Life lives on life—it is cruel, but it is God's will." Living organisms can survive only at the expense of other living organisms. The English poet Alfred Lord Tennyson called nature "red in tooth and claw." The ability to embrace the totality of existence with full awareness and acceptance of the nature and depth of its dark side is one of the most difficult challenges of the spiritual journey.

In many instances, inner experiences of encounter with evil are accompanied by various manifestations that can be perceived by external observers. They involve strange grimacing, evil expression in the eyes, spastic contractions of various parts of the body, change of voice, projectile vomiting, and many others. In a therapeutic context, such episodes can have remarkable healing and transformative effect. I have had many encounters with various forms and degrees of demonic phenomena in the course of my professional life, but none of them was as dramatic and extreme as my experience with Flora, a patient I treated with psychedelic therapy at the Maryland Psychiatric Research Center in Baltimore in the late 1960s.

For better understanding of what happened, I have to say a few words about the larger context of this extraordinary episode. Our research center was a brand-new, four-story building with state-of-the-art laboratories and treatment rooms, situated on the premises of Spring Grove State Hospital. However, it did not have any hospital beds, and the patients participating in our research were housed in the wards of the state hospital. The relationship between the staffs of the two institutions was distant and somewhat uneasy because the hospital personnel looked at us as more fortunate cousins. It came, therefore, as a surprise when Dr. Charles Savage, director of clinical services, and I were one day invited to a staff meeting at the Spring Grove State Hospital.

As the staff meeting unfolded, we began to understand how this had come about. One of the Spring Grove psychiatrists was presenting the case of Flora, a twenty-eight-year-old single patient who had been hospitalized for more than ten months in a locked ward. All available therapy, including tranquilizers, antidepressants, psychotherapy, and occupational therapy, had been tried but failed. Flora was facing transfer to the chronic ward, which meant spending the rest of her life among chronic psychotics and geriatric patients.

Flora had one of the most complicated and difficult combinations of symptoms and problems I have ever encountered in my psychiatric practice. When she was sixteen years old, she was a member of a gang that conducted an armed robbery and killed a night watchman. As driver of the getaway car, Flora spent four years in the penitentiary and was then placed on parole for the rest of her sentence. During the stormy years that followed, she became an alcoholic and multiple-drug addict. She was addicted to heroin and used high doses of psychostimulants and barbiturates. Her severe depressions were associated with violent suicidal tendencies; she frequently had impulses to drive her car over a cliff or collide head-on with another automobile.

She also suffered from hysterical vomiting, which often occurred in situations where she became emotionally excited. Probably the most agonizing of her complaints was a painful facial cramp, *tic douloureux*, for which a Johns Hopkins neurosurgeon had suggested a brain operation consisting of severing intracranially her trigeminal nerve. Flora was a lesbian and had never had heterosexual intercourse in her life. She had a severe psychological conflict and guilt about her sexual orientation and on occasion contemplated suicide, "to end it all." To further complicate the situation, she was court-committed because she had severely wounded her girlfriend and roommate while trying to clean a gun under the influence of heroin.

At the end of the Spring Grove case conference, Flora's attending psychiatrist asked Dr. Savage and me if we would accept her into our program of LSD psychotherapy. We found this to be an extremely difficult decision, not only because of the seriousness and complexity of her psychiatric problems, but also because of the national hysteria in regard to LSD that raged in the country at the time. In addition, our protocol dictated by the National Institute of Mental Health (NIMH) limited the number of LSD sessions we could administer to our patients to three. And this was naturally a great disadvantage, particularly in such a difficult case.

Flora already had a criminal record, access to weapons, violent fantasies and impulses, and severe suicidal tendencies. We were well aware that the atmosphere regarding psychedelics was such that if we gave her LSD, whatever would happen after that point would automatically be blamed on the drug and our treatment, without regard to her past history. On the other hand, everything else had been tried without success, and Flora was facing a lifetime in a chronic ward. After some deliberation, we decided to take a chance and accept her into the LSD program, feeling that her desperate situation justified the risk.

Flora's first two high-dose LSD sessions were not much different from many others I had run in the past. She had to confront a number of situations from her stormy childhood, including alcoholism, violence, and incest in her family of origin. Her birth was very difficult, and she repeatedly relived sequences of her struggle in the birth canal. She was able to connect her violent suicidal tendencies and painful facial cramps to certain aspects of the birth trauma, and to discharge large amounts of intense emotions and physical tensions. In spite of it, the therapeutic gains of all these efforts seemed to be minimal.

In her third LSD session, nothing extraordinary happened during the first two hours; her experiences were similar to those of the previous two sessions. And then the session suddenly took an unexpected turn. Flora started to cry and complained that the painful cramps in her face were becoming unbearable. Before my eyes, the facial spasms were grotesquely accentuated, and her face froze into what can best be described as a mask of evil.

She started talking in a deep, male voice, and everything about her was so different that I could not see much similarity between her present appearance and her former looks. Her eyes had an expression of indescribable malice reminiscent of the last scene of the movie *Rosemary's Baby*, which showed a close-up of the infant conceived by the devil. Her hands, which were now spastic and looked like claws, completed the picture. Then the energy that took control over her body and voice assumed a personified form and introduced itself as the Devil.

"He" turned directly to me, ordering me to stay away from Flora and give up any attempts to help her. He asserted that she belonged to him and threatened that he would punish anybody who would dare to invade his territory. What followed was a barrage of explicit blackmail, a series of intimidations describing what would happen to me, my colleagues, and to our program if I would not obey. It is difficult to describe the uncanny atmosphere that this scene evoked; one could actually feel the tangible presence of evil in the room.

The power of the blackmail was further increased by the fact that it involved certain concrete information to which the patient in her everyday life could not possibly have access. Some of it involved me personally, but much of it referred to my Spring Grove colleagues. When I later shared with them what transpired, they were astonished, because there was no conventional way through which I or the patient could have obtained such knowledge of those specific aspects of their private lives.

Although I had occasionally seen various demonic manifestations in LSD sessions before, they had never been so extreme, realistic, and convincing. I found myself under considerable emotional stress and experienced fear that had metaphysical dimensions. I was struggling, on the one hand, with my anxiety and, on the other, with a tendency to enter into an active psychic combat with the evil presence. I found myself thinking fast, trying to choose the best strategy for the situation. At one point, I caught myself seriously considering that we should have a crucifix in our therapeutic armamentarium. My rationalization for this idea was that what we were witnessing was manifestation of a Jungian archetype and that in this situation the cross would be the appropriate archetypal remedy.

It soon became clear to me that my emotions, whether it was fear or aggression, were making it more believable to me that I was dealing with a powerful metaphysical entity. I could not help thinking of scenes from an episode of *Star Trek*. The episode featured an alien intruder on starship Enterprise that fed on the crew's emotions. The creature was finally overcome when the starship physician, Dr. McCoy, administered tranquilizers to the entire crew. I realized that it was essential for me to remain calm and centered, no matter what I was witnessing.

I decided to put myself into a meditative mood and visualize a capsule of white light enveloping both of us. One thing I remembered from spiritual literature about evil entities was that they do not like light. While meditating on light, I held Flora's cramped hand, focused on her disfigured face, and tried to imagine her in the form in which I had known her before. The situation lasted over two hours of clock-time; in terms of subjective time-sense these were the longest two hours I have ever experienced outside of my own psychedelic sessions.

After this time, Flora's hands relaxed, and her face returned to its usual form. These changes were as abrupt as the onset of this peculiar condition. I soon discovered that she did not remember anything that had happened during the preceding two hours. Later, in her write-up, she described the first hours of the session and continued with the period following the "possession state." I seriously questioned if I should discuss with her the events that had occurred during the time covered by her amnesia, and decided against it. She was radiant and felt wonderful. There did not seem to be any reason to introduce such a macabre theme into her conscious mind.

To my great surprise, this session resulted in an astonishing therapeutic breakthrough. Flora lost her suicidal tendencies and developed a new appreciation for life. She gave up alcohol, heroin, and barbiturates and started zealously attending the meetings of a small religious group in Catonsville. For most of the time she did not have any facial cramps; the energy underlying them seemed to have exhausted itself in the "mask of evil" that she had maintained for two hours. This made it possible to cancel the neurosurgery suggested by the Johns Hopkins neurosurgeon. The occasional recurrence of the pain was of negligible intensity and did not even require medication.

Flora also started experimenting with heterosexual relations and eventually got married. However, her sexual reorientation clearly was temporary and superficial; she was able to engage in sexual intercourse with her husband, but found it painful and unpleasant. The marriage ended three months later, and Flora returned to lesbian relationships, this time, however, with much less guilt. Her condition was so improved that she could be released from the hospital and started working as a Baltimore taxi driver. Although in the following years she had her ups and downs, she did not need hospitalization and did not have to return to the psychiatric hospital that could have become her permanent home.

I have never in my fifty-some years of practicing psychiatry seen a more dramatic, lasting improvement than the one I witnessed in Flora's case. I cannot help but see a great irony and even a touch of cosmic humor in the fact that, after years of studying and practicing medicine and psychiatry, the most dramatic therapeutic result I have ever encountered in my life was not achieved by officially accepted respectable psychiatric treatment. It was the result of a process that resembled more a medieval exorcism or an intervention of a witchdoctor than a respectable rational therapeutic procedure based on discoveries of modern science.

EMBODYING THE
DAPHNE ARCHETYPE

The Story of Martha

The rich spectrum of transpersonal phenomena includes experiences of identification with other life forms, including plants and botanical processes associated with them. On occasion, such experiences show deep connection with various emotional and psychosomatic problems. In those instances, full emergence of such experiences from the unconscious into consciousness is a necessary prerequisite for healing. This can be illustrated by the case history of Martha, a 32-year-old client of mine, who was accepted into the experimental program of LSD psychotherapy after many months of unsuccessful treatment by various psychopharmacological substances and other conventional methods.

Martha's psychiatric diagnosis included terms like "bizarre hypochondriacal complaints" and "borderline psychosis with vague distortions of the body image." The most striking of her complaints involved very strange sensations in her legs and body that she had great difficulty describing. She said about it: "Something is just terribly wrong about how my body feels." These symptoms began after what she described as "repeated sexual harassment" by one of her co-workers, a handsome young man. Martha was very attractive herself and had many suitors, but felt strong resistance to the idea of a committed relationship and marriage. She attributed her sexual problems to her childhood history of repeated abuse by her older cousin.

Several of Martha's initial LSD sessions had a relatively normal course; they focused on her traumatic childhood experiences and on various aspects of her birth. In one of her later sessions, the content of her experiences suddenly dramatically changed. She felt an abrupt increase of the strange sensations in her legs that eventually reached such intensity that they seemed absolutely unbearable. Martha decided to have her session terminated and asked me for an injection of Thorazine, something we tried to avoid in psychedelic therapy at any cost. Administration of tranquilizers in the middle of a "bad trip"—unfortunately, a common practice among mainstream professionals—tends to freeze the experience in a difficult stage. It prevents positive resolution of the underlying problem and makes successful completion of the session impossible.

Talking to Martha, I was able to find out why she did not want to continue. "This is absolutely crazy," she said. "I think that if I continue, I will turn into a tree." I assured her that she would not turn into a tree, regardless of how believable and convincing her concerns that this would happen. The worst that could happen to her was that she would *experience* herself as a tree. I told her that experiences of identifying in a very convincing way with various aspects of nature were very common in psychedelic sessions and did not pose any danger. After a while, Martha calmed down and agreed to continue with her LSD session.

As she closed her eyes and turned her attention inside, the bizarre sensations in her body and her legs continued to intensify, but this time she was able to endure them. As she allowed them to fully develop, she realized that what she had considered weird feelings and distortions of her human body image were perfectly normal and very authentic experiences of being a tree. She stood up, stretching her arms toward the sky, and maintained that position for a long time. She had an ecstatic expression on her face, and it was obvious that she had actually started to enjoy the session.

Martha sensed that her fingers were now extended and had become branches with rich foliage. She had a powerful vision of the sun and was receiving its light, experiencing on a cellular level the mysterious process of photosynthesis—the basis and secret of life on our planet. Her body became the trunk of the tree; she experienced the cellular activity in the cambium and felt the flow of the sap through the system of veins traversing the sapwood. Her feet and toes were growing and branching until they became the convolution of roots penetrating deep into the earth. Martha was now able to sense the exchange of water and minerals in the tiny feeder roots and root hairs of the tree. She was amazed by the authenticity of the insights concerning the anatomy and physiology of trees that she was receiving through this experience

However, her insights were not limited to the botanical aspects of this experience; they had a profoundly numinous quality and distinct mythological and spiritual dimensions. What at first appeared to be just the astronomical sun, the source of physical energy supporting all life on our planet, became also the Cosmic Sun, the source of creative power and Logos in the universe. Similarly, the soil in which the tree grew became Gaia, a fantastic mythological figure of Mother Earth. The tree itself assumed a mythological meaning and became the Tree of Life. The experience that was at first difficult and frightening thus became ecstatic and mystical.

Later in the session came another experience that revealed the deep archetypal meaning of Martha's symptoms. She identified with Daphne, a young, beautiful nymph, daughter of the river god Peneus. According to Greek mythology, Daphne dedicated herself to Artemis and, like the goddess, refused to marry. She was pursued by many admirers, but rejected every lover, including the god Apollo. When the god pursued her, Daphne prayed to the Earth and to her father to rescue her, whereupon she was transformed into a laurel tree. This insight made a lot of sense in view of Martha's resistance to marriage and of the fact that her symptoms had started after unwanted advances from her very attractive co-worker. Martha emerged from the session without the disturbing distortions of her body image and open to the idea of getting married and starting a family.

HEALING DEPRESSION BY A
SEPHARDIC PRAYER

The Story of Gladys

Although reading Sigmund Freud's *Introductory Lectures to Psychoanalysis* and my enthusiasm about it was what inspired me to study psychiatry, my excitement about Freud's theories and his method of therapy has been seriously undermined by my later clinical experience. While I continue to admire Freud as a great pioneer of depth psychology, I believe that most of his theoretical concepts have not withstood the test of time and require substantial revisions. I have even stronger reservations about his therapeutic strategy.

During my psychiatric practice, I have seen many patients who, after years of psychoanalysis, were able to give lectures about their emotional and psychosomatic symptoms and their connection with various postnatal biographical issues, such as oral cannibalism, toilet training, primal scenes, or Oedipal and Electra complexes. However, their intellectual discoveries did not produce equally impressive clinical results. My experience with therapeutic use of holotropic states was exactly the opposite. After powerful psychedelic experiences and sessions of Holotropic Breathwork, we have often seen dramatic therapeutic changes, but had no idea why and how they came about.

A salient example of this kind is the story of Gladys, a young woman who participated in one of our five-day workshops at Esalen. As she told the group at the beginning of the workshop, she had suffered for about four years from serious attacks of depression accompanied with intense anxiety. These episodes started daily early in the morning and lasted as a rule several hours. During this time, she had to struggle to accomplish the most elementary tasks—to take a shower, brush her teeth, and get dressed. From a traditional point of view, these features characterized her depression as *endogenous* (literally "generated from within") rather than *reactive* (caused by external life circumstances).

In our five-day Holotropic Breathwork workshops, participants typically had two sessions each in the role of breathers and functioned as "sitters" in two sessions of their peers. In her first session of holotropic breathing, Gladys had a powerful experience in which she encountered various traumatic experiences from her childhood and infancy. She also relived several sequences of her biological birth. She had very good feelings about the session, although it did not bring her any noticeable relief from her morning depression.

The second session she had, two days later, took her deeper into her unconscious and consisted almost entirely of the reliving of her birth. It resulted in an extraordinary activation of physical energy, which is an important step in the work on depression, a condition characterized by major blockage of emotional and physical energy. However, in spite of intense bodywork in the termination period, she did not reach a satisfactory resolution. This is a situation that is quite exceptional when systematic effort is used to facilitate the integration of the session.

The next morning, her depression came as usual, but was considerably more pronounced. It also took a different form than it had before. Instead of the usual inhibition, lack of initiative, and apathy, Gladys was agitated. We had originally planned for the morning session an open forum, a group discussion during which participants could ask any questions about their process, the method of Holotropic Breathwork, or theory. However, seeing the condition Gladys was in, we decided to change our program and do experiential work with her without delay.

We asked her to lie down in the middle of the group, do some deep breathing, surrender to the flow of the music we were playing, and accept any experience that might emerge under these circumstances. For about fifty minutes, Gladys experienced violent tremors, choked and coughed, made loud noises, and seemed to fight some invisible enemies. Retrospectively, she reported that this part of her experience involved the reliving of her difficult birth, but this time more deeply than before.

Later in the session, her screams became more articulate and started resembling words in an unknown language. We encouraged her to let the sounds come out in whatever form they took, without censoring them or judging them, even if they made no sense to her. Gradually, her movements became extremely stylized and emphatic and her words clearly recognizable. However, what was coming out was in a language that we did not understand or recognize. At one point, she sat up and began chanting a haunting repetitive sequence that sounded like some kind of prayer. This went on for quite some time.

The impact of this event on the group was extremely strong. Without understanding the words or knowing what Gladys was experiencing internally, most participants felt deeply moved and started to cry. Some assumed a meditative posture and joined their hands as if in prayer. When Gladys completed her chant, she quieted down and resumed a horizontal position on her back. She moved into a state of bliss and ecstatic rapture in which she stayed for more than an hour, entirely motionless. Later, when giving a retrospective account of her experience, she described that she had felt an irresistible urge to do what she did. She did not understand what had happened and indicated that she had absolutely no idea what language she was using in her chant.

Carlos, an Argentinian psychoanalyst from Buenos Aires, who participated in the group, recognized that Gladys had chanted in perfect Sephardic language, which he happened to know. This language, also called Ladino, is a Judeo-Spaniolic hybrid that is a combination of medieval Spanish and Hebrew. By strange coincidence, Carlos, who was Jewish, had studied the Sephardic language for many years as his personal hobby. Gladys was not Jewish and did not know any Hebrew or Spanish. She had never heard about Ladino and did not know that it existed and what it was. Carlos translated for us the words of Gladys's repetitive chant, which had had such a powerful effect on the group. The literal translation was: "I am suffering, and I will always suffer. I am crying, and I will always cry. I am praying, and I will always pray."

During this dramatic finale of her experience in the group, when she chanted the Sephardic prayer, Gladys broke through the depression and her condition stabilized in a psychologically comfortable place. Since the Esalen group, we have seen Gladys on two different occasions and found out that her depression has not returned. It was one of the most powerful healings I have observed during my entire psychiatric career. Yet, this episode and the profound influence it had on Gladys have remained a mystery for her, as well as for us, until this very day.

THE STORMY SEARCH
FOR THE SELF

The Story of Karen

I t seems to have been my destiny or karma in this lifetime to get involved in controversial projects and activities. That is certainly true for my lifetime passionate interest in psychedelics and non-ordinary states of consciousness in general. Years of research in this area have convinced me that current beliefs of mainstream psychiatrists concerning the nature of the human psyche and consciousness are deeply erroneous and require a radical revision. I also came to the conclusion that many of the findings from consciousness research seriously challenge the materialistic worldview of Western science, particularly in regard to the relationship between consciousness and matter.

I have expressed my ideas and reservations quite openly in many articles and books. None of the implications of the new findings generated more controversy than the concept of spiritual emergency, which I developed jointly with my wife, Christina. Over the years, we had come to the conclusion that many of the conditions that are currently diagnosed as psychotic and indiscriminately treated by suppressive medication are actually difficult stages of a radical personality transformation and of spiritual opening. If they are correctly understood and supported, these psychospiritual crises can result in emotional and psychosomatic healing, remarkable psychological changes, and consciousness evolution.

The term "spiritual emergency" describes the problematic nature of these states, but, at the same time, alludes to their positive potential. It is a play on words suggesting a crisis, but—because of its Latin root *emergere* (to emerge)—also an opportunity to rise to a higher level of psychological functioning and spiritual awareness. We often refer in this context to the Chinese pictogram for "crisis," which illustrates the basic idea of spiritual emergency. This character is composed of two images, one of which represents "danger" and the other "opportunity." We described and discussed this concept in our books *The Stormy Search for the Self* and *Spiritual Emergency* (Grof and Grof 1989, 1991).

The nature and the healing potential of psychospiritual crises can be demonstrated with the following story of Karen, with whom we had the chance to work at Esalen. I will use here a slightly modified description of our work with Karen that Christina wrote for our joint book on spiritual emergency. Karen was a graceful young woman in her late twenties, blonde and lithe, who exuded a soft, dreamy beauty. Externally, Karen seemed rather shy and quiet, but she was very bright and physically active. She had had an unusually difficult childhood. Her mother committed suicide when she was three years old, and Karen was alone with her at home when it happened. She then grew up with her alcoholic father and his physically and emotionally abusive second wife. Having left home in her late teens, she lived through episodes of depression and struggled periodically with compulsive eating.

She traveled, studied, and fell in love with jazz dancing, becoming an accomplished dancer and occasional teacher of dance. She liked to sing and developed a professional competence as a skilled massage practitioner. Karen settled in the country, where she met and began living with Peter, a gentle and caring man. Although they remained unmarried, they had a three-year-old daughter, Erin, to whom they were both devoted.

Karen's story represents the most dramatic end of the continuum between a gradual, gentle spiritual emergence and the extreme crisis of spiritual emergency. Even so, many of the issues surrounding her experience apply to anyone undergoing a transformational process. Karen's crisis contained all the elements of a true spiritual emergency. It lasted three and a half weeks and completely interrupted her ordinary functioning. The experiences were so intense that she needed twenty-four-hour care. After she had been in her spiritual emergency for a few days, some of her friends, who knew of our interest in this area, asked us to become involved in her care. We saw her almost every day during the last two and a half weeks of her episode.

As is the case with many spiritual emergencies, the onset of Karen's crisis was rapid and unexpected, and Karen became so absorbed in it and over-whelmed by her experiences that she could not take care of herself or Erin, who stayed with her father. Karen's friends from Esalen, where she lived, de-cided that instead of hospitalizing her, they would take turns caring for her twenty-four hours a day. Karen was moved from her house to a special room in the community. Her friends then set up a "sitters' service": two people at a time signed up for two- to three-hour shifts throughout each twenty-four period. A notebook was placed just outside the door so that sitters could sign in and out and write down their impressions of Karen's condition. They kept records of what she had said or done, what liquids or food she had consumed, and what kinds of behavior the next couple should expect.

On the first day of her episode, Karen noticed that her vision was sudden-ly clearer, not as "soft and fuzzy" as it usually was. She heard women's voices telling her that she was entering into a benign and important experience. For many days, tremendous heat radiated throughout her body, and she saw visions of fire and fields of red, at times feeling herself consumed by flames. To quench the extreme thirst, which she felt was brought about by the burn-ing feelings, she drank great quantities of water. She seemed to be carried through her episode by an enormous energy that poured through her, taking her to many levels of her unconscious and to the memories, emotions, and physical sensations stored there. In deep age regression, she relived many traumas from her early life, such as her mother's suicide and subsequent physical abuse from her stepmother. Once, a childhood memory of being beaten with a belt suddenly shifted, and she felt herself to be a suffering black African, being repeatedly brutally whipped on a crowded slave ship.

She struggled through the physical and emotional pain of her own biologi-cal birth and repeatedly relived the delivery of her daughter. She experienced death many times and in many forms; her preoccupation with dying caused her sitters to become concerned about the possibility of a suicide attempt. However, such an occurrence was unlikely, because of the safety of her environment and the close scrutiny of the helpers. Everyone involved kept a particularly close watch on her, staying with her constantly and encouraging her to keep the experiences internalized rather than acting them out.

Periodically, Karen felt that she was in connection with her dead mother, as well as with a friend who had died in an accident just a year before. She said she missed them and yearned to join them. At other times, she had visions of dying people or felt that she herself was dying. We explained to her that it was possible to experience death symbolically without actually dying physically. Such an experience is typically followed by an experience of psychospiritual rebirth. We then asked her to keep her eyes closed and encouraged her to fully experience these sequences of dying inwardly and to express the difficult emotions involved. She complied and, in a short time, she moved past the intense confrontation with death to other experiences.

For a couple of days, Karen was swept by sequences involving elements of evil. At times she felt as though she were an ancient witch, participating in magic sacrificial rituals. At other times, she sensed that there was a terrible monster within her. As the diabolical beast expressed its demonic energies, she flooded the room with angry expletives and rolled on the floor, making ferocious faces. Her sitters, realizing that the outpouring was not directed at them, protected her from self-injury and encouraged full, safe expression of these impulses.

Sometimes her experience centered on sexuality. After reliving some traumatic memories from her own sexual history, she felt a strong source of energy in her pelvis. She had always regarded sexuality as a lowly instinctual drive that we share with animals. In one of her profound spiritual experiences during this episode, she had the insight that is part of some esoteric traditions, particularly Tantra: the sexual impulse is not simply a biological drive, but an expression of a divine spiritual force. She felt that she was the first woman to have been granted such an awareness, and she expressed a new reverence for her mystical role as a life-giving mother.

During another experience, Karen felt united with the Earth and its people, both of which she feared were about to be destroyed. She envisioned that the planet and its population were heading toward annihilation and was putting forth clear and sophisticated insights about the world situation. She saw images of Soviet and American leaders with their fingers "on the button," and offered accurate and often humorous comments about international politics.

For several days, Karen tapped directly into a powerful stream of creativity and kept expressing many of her experiences in the form of improvised songs. It was remarkable to witness her performance. As soon as an inner theme would surface into her awareness, she would either make up a song about it or recall an appropriate one from memory, lustily singing herself through that phase of her process. The speed and artistic quality of this process were astonishing.

Karen was also extremely psychic, highly sensitive, and acutely attuned to the world around her. She was able to "see through" everyone around her, often anticipating the comments and actions of her helpers. Much to the discomfort of those involved, Karen commented very frankly about any interpersonal games that she saw being played and immediately confronted anyone who was too controlling or rigid, refusing to cooperate with them. At one point, two people coming to take a shift talked about Karen on the way to her room. When they entered, Karen seemed to know what they had said and joined their conversation as if she had been part of it from the very beginning.

After about two weeks, some of the difficult, painful states started to subside and Karen received increasingly benevolent, light-filled experiences, feeling more and more connected with a divine source. She saw within herself a sacred jewel, a radiant pearl that she felt symbolized her true center, and she spent a lot of time tenderly speaking to it and nurturing it. Karen also received instructions from an inner source about how to love and care for herself, and she felt the emotional wounds that she had carried in her heart and body being healed. She said she had passed through a "second birth" and summed up her feelings in the sentence: "I am opening to life, to love, light, and self."

As Karen began to emerge from her experience, she was less and less absorbed by her inner world and more interested in her daughter and the other people around her. She began to eat and sleep more regularly and was increasingly able to care for some of her daily needs. She wanted to finish her experience and return to her home. It became clear to her that the people around her were also ready for the episode to end. Karen and her helpers reached the agreement that she would move from her special room to her home and resume the responsibilities of daily care for herself and her daughter.

We have had a chance to talk to Karen on a number of occasions since her episode and were very pleased to see that many positive changes that had taken place in her during her episode have persisted. Her mood was greatly improved, and she was much more self-assured and outgoing. Her increased self-confidence made it possible for her to use her beautiful voice and perform as a singer in public events. Her experiences, which could have lead to psychiatric hospitalization, a stigmatizing diagnostic label, and years of tranquilizing medication, thus turned out to be a profoundly healing and transformative experience.

WHEN HEARING VOICES
IS NOT SCHIZOPHRENIA

The Story of Eva

In the late 1960s, my brother, Paul, and his then wife, Eva, who are both psychiatrists, emigrated from Czechoslovakia to Canada. They settled down in Hamilton, Ontario, and started working at the psychiatric department of McMasters University. To obtain Canadian medical licenses, they had to pass the required examinations. Because they both also had to work in the psychiatric hospital to support themselves financially, they had to study in the evenings and on weekends, often until the small hours, to prepare for these exams.

Many weeks of intense stress and very little sleep seemed to take their toll on Eva. One day, while working very late at night, she started hearing a human voice. Hearing voices means very bad news for a psychiatrist because this symptom immediately brings the threatening prospect of serious mental illness, more specifically paranoid schizophrenia. After overcoming her initial fears, Eva realized that the voice did not speak in Czech, her native language, or in English, the language she spoke fluently and could understand, but in a foreign tongue unknown to her. This is not typically the case in schizophrenia, where the voices convey specific understandable messages to the patients, usually giving them orders, threatening them, or humiliating them.

Although Eva did not understand what the voice was saying and was not able to identify the language it was using, it clearly sounded like a structured language and not just inarticulate gibberish. Because she had a strong feeling that what was coming was a meaningful communication, she decided to write down the messages and seek consultation with some linguists. Czech, unlike English, is a phonetic language, which makes it possible to write down phonetically any words that one hears and reproduce them later with great accuracy.

By a fortunate synchronicity, Paul had at that time met Asaf, a Croatian physician who had recently come to Canada and turned out to be an extraordinary man. Among other things, he had a photographic memory, was a Sufi sheik, and was able to teach in several languages. Eva decided on an impulse to share with Asaf what was happening to her and read him a few passages from her notebook. Asaf was astounded because Eva's reproduction of the voice she was hearing was accurate enough for him to understand her. The messages were in ancient Arabic, and it was an esoteric Sufi text of his order that was part of a secret oral tradition.

Having recognized this, he immediately accepted Eva as his student. Several months later, he sent her to Yugoslavia to spend three weeks in one of the centers of his order to undergo special training. The Yugoslavian Sufi teachers then sent her farther, to the headquarters of their order in Konya, Turkey, and arranged a visit with the head of the order, Sheik Dede Lorejn. Eva traveled to Turkey all by herself, and the exact time of her arrival was not announced to the Konya Sufis. As she traveled by bus to Konya on the last leg of her journey, she noticed a stately old man with a gray beard who boarded the bus at the same time with her. He had a beautiful, expressive face and serene eyes; during the drive, which lasted several hours, Eva became increasingly fascinated by him. As they arrived in Konya, he left the bus at the same station as Eva and disappeared in the crowd.

Eva found the Sufi headquarters, and when she announced her arrival, she was given the time for the audience with the sheik. The long-awaited time came and she knocked on the door of the sheik's quarters. She was astounded when she realized that Sheik Dede, who answered the door, was the old man from the bus, whose striking presence had captivated her for several hours on her journey to Konya. It was an extraordinary coincidence that the sheik happened to travel on the same bus with Eva because nobody in the order knew the exact time of her arrival. The next surprise came when the sheik told her that he had been waiting for her for many years. He told her that he had known she would come long before her inner voice had brought her to the Sufi teacher in Toronto. Eva has not shared with us the details of her visit with the sheik and the exact content of their interactions because these were supposed to remain secret. At the end of Eva's stay in Konya, the sheik taught her Sufi spiritual exercises, which, after her return to Canada, she used very successfully with her patients.

In the early 1970s, I had another experience that profoundly changed my attitude toward the phenomenon of "hearing voices," which according to my psychiatric training was a symptom of serious mental illness. I was conducting a workshop at the Westerbeck Ranch in Sonoma, California, a beautiful human potential center, one of many such centers inspired by the Esalen Institute. During the lunch break, Pat Westerbeck, the owner of the ranch and our host, introduced me to Helen Schucman and Bill Thetford, two psychologists from New York City who happened to be visiting her at the time. Helen was a clinical and research psychologist and tenured associate professor of medical psychology at Columbia University in New York City. Bill was a tenured professor of medical psychology at the medical center where they both worked and the head of Helen's department.

During our joint lunch, Helen shared with me her fascinating story. At a time of great emotional stress and interpersonal tensions between her and Bill, she started experiencing highly symbolic dreams and images and what she referred to as "the Voice." It seemed to be giving her a rapid inner dictation, not in words but by some form of telepathic transmission. To Helen's great surprise and consternation, the Voice introduced himself as Jesus. Helen, who was Jewish, an atheistic scientist, psychologist, and educator working in a highly prestigious academic setting, was initially horrified, suspecting like Eva that this was the onset of a psychotic break. But then she noticed that the Voice was accurately quoting long passages from the Bible, which she had not read, and was making very specific linguistic references to errors that had been made in various translations of these passages. And she was also able to verify the accuracy of this information.

At Bill's suggestion and encouragement, Helen started recording all the communications in her notebook, jotting them down in shorthand; the next day she read her notes to Bill, and he typed them. As she pointed out to me, the writing was never automatic; she could interrupt it at any time and pick it up again later. As she decided to embark on this giant project, Helen surprised herself by beginning her writing with the sentence: "This is a course in miracles." She felt that this was a special assignment that she had "somewhere, sometime, somehow, agreed to complete."

After lunch, Helen showed me the result of this collaborative venture with Bill, a thick manuscript entitled *A Course in Miracles*. She shared with me a major dilemma she was experiencing: she felt a strong urge to publish her manuscript and share it with the public. However, she was afraid that she would be considered crazy and that it would destroy her academic reputation. After lunch, she asked me if I would give her an hour with the participants of my group and let her share her story with them. "People who come to your workshops are more open-minded than most, and I would like to give it a try. It would be an important test for me," she explained her request.

I wholeheartedly agreed, and the response of the group (as well as my own) was so enthusiastic and encouraging that it seemed to tip the balance of Helen's decision-making process, and she left the ranch determined to take a chance and come out of the closet with her remarkable opus. When *A Course in Miracles* was published, it quickly became a bestseller and a sensation not only among transpersonal psychologists, but also for the general public. It was soon followed by the *Workbook for Students*, a volume consisting of 365 lessons, each offering an exercise for one day of the year, and the *Manual for Teachers*. This three-volume set has now been translated into more than thirty languages and sold a million and a half copies.

Psychiatric Heresy That Brought Fruit

The Story of Milada

I have described earlier, in the Preface and in the introduction to the story of Karen, our concept of "spiritual emergency." This new approach to spontaneous episodes of holotropic states of consciousness replaces indiscriminate pharmacological suppression of symptoms with psychological support and encouragement to "go through the process." This therapeutic strategy does not have to be limited to conditions with strong spiritual emphasis. We have been able to extend it to many individuals whose nonordinary experiences did not include manifest spiritual elements.

The extreme heresy I have committed in the course of my professional career took this strategy even a step further. During my work at the Psychiatric Research Institute in Prague, I used in several patients with the diagnosis of psychosis a strategy diametrically opposite to the conventional suppressive therapy with tranquilizers. I employed a series of LSD sessions to activate and deepen the process, utilize its intrinsic healing potential, and bring it to a positive resolution. An example of this approach is the following story of Milada.

Milada was a thirty-eight-year-old psychologist who for many years before starting LSD treatment had suffered from a complicated neurotic disorder, involving a variety of obsessive-compulsive, organ-neurotic, and hysterical conversion symptoms. She had started long-term psychoanalytic therapy with the nestor of Czech psychoanalysis, seeing him three times a week for fifty-five minutes at a time. In the fifth month of her analysis, she had to be hospitalized because she developed acute psychotic symptoms.

An important part of her clinical symptomatology was an erotomanic delusional system. Milada fell deeply in love with the chief of her department and felt irresistible affection and sexual attraction toward him. She was convinced that this was not a one-sided affair and that he shared her passion. According to her, this strong erotic and spiritual communion existing between them could not be expressed overtly and had to be experienced intrapsychically, beyond the facade of their rather formal social interaction. She felt that her boss, who was married and had children, could not express his feelings openly, at least initially.

Several weeks later, she started hallucinating the voice of her imaginary lover. In these hallucinations, she heard him describe in detail his passionate feelings for her, promise a beautiful shared life in the future, and give her advice and even specific suggestions. During the evening and night hours, Milada experienced powerful sexual sensations, which she interpreted as intercourse at a distance, magically performed by her secret lover. Although in actual sexual situations with her own husband she had never been able to reach an orgasm, during these episodes she experienced orgiastic feelings of cosmic proportions.

Gradually, the nature of the communications changed. Her boss now conveyed to her that divorces had been arranged for both of them and that they now would be able to live together. Milada's hospitalization became unavoidable when she started acting under the influence of her delusions and hallucinations. One day in the morning, she left her husband and made an attempt to move into her employer's apartment with her children and several suitcases. She actually got into a fierce physical fight with her boss's wife, who refused to let her in. After many months of unsuccessful treatment with a variety of tranquilizers and antidepressants, as well as individual and group psychotherapy, she began an experimental program of therapy with serial LSD sessions.

After twelve LSD sessions with medium dosages, her psychotic symptoms completely disappeared, and Milada developed full insight into her irrational behavior in the past. She now interpreted her erotomanic delusion concerning her boss as transference of her feelings for her father, who was very cold and whom she never had been able to reach. In a series of subsequent sessions, she worked on a variety of complicated neurotic and psychosomatic problems.

While reliving various traumatic memories from different periods of her life, she was able to trace many of her present problems to their emotional sources in her unhappy infancy and childhood. She also spent much time on her complicated marital situation. Her husband was insensitive, cruel, and emotionally, as well as physically, abusive. He was an ardent member of the Communist Party, completely immersed in the pursuit of his political career, and provided no emotional support for her. In addition, both of their children were showing signs of serious emotional disturbances that required professional assistance.

Then the LSD sessions moved into the perinatal realm, and Milada was reliving various aspects of her difficult biological birth. She experienced a rich spectrum of experiences characteristic of the death-rebirth process. The emotions and physical sensations associated with the reliving of her difficult birth, during which her twin brother had died, were so abysmal that she referred to these sessions as a "psychological Hiroshima." When she finally completed the birth process and experienced the final ego death, I expected a marked improvement, as was the case in most neurotic patients.

However, to my great surprise I witnessed instead a sudden and complete reappearance of the original psychotic symptomatology, which Milada had not shown for many months. The only difference was that this time I replaced her boss in the role of the main target of all erotomanic fantasies and experiences. In the process of LSD psychotherapy, Milada had developed a transference psychosis. She now believed that she was under my hypnotic influence and felt in constant rapport with me, in the LSD sessions, as well as during the free intervals between them. She experienced a mutual exchange of thoughts and even verbal communication between us.

It was interesting that in some of these hallucinated interviews we "continued psychotherapy." At one point, I spent a week in Amsterdam, Holland, attending a conference on LSD psychotherapy. During that time, Milada, who was hospitalized in the Psychiatric Research Institute in Prague, continued having her imagined psychotherapeutic sessions with me. We "discussed" various aspects of her life, and she carried out activities suggested by my illusory voice. This involved several hours of bathing and physical training every day and practicing feminine crafts, such as knitting and embroidery.

Eventually, I told her in these hallucinated conversations that I had decided to drop the therapeutic game and to become her lover and husband. I encouraged her not to address me as "Dr. Grof," but as "Stanya" (an affectionate form of my first name), and to employ the informal grammatical version of the second person used among relatives, close friends, and lovers. In Czech, as in many other languages, the difference between an intimate and more formal relationship finds its expression in the language used (as in the French tu versus vous, German du versus Sie, or Spanish tu versus Usted).

I also gave Milada the permission to use my last name instead of her husband's name. I repeatedly assured her of my love, told her that her divorce had already been arranged, and asked her to move with her children into my apartment. Among other things, Milada was now referring to "hypnogamic sessions" that she was getting from me in the evening and night hours. She interpreted the sexual sensations and hallucinations of intercourse she had at this time as arranged lessons in enjoying sex that I had decided to give her in order to accelerate her therapy. From the context of her LSD sessions, it became clear that, on the deepest level, Milada's wishful magical thinking was a transference phenomenon reflecting her early symbiotic relationship with her mother.

At one point, Milada spent many hours a day assuming bizarre postures, sometimes lying on the bed, other times standing. Once the nurses told me that they found her standing for a long time on the tips of her toes with her arms stretched forward and clasped together. When they asked her what she was doing, she brushed them away, saying: "Leave me alone, I am embracing him (meaning me)." Inevitably, I became a target of the nurses' jokes; they teased me by pointing out that Milada had my size down and was holding her arms at just the right distance from the floor.

Externally, Milada's postures resembled those I used to see in the chronic ward in catatonic schizophrenics, who manifested the symptom called "waxy flexibility" (*flexibilitas cerea*). Like Milada, they maintained for long periods of time strange and often bizarre postures. However, Milada's "catatonia" differed significantly from the stupor of schizophrenic patients in one significant way: it was always possible to reach her verbally and bring her out of these positions just by addressing her and engaging her in interaction. She would then resume a normal posture and be able to carry on a reasonable conversation.

She also understood what she was doing and offered for it a fascinating explanation. She shared with us that, at this time, her emotional and psychosomatic condition was critically dependent on the position of her body. In some postures, she experienced ecstatic bliss, oceanic feelings, and a sense of cosmic unity. In others, she felt deep depression, nausea, and metaphysical anxiety. She felt that this repeated the situation in her prenatal life, when she had to compete with her twin brother for their mother's womb.

On the basis of previous experiences with other clients, I continued with regular weekly administrations of LSD, despite Milada's persisting psychotic symptoms. These sessions consisted almost entirely of negative experiences of a transpersonal nature. There was an important emphasis on reliving unpleasant intrauterine memories, which she related to the emotional stresses and illnesses of her mother during pregnancy, various embryonal crises, and the mechanical discomfort of having to share the uterus with her twin brother. This was accompanied by challenging karmic sequences and archetypal experiences of a demonic nature.

In the final phase of treatment, a most unusual phenomenon occurred during one of Milada's sessions. This time, the LSD had a paradoxical effect; instead of inducing holotropic experiences, it brought her back to normal. As soon as it took effect, she started addressing me in a formal way appropriate at that time in Czechoslovakia for a doctor-patient relationship. She distanced herself from her psychotic world and offered interesting psychological insights about it. However, when the effect of the drug started to wear off, the symptoms of transference psychosis returned.

In the following session, she experienced for several hours profound ecstatic feelings, with the sense of cosmic unity as the prevailing pattern. They were associated with a sense of being the Divine Child in the womb of the Great Mother Goddess. To my surprise, she emerged from this session without the previous psychotic and neurotic symptoms and with a completely restructured personality. According to her own description, she was now able to experience herself and the world in a way completely different than ever before. She had zest for life, a new appreciation of nature and art, a totally transformed attitude toward her children, and the ability to give up her previous unrealistic ambitions and fantasies. She was able to resume her job and perform it adequately, obtain a divorce from her husband, and live independently while taking care of her two children.

Many years later, after the liberation of Czechoslovakia, I was able to see her during my visits and find out that this remarkable improvement was lasting. Milada was able to cope with emotional crises in the lives of her two children, who were both severely affected by their parents' stormy marriage. She did not even experience an emotional breakdown or require hospitalization at the time when her daughter committed suicide by throwing herself under a train. Although she was experiencing deep grief and struggled with feelings of guilt about her daughter's death, she was able to function in everyday life.

After the liberation of Eastern European countries, when our training in Holotropic Breathwork and transpersonal psychology extended to that part of the world, Milada completed the training and became certified as a facilitator. The highly controversial and heretic therapeutic strategy thus produced one of the most dramatic improvements I have ever experienced during the fifty-some years of my psychiatric practice.

THE MAGIC OF SANDPLAY
When a Kitten Can Be Therapist

We have seen repeatedly that the use of therapeutic methods inducing holotropic states of consciousness, such as psychedelic therapy or Holotropic Breathwork, tends to greatly increase the incidence of synchronicities. Synchronicities are also extremely frequent in the work with people undergoing spiritual emergencies. Initially, I thought that this reflected a special relationship between synchronicity and holotropic states of consciousness, but with time I came to the conclusion that it was associated with the transpersonal set and setting rather then a special state of consciousness.

We have often observed in our workshops that extraordinary synchronicities occurred before the Holotropic Breathwork sessions started, when participants were choosing their partners, or even on their way to the workshop. We have also witnessed an unusually high incidence of synchronicities in association with sandplay, an extraordinary therapeutic technique developed by our dear friend, the late Dora Kalff. Christina and I had frequent contact with Dora because we used to stay as guests in her beautiful old house in Zollikon, near Zürich, practically every time we visited Switzerland. We both had a chance to experience sandplay under her guidance, using her extraordinary collection of sandplay paraphernalia.

As Dora told us, it was C. G. Jung himself who had given her the idea for the sandplay. Dora was married to a Dutch baron who was much older than she, and lived with him in Holland. After the death of her husband, she returned with her children to Switzerland, desperately looking for a new perspective and orientation in her life. It just so happened that she liked to visit with her children a small village, which also was the favorite vacation place for Jung and his relatives. Dora and Jung met there, and she shared with him that she was looking for a vocation for herself. And Jung responded by suggesting that she might enjoy experimenting with therapeutic use of sandplay and gave her the basic instructions for how to do it.

The technique of sandplay is very simple. It uses a box of prescribed size (about two feet by two-and-a-half feet), partially filled with clean sand, and a large collection of objects displayed on shelves. These include human figures of different races and professions, animals, trees, and characteristic dwellings from various countries, natural objects, such as stones or shells, and mythological characters and symbols. The task of the client is to shape the surface of the sand and create a scene with the use of any figures and objects they choose. The sandplay does not use a standard set of items; each therapist creates his or her own collection. Dora had an extraordinary assembly of objects and figures from all over the world.

Christina and I fell in love with this technique after we had experienced its power, and we incorporated it into our monthlong workshops at Esalen. One room in the Big House, where our workshops were held, was regularly designated as a sandplay room. The sandplay toys came partially from our own personal collection, partially from the traveling kits of our guest faculty. Besides rare guest appearances of Dora herself and her son Martin, the resident sandplay therapist for the monthlongs was Jungian psychologist and Dora's senior student, Cecil Burney.

One of the most remarkable and hilarious synchronicities we have observed in connection with the sandplay happened during a monthlong in which Mary, one of the participants, was "pushing the buttons" of all the participants. She was almost manic and talked incessantly, extolling her marriage, her intimate life, and the sexual prowess of her seventy-year-old husband. She had "the most incredible orgasms, fantastic breathwork experiences, the greatest mandalas," and so on. When Emmett Miller, a hypnotist who came to the group as guest faculty, asked participants to introduce themselves with an appropriate movement or gesture, she went outside, ran into the room through an open door, made a wild pirouette screaming her name, and then ran out through the door in the opposite wall.

It was all too obvious to everybody in the group that her inflated panegyrics were desperate attempts to cover up a very different reality. When it was her time to do the sandplay, she created a complex ornate scene representing her idealized life and romanticized marriage. She was very excited by her creation and went to find Cecil, Christina, me, and Al Drucker, an Esalen rolfer and acupuncturist, to show us her unparalleled creation. When she got us all together, she insisted that we had to go and see the "fantastic sandplay" she had made. She practically dragged us to the Big House and up the stairs to the sandplay room.

When we arrived, she was in for a major shock. On her way out of the room, she had left the door open and, during her absence, a kitten walked inside and used the sandbox as his kitty litter. He jumped up into the box, knocked over some of the key figures, and left a big turd in the part of the sandplay that represented the biggest distortion of reality. Seeing what happened, Mary was devastated and heartbroken. We left, and she stayed alone with her ruined sandplay scene. She had to take out the turd and the sand that was defiled and wash some of the figures. As she was doing it, she thought a lot about what had just happened. In the process, she removed some of the figures and replaced others. The result was a very different sandplay, much more realistic and honest than the first one.

Several months later, during a dinner at the ITA conference in Phillip Island, Australia, we were talking about synchronicities. On this occasion, Cecil Burney related this sandplay story in front of anthropologist Michael Harner, who was known for his incisive humor and his ability to respond very quickly to social situations. Michael and Cecil often got involved in verbal fencing. "What it tells me, Cecil," Michael charged without losing a second, "is that cat is a better therapist than you are."

PART 7

TRANSPERSONAL PSYCHOLOGY AND MAINSTREAM SCIENCE

WHEN SCIENCE
BECOMES SCIENTISM
Carl Sagan and His Demon-Haunted World

The challenging observations from consciousness research amassed in the second half of the twentieth century and the basic tenets of transpersonal psychology encountered incredulity and strong intellectual resistance in academic circles. Transpersonal psychology, as it was born in the late 1960s, was culturally sensitive and treated the ritual and spiritual traditions of ancient and native cultures with the respect they deserve in view of the findings of modern consciousness research. It also embraced and integrated a wide range of anomalous phenomena, paradigm-breaking observations that academic science has been unable to account for. However, although comprehensive and well substantiated in and of itself, the new field represented such a radical departure from academic thinking in professional circles that it could not be reconciled with either traditional psychology and psychiatry or with the Newtonian-Cartesian paradigm of Western science.

As a result of this, transpersonal psychology was extremely vulnerable to accusations of being irrational, unscientific, and even "flaky," particularly by scientists who were not aware of the vast body of observations and data on which the new movement was based. These critics also ignored the fact that many of the pioneers of this revolutionary movement had impressive academic credentials. These pioneers generated and embraced the transpersonal vision of the human psyche not because they were ignorant of the fundamental assumptions of traditional science, but because they found the old conceptual frameworks seriously inadequate in accounting for their experiences and observations. Much of the resistance came from representatives of the academic community, who saw the current scientific worldview as an accurate and definitive description of reality and clung to it with stubborn determination, impervious to any evidence countering it.

The nature and intensity of some of the mainstream scientists' reaction to any form of spirituality, in general, and to transpersonal psychology, in particular, seems to mirror the fanaticism of religious fundamentalists. Their attitude lacks solid scientific grounding, ignores or distorts all existing evidence, and is impervious to facts of observation and logical arguments. Closer scrutiny reveals that what they present as an image of reality that has been scientifically proven beyond any reasonable doubt is a colossus on clay feet supported by a host of a priori metaphysical assumptions.

One of the most salient examples of this category of scientists was Carl Sagan, professor of astronomy and space sciences at Cornell University in New York City. An outstanding representative of his field, he achieved worldwide acclaim by his participation as experimenter in most of the unmanned planetary probe missions, by founding the project SETI (Search for Extraterrestrial Intelligence), and creating the highly acclaimed TV series *Cosmos*. He also designed, jointly, with Frank Drake, the gold plaque with the message of Earthlings for extraterrestrial civilizations carried by Pioneer 10, the first spacecraft to leave the solar system. Shortly before Sagan's death, of myelodysplasia, his science fiction novel *Contact* inspired a widely acclaimed movie with the same name.

However, instead of enjoying his professional success and reputation in the area of his expertise, Carl Sagan embarked for unknown reasons with unusual emotional charge and determination on a crusade against everything he considered irrational, unscientific, and occult. He assumed a highly authoritative position of an arbiter and judge of observations reported by a variety of experts from several other disciplines, including parapsychology, thanatology, psychedelic research, anthropology, and comparative religion.

To accomplish his goal of sanitizing the culture from the pollution by occultism and superstition, Carl Sagan became one of the founding members of an organization called CSICOP (Committee for the Scientific Investigation of Claims of the Paranormal), associated himself with the journal entitled *The Skeptical Inquirer*, and employed the services of magician James Randi to help him prove that all claims of the paranormal were fraudulent. The epitome of his efforts was his book of passionate philippics against the dangers of irrationality, *The Demon-Haunted World* (Sagan 1997).

My first contact with Carl was through an enthusiastic letter I received from him shortly after the publication of my book *Realms of the Human Unconscious* (Grof 1975). In this book, I described that my patients undergoing LSD psychotherapy often experienced deep regression, in which they relived with intense emotions and physical feelings the memory of their biological birth. I was able to distinguish four experiential patterns that were associated with this process, reflecting the consecutive stages of childbirth, and referred to them as basic perinatal matrices (BPMs).

BPM I is related to prenatal existence in an advanced stage of pregnancy before the onset of delivery. BPM II reflects the experience of claustrophobic terror and hopelessness experienced by the fetus during the stage of childbirth when the uterus is contracting, but the cervix is not yet open. BPM III is associated with the difficult passage through the birth canal that begins after the cervix is sufficiently dilated. And, finally, BPM IV reproduces the experience of the moment of birth and the immediately following period of reconnection with the mother. Full conscious reliving of birth is then experienced as psychospiritual death and rebirth.

Carl was particularly fascinated by my description of the fourth perinatal matrix, which typically involves visions of brilliant light and of various archetypal figures appearing in this light. In his opinion, expressed in an article published in 1979 in the *Atlantic Monthly* magazine (Sagan 1979a), this observation rendered a mortal blow to the claims of the mystics, who often report visions of divine light and of celestial beings. He concluded that what mystics consider to be supernatural light and angelic beings is actually the infantile memory of emerging into the light of the operation room and seeing cloaked obstetricians and nurses. The misperception of this situation as numinous is thus a result of the immature eyesight and cognition of the newborn.

Carl's interpretation of perinatal visions taken from my book was in sharp conflict with my own description of this phenomenon. After having observed literally hundreds of experiences of psychospiritual death and rebirth, I realized that the reliving of birth functions as a gateway to the Jungian collective unconscious and that the archetypal visions that accompany it are ontologically real and cannot be derived from our experiences of the material world. This is an issue of great theoretical relevance in view of Carl's provocative statement about the nature of reality that opened *Cosmos*, his magnum opus: "The Cosmos is all that is or ever was or ever will be" (Sagan 1983).

Carl later repeated his argument in his book *Broca's Brain* (Sagan 1979b), in which he dedicated to this issue an entire chapter entitled "The Amniotic Universe." He certainly had the right to draw his own conclusions from my observations. However, disregarding my own interpretation and hallowing me as a debunker of mysticism was another matter. In doing this, he also discounted the fact that the entire second half of *Realms of the Human Unconscious*, the book he was referring to, was dedicated to a detailed description of spiritual experiences with many clinical examples. The material in it was actually one of the sources of transpersonal psychology, a discipline seeking a synthesis of genuine spirituality and science.

As transpersonal psychology, with its efforts to legitimize spirituality, continued to grow and gain more ground in the academe, it became a major irritation for Carl and the CSICOP group. Carl finally asked me, as a surviving member of the small group of professionals who had founded transpersonal psychology, to meet with him in a session of open confrontation and discuss theoretical issues related to this discipline. I accepted his invitation and met him in his hotel room in Boston. Other participants in this meeting included my wife, Christina, Carl's wife, Ann Druyan, and Harvard psychiatrist and researcher John Mack, our mutual friend.

Carl started the session by reminding me of my responsibility as a professional trained in medicine and psychology to be careful what information I release to the public because the words of educated people with academic titles are taken more seriously by lay audiences. He emphasized that it was essential for scientists to offer seasoned and unadulterated scientific truth to those who are unable to make their own independent judgment. He then began citing a series of instances in which people were deceived by various hoaxes, scams, and frauds. He brought up the case of the German horse named "smart Hans" ("der kluge Hans"), which, according to the claims of his owner, was able to perform mathematical computations; a fraud involving a figure excavated in Italy that allegedly was a petrified giant; and a few other instances. At this point, I interrupted Carl and told him I felt that what he was describing had no relevance for the subject we were supposed to discuss.

"What do *you* think is relevant for our discussion?" he asked.

"It is the problem of the ontological status of transpersonal experiences," I answered, "such as experiential identification with other people and other life forms, veridical out-of-body experiences, visions of archetypal beings and realms, or ancestral, racial, karmic, and phylogenetic memories. Are they hallucinations and fantasies without any basis in reality or instances of authentic connection with dimensions of reality and sources of relevant information that are normally inaccessible for our consciousness?"

"Give me examples!" he urged me, appearing puzzled and confused.

I described several instances in which individuals in non-ordinary states of consciousness identified experientially with various aspects of the material world or experienced the historical and archetypal domains of the collective unconscious and were able to gain access to information that was clearly far beyond what they had acquired through the conventional channels in their present lifetime. Three of these examples involved experiential identification with animals (eagle, whale, and lion), two of them historical events (see the stories of Renata and Karl), and one the obscure archetypal vision of the Terrible Mother Goddess of the Malekulans in New Guinea (see the story of Otto).

Listening to my stories, Carl regained his composure and assumed an authoritative teaching role. "Oh, this is what you are talking about? Well, that's easy to explain; not a big mystery there," he said. "American children watch television on average about six hours a day. They see a lot of various programs, including those that contain scientific information, such as Nova or the Discovery Channel. They forget much of it, but their brains, being the miraculous organs they are, record it all. In non-ordinary states of consciousness, then, this information is used to generate what appears to be new relevant information. But, as you know, there is no way we can access information that did not enter our brain through the senses. If such information emerges, they must have received it somewhere at some time during this life."

I felt frustrated. Carl was using here the old dictum of British empiricist philosophers that had become a popular tenet of monistic materialistic science: "*Nihil est in intellectu quod non antea fuerit in sensu*" (Nothing is in the intellect that prior to that was not in the sensory organs). If my subjects' experiences contained some seemingly new information, they must have acquired it sometime, somewhere, somehow during this lifetime through sensory input. This should be clear to anybody who has studied natural sciences; how could any educated person see it differently?

Feeling that we were facing a blind alley, I resorted to thanatology, a discipline studying death and dying. In the last few decades, researchers in this field had accumulated some fascinating observations concerning out-of-body experiences in near-death situations. Unlike many other transpersonal phenomena, these experiences are easily subjected to objective verification. Since this material had been widely publicized in best-selling books, television talk shows, and even a number of Hollywood movies, I expected that it would not be difficult to make my point.

I referred to a number of thanatological studies that had independently confirmed that during out-of-body experiences in near-death situations, disembodied consciousness is capable of perceiving the immediate environment, as well as various remote locations, without the mediation of senses. In a fascinating study described in Ken Ring's book entitled *Mindsight* (Ring and Cooper 1999), the capacity of disembodied consciousness to perceive the environment appeared even in people who had been congenitally blind for organic reasons. They were not only able to see for the first time in their lives, but what they saw could be consensually validated. In Ken's terminology, they had "veridical out-of-body experiences."

In this context, I also quoted an example from the book *Recollections of Death*, written by Michael Sabom, a cardiosurgeon who had studied near-death experiences of his patients (Sabom 1982). I told Carl that one of Michael Sabom's patients was able to describe in detail the procedure of his resuscitation following cardiac arrest during an operation. He reported that his disembodied consciousness first watched the procedure from a place near the ceiling. Later, it became interested in the procedure and floated down to a position where it could observe from close up the gauges on the equipment. During the interview following successful resuscitation, the patient was able to reconstruct to Michael Sabom's surprise the entire procedure, including the movements of the little hands on the measuring devices in correlation with the interventions of the surgical team.

Having described this case to Carl, I asked him how he would explain this event in the context of the worldview to which he subscribed. He paused for a while, and then he said assertively: "This, of course, did not happen!"

I shook my head incredulously, not believing what I just had heard. "What do you mean, this did not happen? Cardiosurgeon Michael Sabom reported this in his book based on the research he had conducted with his patients. What is your explanation for what I just have described to you? What do you think all this is about?" I asked. This time the pause was even longer; Carl was clearly thinking very hard, struggling to find the answer. "I'll tell you," he finally broke the long silence. "There are many cardiosurgeons in the world. Nobody would have known the guy. So he made up a wild story to attract attention to himself. It's a PR trick!"

I was shocked. Carl's last words seriously undermined the respect I had had for him. I realized that his worldview was not scientific, but scientistic. It had the form of an unshatterable dogma that was impervious to evidence. It was also clear to me that our discussion had reached an insurmountable impasse. I saw that Carl was willing to question the integrity and sanity of his scientific colleagues before considering that his belief system might require revision or modification to fit the new data. He was so convinced that he knew what the universe was like and what could not happen in it that he did not feel the slightest inclination to examine the challenging data.

My experience with Carl's determination to preserve his scientific beliefs was later further confirmed by a scandal involving CSICOP and the so called "Mars effect." In their studies, originally designed to debunk astrology, French statisticians Michel and Louise Gauquelin demonstrated that in the birth chart of prominent athletes Mars appeared with statistically significant frequency in the ascendent or zenith (Gauquelin 1973). To their surprise, their study thus supported rather than refuted astrological prediction. The statistical probability that this could have happened by chance was one in five million. In later years, the Gauquelins tested astrological predictions involving five planets and eleven professions and found significant results; their data were later replicated independently by other researchers.

After the results of the Gauquelin study had been published, three CSICOP members, Paul Kurtz, George Abell, and Marvin Zelen, incensed by this report, got involved in the controversy, first by a critical response and later by their own study. After a number of heated exchanges, rather than admitting that they essentially confirmed the Gauquelin results, they resorted to conscious falsification of their own data. This fraud was exposed in an article entitled "Starbaby" by Dennis Rawlins, cofounder of CSICOP and a member of its ruling executive council (Rawlins 1981). When Rawlins realized that the organization was committed to perpetuating its ideological position and not to discovering the truth, he concluded that honesty was more important than an indiscriminate witch-hunt against the paranormal.

In 1984, when I was invited to lecture at the World Congress of Astrology in Luzern about my research related to the psychological importance of the trauma of birth and about the Basic Perinatal Matrices, the program actually featured Michel Gauquelin as one of the presenters. It also included another convert to astrology, Hans Eysenck, the famous fierce critic of Freudian psychoanalysis.

JOURNEY TO THE EAST

Bringing LSD to the Soviet Union

Between 1960 and 1967, I worked in the Department for the Study of Interpersonal Relations at the Psychiatric Research Institute in Prague. For all these years, my primary responsibility was research of the therapeutic and heuristic potential of psychedelic substances. Besides Switzerland, Czechoslovakia was at the time the only country that officially produced pharmacologically pure LSD. As principal investigator of the psychedelic research program, I had unlimited access to the substance.

In 1964, Zdenek Dytrych, my co-worker, and I were invited to spend six weeks in the Soviet Union as exchange visitors to study Soviet research of neuroses and psychotherapy. Soviet psychiatry was at the time dominated by Communist ideology, and the only acceptable theory of neuroses was based on I. P. Pavlov's experiments in dogs. Treatment was limited to administration of a bromine-caffeine mixture, sleep therapy, hypnosis, and tranquillizers. Depth psychotherapy of the kind we were researching and interested in was practically nonexistent in the Soviet Union.

It was not easy to design an itinerary for our trip that would be interesting and educational. However, we found out that there was a group in the Bekhterev Psychoneurological Institute in Leningrad that was conducting under the leadership of Professor Myasischev its own variety of dynamic psychotherapy, and we included in our travel plan four weeks in this facility. After all, Leningrad was a beautiful city, and the Hermitage, with its incredible art collection, was a sufficient reason to visit! We also incorporated into our itinerary a stop in Suchumi, Georgia, to spend some time in the large monkey farm on the Black Sea that was conducting research in experimental neuroses of the hamadryas baboons. And in view of the political situation, it was absolutely mandatory to pay a visit to the utterly uninteresting facility of academician Andrei Snezhnevsky, head of the Moscow Institute of Psychiatry of the U.S.S.R. Academy of Medical Sciences and chief ideologist of Soviet psychiatry.

Going to the Soviet Union, we decided to take with us 300 ampoules of LSD-25, each containing 100 micrograms of the substance. It was a product of the Czechoslovakian pharmaceutical industry, listed in the official pharmacopoeia jointly with respectable drugs, such as tetracycline antibiotics, insulin, and aspirin. This was the time before the Harvard scandal stigmatized this substance, and there was nothing illegal about what we were doing. During the first staff meeting we attended at the Bekhterev Institute, we gave a report about our work with psychedelics and offered to conduct LSD sessions with any interested members of the staff.

The team of the Department for the Study of Neuroses, headed by Dr. Straumit, was conducting a superficial form of dynamic psychotherapy. Although the psychologists and psychiatrists of the department, particularly the young ones, were interested in psychoanalysis, they had to keep this very private. Freud's books were forbidden in the Soviet Union because his model of the psyche portrayed humans as dominated by egotistic base instincts and thus incapable of creating the ideal Communist society of the future. It also denigrated the proletarian revolutionaries by attributing their fervor to overthrow the ruling class to unresolved Oedipal issues. The Bekhterev group had to be very careful not to be accused of succumbing to this heresy.

The members of the therapeutic team were very excited by the opportunity to undertake a journey into the deep recesses of their psyches in a way that did not carry the stigma of Freudianism. My colleague and I were spending our time in Leningrad attending and observing the individual or group sessions of the therapists of the Bekhterev Institute, conducting LSD sessions with the staff members of the institute, and visiting the famous Hermitage Museum.

During my stay, I gave a lecture on LSD psychotherapy in the auditorium of the Bekhterev Institute that was open to the public. In those years, I spoke fluent Russian, which made my talk accessible to a large audience without the need for translation.

At the time, there was no clinical research with psychedelics anywhere in the Soviet Union. There were some projects of basic laboratory research, one of them actually at the Bekhterev Institute. Biochemist Lapin was studying the effects of psilocybin, an LSD-like substance, on the vessels in the rabbit's ear. And there were some rumors that mescaline and LSD were being used by the KGB for interrogation and brainwashing. Russian people, deprived of information about the world at large by their strict censorship, were eager to get information about anything coming from the outside. The interest was enormous, and I spoke to a packed auditorium.

On the day of my lecture, I conducted an LSD session with Dr. Straumit, the head of the department. He insisted that he wanted to be part of my presentation and share at the end of my talk his experience with the audience. My lecture was scheduled early in the afternoon; Dr. Straumit had a very deep and meaningful experience, and when he gave his account of it he was still in what we call "psychedelic afterglow." His articulate presentation made a great impression on the audience, and the event was a definite success.

Thanks to the timing of our visit to Russia, we were able to witness as a fringe benefit a very interesting political-scientific development. During our stay in Leningrad, a rumor spread about the 1958 historic "Operation Sunshine," during which the American submarine *Nautilus* traveling under the Arctic ice accomplished the first crossing of the North Pole by a ship. In 1959, in the middle of the cold war, French journalists splashed a sensational story that *Nautilus*, cut off from the conventional means of electronic communication by a thick layer of polar ice, was able to successfully exchange telepathic messages with its base.

Shortly before our arrival in Leningrad, academician Leonid Vasilyev, an internationally recognized physiologist and holder of the Lenin Prize, mentioned this American success at a conference of Soviet scientists commemorating the discovery of radio. He predicted that the harnessing of the energy underlying ESP would be equivalent to the discovery of atomic energy. Vasilyev's comment generated great excitement and attracted attention not only among professionals, but also in the military circles.

The Soviet government was alarmed by the possibility that the United States might be gaining military advantage. Within a year following his lecture, Vasilyev was heading a special laboratory for parapsychology at the University of Leningrad. This launched the golden era of Soviet parapsychological research, conducted under the aegis of the Soviet military and the Soviet secret police and supported by an annual budget estimated at about twenty million rubles. This was at the time equivalent to a little more than the same amount in U.S. dollars. However, this development benefited also American parapsychologists, because Soviet focus on parapsychology made this field important for national security and thus deserving the support of the U.S. government.

During the four weeks of our stay in Leningrad, the deep personal sharing around the psychedelic sessions of the staff and parties enlivened by Starka, or Starinnaya vodka, prepared according to an old Czarist recipe, created between us bonds of deep friendship. When we were leaving to continue our trip to Moscow and Suchumi, we left a substantial number of the remaining LSD ampoules with our Leningrad colleagues so that they could continue their inner explorations. After a visit to Moscow, certainly more interesting culturally than professionally, and a lovely visit in the subtropical coast of Georgia, we returned to Prague.

This experience had an interesting sequel three years later, when I began my fellowship at Johns Hopkins University in Baltimore. The Henry Phipps Psychiatric Clinic, where I taught students psychotherapy, had regular Wednesday seminars with lectures by visiting teachers. One of these guests was Dr. Isidor Zifferstein, an American psychiatrist born in Byelorus. Taking advantage of the fact that he spoke fluent Russian, he was paying regular annual visits to the Bekhterev Institute and participated, as we had, in their individual and group therapy sessions. Because the Bekhterev Institute was the only place in the Soviet Union that had a school of psychotherapy with a definable therapeutic approach, Dr. Zifferstein soon became an official U.S. expert on Soviet psychotherapy. He traveled around the country, giving lectures and writing articles on this subject.

His visit to Henry Phipps Clinic was one of the stops on his lecture tour. After describing as usual the work of the Leningrad school of Professor Myasischev, Dr. Zifferstein shared with us an observation that he found very puzzling. He had been visiting the Bekhterev Institute annually for a number of years, he said. But during his last visit he found a situation that was new and surprising. The intellectual atmosphere in the institute had radically changed. During his past visits, most of his discussions with staff had revolved around Ivan Petrovich Pavlov, a Russian Nobel-prize winning physiologist and citizen of Leningrad. The therapists had tried to justify their theoretical concepts and therapeutic strategies by references to Pavlov's work.

To Zifferstein's surprise, during his last visits, that was not the case. All the young psychologists and psychiatrists kept talking about Oriental philosophy, various schools of yoga, and Zen Buddhism. They were mentioning books like Aldous Huxley's novels *Brave New World* and *Island,* and Hermann Hesse's *Journey to the East.* This was a long time before "perestroika" and "glasnost." Knowing that pointing out the possible connection between the psychedelic sessions of the staff and the change of their interests could have had unpleasant consequences for them, I refrained from suggesting a plausible explanation for Dr. Zifferstein's mysterious observation.

For me, this was just another proof for what I have seen repeatedly in my own work: intelligent psychiatrists and psychologists with good academic credentials, who have the opportunity to experience holotropic states find the materialistic scientific worldview inadequate to explain these states, and they open up to spiritual philosophies of the East and to mystical traditions of the world as a more appropriate alternative.

PSYCHE AND COSMOS
What the Planets Can Reveal about Consciousness

One of the greatest surprises I have experienced during the fifty years I have been involved in consciousness research was the discovery of the predictive power of astrology. Working with holotropic states of consciousness and experiencing them personally tends to undermine one's materialistic worldview and creates more openness to various esoteric teachings. However, my skepticism concerning astrology was very strong and persistent and survived many years of my consciousness research. The idea that stars could have anything to do with states of consciousness, let alone events in the world, seemed absurd and preposterous long after I had opened up to the Eastern spiritual philosophies, acupuncture, and the I Ching.

My journey of discovering astrology extended over many years. My first encounter with it happened in 1966 during my guest appearance on a Czechoslovakian TV program, when I was invited by a talk-show host to discuss the psychedelic research project that I was heading at the Psychiatric Research Institute in Prague. The same program featured a Slovak colleague, psychiatrist Eugene Jonás. Eugene was deeply interested in astrology, which he had studied for over twenty-five years, including its Babylonian, Assyrian, Egyptian, and Indian versions. Because of the Marxist censorship, he was not using the term astrology and referred to his work as study of "cosmobiological influences."

In the TV program, in which both of us participated, he discussed his research on cosmobiological influences on female reproductive functions.

Using clues that he found in an ancient book of Vedic astrology, he was trying to predict the sex of the fetus and to explain the occasional failure of the Ogino-Knauss rhythm method of contraception. In a research project, conducted in cooperation with the universities in Bratislava and Heidelberg, he had been able to correctly predict the gender of the fetus from the horoscope of conception in seventeen consecutive cases. The statistical significance of these findings was enormous. It is important to emphasize that this was many years before gender assessment of the fetus became possible thanks to the development of ultrasound analysis.

Eugene and I had a chance to chat in the meeting room before the show and, after a brief discussion about our respective research projects, we decided to have dinner on the way home from the TV station. While we were eating, Eugene shared with me his enthusiasm and passion concerning astrology and was trying to convince me that natal and transit astrology could be an extremely useful tool in our psychedelic research. At a later date, he was actually able to give me some interesting feedback about several of my LSD patients, based solely on their natal charts and current transits. I found it very interesting, but my skepticism about astrology, reflecting my scientific training, was too strong to allow me to pursue Eugene's suggestion and get involved in serious study of this discipline.

This episode, although not convincing enough to turn me into an astrology aficionado, planted a seed in me that had to wait many years to sprout. In 1973, after seven years of conducting psychedelic research at the Maryland Psychiatric Research Center in Baltimore, I was offered the position of Scholar-in-Residence at the Esalen Institute in Big Sur and moved to California. Several months later, I connected with Richard Tarnas, a Harvard student who came to Esalen to write his dissertation on LSD psychotherapy. He had heard about my research and came to ask me to be on his dissertation committee. The only place available at Esalen at that time was a little studio in the basement of the house in which we lived. Rick moved in, and our initial working relationship quickly developed into close friendship.

And this began the next chapter of my interest in astrology. At Esalen, Rick and I met Arne Trettevik, a man whose life was completely dedicated to astrology. He walked around with the *American Ephemeris* book, which he consulted on a daily or even hourly basis, monitoring the correlations between planetary transits and the events in his life. Arne's strategy was different from Eugene's; instead of just sharing with us his observations, he taught us how to calculate transits and discussed with us the principal characteristics of the planetary archetypes so that we could verify for ourselves the basic tenets of astrology.

Arne's strategy worked, and both Rick and I emerged from this initial experience convinced about the value of astrology. Rick's interest in astrology was deep enough to turn into his lifetime passion and vocation. I continued my research in non-ordinary states of consciousness, but now with astrology as an important tool and an integral part of the study. Over the years, Rick and I have functioned as a team, complementing each other. My function has been to collect interesting clinical observations from psychedelic sessions, Holotropic Breathwork workshops and training, mystical experiences, spiritual emergencies, and psychotic breaks. Rick, using his astrological expertise and extraordinary knowledge of cultural history, has been studying the astrological correlations involved.

Working this way, we have amassed over the years convincing evidence that quite specifically supports important basic assumptions of astrology. This material has revealed the existence of systematic correlations between the nature and content of holotropic states of consciousness and planetary transits of the individuals involved. The first indication that there might be some extraordinary connection between astrology and my research of holotropic states was the realization that my description of the phenomenology of the four basic perinatal matrices (BPMs), experiential patterns associated with the stages of biological birth, showed astonishing similarity to the four archetypes that astrologers link to the four outer planets of the solar system. My description of the BPMs was based on clinical observations made quite independently many years before I knew anything about astrology.

The positive aspect of the first perinatal matrix (BPM I)—the reliving of episodes of undisturbed intrauterine existence, as well as the concomitant experiences of dissolution of boundaries, oceanic ecstasy, cosmic feelings of unity, transcendence of time and space, and awareness of the mystical dimensions of reality—is unmistakably reflective of the archetype that astrologers link to Neptune. The same is true for the negative aspect of BPM I, associated with regressive experiences of prenatal disturbances. Here the dissolution of boundaries is not mystical but psychotic in nature; it leads to confusion, delusional thinking, a sense of chemical poisoning, and paranoid perceptions of reality. This matrix also has a psychodynamic connection with alcoholic or narcotic intoxication and addiction. All these are qualities that astrologers describe as the shadow side of the Neptune archetype.

Prominent features of BPM II—related to the "no exit" stage of birth, during which the uterus contracts and the cervix is still closed—are preoccupation with aging and death, difficult ordeal and hard labor, depression, oppression, constriction, and starvation. This matrix also brings feelings of inadequacy, inferiority, and guilt. It is associated with skepticism and a profoundly pessimistic view of existence, a shattering crisis of meaning, inability to enjoy anything, and loss of any connection with the divine dimension of reality. In astrology, all these qualities are attributes of the negative side of the Saturn archetype.

The precise astrological correspondence with the experiential aspects of BPM III is particularly extraordinary and surprising because this matrix represents an unusual combination of elements characteristic of the final stage of biological birth. Here belong unrelenting thrust of an elemental driving force, clash of titanic energies, Dionysian ecstasy, birth, sex, death, rebirth, elimination, and scatology. We can further mention the experiences of life and death relevance and the motifs of volcanic eruptions, purifying fire, and of the underworld—urban, criminal, psychological, sexual, and mythological. Astrologically, all these are attributes of the archetype of Pluto.

And finally, the phenomenology of BPM IV—the experience of emerging from the birth canal—is closely related to the archetype of Uranus. This is the only planet the archetypal meaning of which considerably deviates from the nature of its mythological namesake. As Rick has convincingly shown in an essay specifically dedicated to this subject, the archetype associated with Uranus actually exactly reflects the basic characteristics of the Greek mythological hero Prometheus (Tarnas 1995). It is characterized by such features as unexpected resolution of a difficult situation, breaking and transcending boundaries, brilliantly illuminating insights, Promethean epiphany, sudden rising to a new level of awareness and consciousness, liberation, and freedom from previous constrictions.

The discovery of these deep similarities between the description of four major planetary archetypes and the phenomenology of the basic perinatal matrices was extraordinary in and of itself, considering that the latter originated quite independently and from completely different sources than the former. However, even more astonishing was Rick's later discovery that in holotropic states the experiential confrontation with these matrices regularly occurs at the time when the individuals involved have important transits of the corresponding planets.

Over the years, we have been able to confirm this fact by thousands of specific observations. Because of these surprisingly precise correlations, astrology, particularly transit astrology, turned out to be the long-sought Rosetta stone of consciousness research, providing the key for understanding the nature and content of present, past, and future holotropic states, both spontaneous and induced.

The correlations concerning past experiences are primarily of theoretical interest and can be used as a basis for longitudinal research. Examining current transits can be extremely useful in the work with individuals undergoing spiritual emergencies, providing a road map for otherwise incomprehensible experiences and their timing. And the possibility of making remarkably accurate predictions based on future transits is an invaluable tool in the planning of psychedelic and holotropic sessions.

Modern Euro-American civilization is under such a strong influence of materialistic science that it usually takes years of research of holotropic states and extensive personal exposure to them before we are able to break its spell and accept the radical revisions that have to be made in our understanding of the human psyche and the nature of reality to accommodate the new data. It is not surprising that this process is so difficult and that it encounters so much resistance. The vast array of challenging observations from holotropic states and astrology cannot be handled by a little conceptual patchwork, occasional cosmetic adjustment using minor *ad hoc* hypotheses. It would require a drastic overhaul, shattering and replacing the most fundamental metaphysical assumptions and beliefs of materialistic science.

The specific implications for psychology and psychiatry go far beyond those I have discussed over the years in my books—the vastly expanded model of the psyche, the much more complex multilevel structure of emotional and psychosomatic disorders, the concept of the inner radar, the existence and therapeutic use of inner healing intelligence, and a few others. Another area that requires radical revision in the light of the new findings is the role of the medical model in psychiatry and the influence it has on clinical practice, particularly in relation to the use of diagnostic labels.

Because the experiences of clients in ordinary, as well as holotropic, states of consciousness show deep correlations with the archetypal fields of the transiting planets at any particular time, they are subjected to constant changes. Clinicians and theoreticians who are trying to establish a fixed classificatory system of psychiatric diagnoses find their work very frustrating. We are currently on the fourth revised version of the official American *Diagnostic and Statistical Manual (DSM-IV)*, and psychiatrists and psychologists keep expressing their frustration concerning the lack of correspondence between the description of the diagnostic categories and the actual clinical pictures they encounter in their patients.

From an astrological point of view, this versatility of the clinical picture reflects the constantly shifting angular relations among the planets and the corresponding archetypal influences. At various periods of history, two or more planets form important aspects in the skies; this is particularly significant and long-lasting if it involves the outer planets from Jupiter to Pluto. The combined archetypal field associated with these planets will give this period a certain experiential flavor, determining its Zeitgeist.

For example, the entire period of 1960 to 1972 coincided with a conjunction involving Pluto and Uranus, the only such conjunction in the twentieth century. This certainly was a very appropriate archetypal combination for a period of sustained major psychospiritual revolution of a Dionysian kind, characterized by social upheaval, the civil rights movement, technological triumph, radical innovations in music and arts, the sexual revolution, the feminist movement, student unrest, and widespread countercultural activity and creativity.

By contrast, the major archetypal influence throughout the 1990s was a Neptune-Uranus conjunction. This was a period of profound, but generally nonviolent, spiritual and social changes, or "velvet revolutions," such as the unification of Germany, liberation of Eastern European countries, and peaceful dissolution of the Soviet Union, a dangerous superpower. At this time, Jungian psychology gained increasing acceptance, and a multitude of spiritually oriented books made the bestseller lists. Transpersonal themes—mythology, near-death experiences, UFO abduction phenomena, instrumental transcommunication (ITC), and virtual reality—attracted the attention of professionals and the general public and many of them have become favorite subjects of movie makers (Tarnas 2006).

At the time of major planetary aspects for the whole world, these planetary combinations also become personalized for individuals as they form major transits to specific planets in their natal charts. These alignments will then be reflected in tendencies toward specific emotional and psychosomatic disorders. As a result, psychiatrists from different historical periods do not see the same phenomena as their colleagues from earlier or later times. This suggests a possible explanation for why the creation of a fixed, universally valid *DSM-IV* seems to be intrinsically problematic.

But that is not the whole story. In the annual courses that Rick Tarnas and I teach at the California Institute of Integral Studies (CIIS) in San Francisco, we discuss the major schools of depth psychology and analyze the astrological charts of their founders. It soon became obvious that these pioneers were not able to study objectively the psyches of their clients and make general conclusions that would remain valid indefinitely. They saw the problems of their clients through their subjective perceptual stencils, or distorting lenses, inherent in the aspects in their own charts and their own transits at the time of the observations.

With the exception of organically determined disorders, psychiatry thus does not have a fixed set of phenomena to study. The result of any research of emotional and psychosomatic disorders that are not organic is thus determined by a complex interplay of a number of factors: the astrological chart of the researcher and his or her transits at the time of observation, the planetary aspects for the entire world that define the Zeitgeist of a particular period, and personal transits that color the experiences of the clients.

The image of psychiatry as a discipline that possesses concise descriptions of fixed and transtemporal pathological conditions and an armamentarium of specific remedies and interventions is an illusion. The only viable approach under these circumstances is to describe psychiatric disorders in terms of relationships and tools that can be used to analyze the situation at any particular time and characterize it in terms of the phenomenology of the experiences of the client and the client's planetary transits. As a corrective, it is also necessary to take into consideration the global planetary aspects and the researchers' own chart and transits.

The connections revealed by astrology are so complex, intricate, creative, and highly imaginative that they leave no doubt of their divine origin. They provide convincing evidence for a deep, meaningful order underlying creation and for a superior cosmic intelligence that engendered it. This raises a very interesting question: is there a comprehensive worldview that could accommodate astrology and assimilate its findings? Over the years, and not without struggle and tribulations, I have come to the conclusion that there is a worldview that can absorb and explain my experiences and observations from consciousness research, as well as embrace astrology. However, it differs diametrically from the belief system that dominates the modern Western civilization.

I have described this worldview in my book *The Cosmic Game: Explorations of the Frontiers of Human Consciousness* (Grof 1998) and presented it also in a condensed form in a chapter of my last book, *Psychology of the*

Future (Grof 2000). This vision of reality is based on experiences and insights from holotropic states and portrays the universe not as a material system, but as an infinitely complex play of "Absolute Consciousness." Ancient Hindu scriptures describe a similar view of the cosmos, referring to the events in the phenomenal worlds as *lila,* the divine play. This way of seeing the universe is becoming increasingly compatible with various revolutionary advances in new paradigm science.

If the cosmos is a creation of superior intelligence and not a supermachine that created itself, it then becomes more readily plausible that astrology could be one of many different orders built into the universal fabric. It could be seen as a useful complement to the field of science, rather than an irreconcilable rival of the scientific worldview. Opening up conceptually to this possibility would make it possible to utilize the great potential that astrology holds as a clinical and research tool in psychiatry, psychology, and psychotherapy, as well as for a variety of other disciplines.

The major difference between the thinking of mainstream scientists and astrologers is that scientists try to apply to astrology principles of linear causality. This can be illustrated by my conversation with Carl Sagan, who was the prime representative of the "scientific" resistance to astrology. When he heard about my interest in this field, he told me: "I can't understand how you, as an intelligent and educated person, can believe this nonsense. Astrology is total hogwash! As I am standing here, I have more influence on you than Pluto." Carl was brilliant, and he carried out in his head a fast computation, taking into account masses, distance, and gravitational fields. This led him to the obvious conclusion that the planets could not have any significant physical influence on the human psyche or the events on earth. And he lacked the imagination to think of another mechanism that could possibly be involved.

Carl's conclusion that astrology does not make sense if we think in terms of physical influence of the planets on the human psyche and events in the world is shared by all well-educated astrologers. They do not think in terms of chains of physical causes and effects, but in terms of synchronistic relations. To accept the worldview of astrology, one would have to abandon the image of the universe as a mechanical and fully deterministic system and replace it with a universe based on a master blueprint created by superior cosmic intelligence. According to the astrological worldview, the universal scheme of things includes systematic correlations between the movements and angular relations of the planets and the dynamics of the archetypal world. And because archetypal dynamics govern and inform the events in the material world, we can infer and predict from planetary positions what kind of happenings we might expect in material reality.

It is important to emphasize that the astrological predictions are archetypal and not concrete. It is not enough to judge astrology on the basis of the fact that it is incompatible with mainstream scientific thinking. Any critic who wants to be taken seriously has to acquaint himself or herself with the theory and practice of astrology and have adequate knowledge of archetypal psychology. The next step is to conduct one's own research and to assess to what extent the actual observations agree with the astrological predictions. I am convinced that if an open-minded researcher conducts such a study, the victim will not be astrology, but the monistic, materialistic worldview of academic science.

EPILOGUE

My experiences and observations during the five decades I have spent researching holotropic states of my own and of thousands of others have profoundly changed my personal and scientific worldviews. The stories collected in this book describe a small but representative sample of the events that have been instrumental in this transformation.

In 1956, at the time of my graduation from the Medical School of Charles University in Prague, I shared with the academic community and with my culture the image of the universe and of the human psyche forged by Western materialistic science. This vision of the world was based on the metaphysical assumption that the universe is a mechanical system that is strictly deterministic and in which matter is primary. Life, consciousness, and intelligence were seen as more or less accidental side-products of matter, essentially flukes that happened in an insignificant section of a giant universe after billions of years of evolution of inert inorganic matter.

In this paradigm, the universe and nature had no guiding intelligence and underlying master blueprint. All the incredible complexity of forms revealed by various scientific disciplines, from astronomy, quantum-relativistic physics, and chemistry to biology and psychology, was seen as resulting from essentially meaningless play of material particles. The universe was a gigantic and fully deterministic mechanical system that was governed by the principle of cause and effect.

In this view, the universe essentially created itself. Particles of inorganic matter just happened to assemble into organic compounds, and these just happened to organize themselves into cells. The entire Darwinian evolution from unicellular organisms to humans was seen as having been guided by accidental genetic mutations and natural selection. According to this worldview, the principal mechanism of evolution in nature was survival of the fittest and the militant strategy of the selfish gene. This seemed to explain and justify what appeared to be characteristic features of human behavior—pursuit of selfish interest in competition with and at the expense of others as it manifests in personal life, as well as on the collective economic, political, and military scene.

This gloomy image of human nature was further reinforced by the findings of depth psychology, pioneered by Sigmund Freud and his followers, which purported that all our behavior is in the last analysis driven by base animal instincts. From this perspective, feelings of love were nothing but a reaction to our innate hostility or desexualized interest in our parents. Ethical behavior was based on fear of punishment, aesthetic interest was psychological defense against powerful anal impulses, and so on. Without societal restrictions, penal institutions, and superegos created by parental prohibitions and injunctions, we would indulge in indiscriminate promiscuous sexual acting out, killing, and stealing, as Freud so eloquently described in his *Civilization and Its Discontents* (Freud 1971a).

Freud and his followers saw religious beliefs and spiritual interests of any kind as reflecting superstition, gullibility, primitive magical thinking, primary process, and obsessive-compulsive behavior resulting from suppression of anal impulses and an unresolved Oedipal or Electra complex. It was again Sigmund Freud who spearheaded this perspective in his writings, such as *The Future of an Illusion* and *Totem and Taboo* (Freud 1971b and 1971c). This sweeping dismissal of legitimacy of anything spiritual did not discriminate between primitive folk beliefs and sophisticated systems based on centuries of profound exploration of the psyche and consciousness, such as various schools of yoga, Buddhism, or Sufism. And direct experiences of spiritual dimensions of reality were seen as manifestations of serious mental disease.

Over the last five decades, my professional observations and personal experiences—along the lines of the ones described in this book—have seriously undermined the above worldview and made me question its basic metaphysical assumptions. Battling considerable intellectual resistance, I have gradually developed an entirely different understanding of the universe, of the psyche, and of human nature. This worldview resembles the systems of thought that Aldous Huxley called perennial philosophy, particularly those of the great Eastern spiritual philosophies. In my current view of reality, consciousness represents a fundamental aspect of existence, equal or possibly supraordinated to matter, rather than its accidental product.

I now believe that the universe was created and is permeated by cosmic consciousness and superior creative intelligence (*anima mundi*) on all its levels and in all its dimensions. The image of the cosmos as a giant supermachine with Newtonian characteristics, consisting of separate building blocks (elementary particles and objects), gave way to a vision of a unified field, an organic whole in which everything is meaningfully interconnected. I now see each individual human psyche as an integral part of the overall field of cosmic consciousness and essentially commensurate with it.

More specifically, to understand the observations and experiences in holotropic states, I had to vastly expand the model currently used by traditional academic psychiatry and psychology. Thinking in terms of biology, physiology, postnatal biography, and the Freudian individual unconscious proved painfully inadequate for that purpose. The new map had to include, besides the postnatal biographical level, two additional domains: the *perinatal* (related to the trauma of birth) and the *transpersonal* (comprising ancestral, racial, collective, and phylogenetic memories, karmic experiences, and archetypal dynamics).

Radical changes occurred also in my thinking in regard to what traditional psychiatrtists call psychopathology. I now see clearly that emotional and psychosomatic disorders that do not have an organic basis (psychogenic psychopathology) cannot be adequately explained from postnatal biographical traumas in infancy, childhood, and later life. The roots of these disorders reach much deeper to include significant contributions from the perinatal level and from the transpersonal domains. While the recognition of the depth of emotional and psychosomatic problems might at first seem very discouraging, it is more than balanced by the discovery of powerful new therapeutic mechanisms operating in the deep unconscious (associated with the reliving of birth, with past-life experiences, experiences of cosmic unity, and many others).

An equally exciting aspect of the new understanding of the human psyche is the discovery of its inner healing intelligence. The goal in traditional psychotherapies is to reach an intellectual understanding as to how the psyche functions, why symptoms develop, and what they mean. This understanding then becomes the basis for developing various techniques that therapists can use to treat their patients. A serious problem with this strategy is the striking lack of agreement among psychologists and psychiatrists concerning the most fundamental theoretical issues and the resulting astonishing number of competing schools of psychotherapy. The work with holotropic states shows us a surprising radical alternative—mobilization of deep inner intelligence of the clients that guides the process of healing and transformation.

The most surprising and exciting feature of the new worldview is that—in contrast with academic science—it recognizes the ontological reality of the ordinarily hidden spiritual dimensions of existence and does not put psychopathological labels on those who experience them. Consequently, it sees serious spiritual quest as an important and fully legitimate activity. However, it is important to emphasize that this statement applies to genuine spirituality based on personal experience and not to dogmatic ideologies of organized religions.

The new worldview that I have briefly outlined above is not an arbitrary construct or result of speculation. It is a philosophical perspective that emerges spontaneously in individuals who have been able to free themselves from the imprints imposed on them by the trauma of their birth and their early life and who have had profound transpersonal experiences. Deep experiential work of this kind has profound implications for the way we conduct our lives. It is not difficult to understand that an important prerequisite for successful existence is general intelligence—the ability to learn and recall, think and reason, and adequately respond to our material environment. More recent research emphasized the importance of "emotional intelligence," the capacity to adequately respond to our human environment and skillfully handle our interpersonal relationships (Goleman 1996). Observations from the study of holotropic states confirm the basic tenet of perennial philosophy that the quality of our life ultimately depends on what can be called "spiritual intelligence."

Spiritual intelligence is the capacity to conduct our life in such a way that it reflects deep philosophical and metaphysical understanding of reality and of ourselves discovered through personal experiences during systematic spiritual pursuit. Buddhist scriptures refer to this kind of spiritual wisdom as *prajña paramita* (transcendental wisdom). Unlike the dogmas of organized church, spiritual intelligence acquired in the process of experiential self-exploration has the power to override the scientistic worldview of materialistic science. At the same time, it is equally effective as a remedy against the fundamentalist misunderstanding and distortion of the spiritual message. The concept of "intelligent design" represents an addition to what science has discovered about the evolution of the cosmos and life, not a primitive and simple-minded alternative to it.

Systematic and responsible self-exploration using holotropic states is conducive to emotional and psychosomatic healing and positive personality transformation. Over the years, I have had the privilege to observe this process in many people who were involved in serious spiritual pursuit of this kind. Some of them were meditators and had regular spiritual practice, others had supervised psychedelic sessions or participated in various forms of experiential psychotherapy; a few had chosen the shamanic path. I have also witnessed profound positive changes in many people who received adequate support during their spontaneous episodes of psychospiritual crises (spiritual emergencies).

Episodes of psychospiritual death and rebirth and experiential connection with positive postnatal or prenatal memories tend to reduce irrational drives and ambitions. They lead to significant decrease of aggression, to inner peace, self-acceptance, and tolerance of others. This is typically associated with a shift of focus from the past and future to the present moment and with increased zest for life—the ability to enjoy and draw satisfaction from simple aspects of life, such as everyday activities, food, lovemaking, nature, and music. Another important result of this process is emergence of spirituality of a universal and mystical nature that is nondenominational and all-encompassing.

The process of spiritual opening and transformation typically deepens further as a result of transpersonal experiences, such as identification with other people, entire human groups, animals, and plants. Additional transpersonal experiences provide conscious access to events occurring in other countries, cultures, and historical periods and even to the mythological realms and archetypal beings of the collective unconscious. Experiences of cosmic unity and one's own divinity result in increasing identification with all of creation and bring the sense of wonder, love, compassion, and inner peace. What begins as psychological probing of the unconscious psyche conducted for therapeutic purposes automatically becomes a philosophical quest for the meaning of life and a journey of spiritual discovery.

One of the most striking consequences of various forms of transpersonal experiences is spontaneous emergence and development of deep humanitarian and ecological concerns and the need to get involved in service for some common purpose. This is based on an almost cellular awareness that the boundaries in the universe are arbitrary and that each of us is identical with the entire web of existence. It becomes clear that we cannot do anything to nature without simultaneously doing it to ourselves. Differences among people appear to be interesting and enriching rather than threatening, whether they are related to sex, race, color, language, political conviction, or religious belief.

Individuals who have undergone this transformation develop a deep sense of being planetary citizens rather than citizens of a particular country or members of a particular racial, social, ideological, political, or religious group. It is obvious that a transformation of this kind would increase our chances for survival if it could occur on a sufficiently large scale. We seem to be involved in a dramatic race for time that has no precedent in the entire history of humanity. What is at stake is nothing less than the future of life on this planet. If we continue the old strategies, which in their consequences are extremely self-destructive, it is unlikely that humankind will survive. However, if a sufficient number of people undergo the process of deep inner transformation outlined above, it would enhance our chances to meet the formidable challenges we are facing and use the enormous creative potential inherent in our species to create a better future.

BIBLIOGRAPHY

Aziz, R. 1990. *C. G. Jung's Psychology of Religion and Synchronicity*. Albany: State University of New York Press.

Bache, C. M. 1988. *Lifecycles: Reincarnation and the Web of Life*. New York: Paragon House.

Franz, M. von. 1980. *On Divination and Synchronicity: The Psychology of Meaningful Chance*. Toronto: Inner City Books.

Freud, S. 1971. *Civilization and Its Discontents. The Standard Edition of the Complete Psychological Works of Sigmund Freud*, Vol. 21. London: The Hogarth Press.

———1971. *The Future of an Illusion. The Standard Edition of the Complete Psychological Works of Sigmund Freud*, Vol. 21. London: The Hogarth Press.

———1971. *Totem and Taboo. The Standard Edition of the Complete Psychological Works of Sigmund Freud*, Vol. 13. London: The Hogarth Press.

Fuller, J. G. 1951. *The Ghost of 29 Megacycles*. London: Souvenir Press.

Gauquelin, M. 1973. *Cosmic Influences on Human Behavior*. New York: Aurora Press.

Goleman, D. 1996. *Spiritual Intelligence: Why It Can Matter More Than IQ*. New York: Bantam.

Grant, J., and D. Kelsey. 1967. *Many Lifetimes.*

Greyson, B., and N.E. Bush. "Distressing Near-Death Experiences." *Psychiatry* 55. (1992):95.

Grof, S. 1975. *Realms of the Human Unconscious: Observations from LSD Research.* New York: Viking Press.

————2000. *Psychology of the Future.*

————1998. *The Cosmic Game: Explorations of the Frontiers of Human Consciousness.* Albany: State University New York Press.

Grof, C., and S. Grof. 1991. *The Stormy Search for the Self: A Guide to Personal Growth through Transformational Crises.* Los Angeles: J. P. Tarcher.

Grof, S., and C. Grof. 1989. *Spiritual Emergency: When Personal Transformation Becomes a Crisis.* Los Angeles: J. P. Tarcher.

Holler, S. A. 1994. *The Gnostic Jung and the Seven Sermons to the Dead.* Wheaton, IL: Quest Books.

Jung, C. G. 1960. *Synchronicity: An Acausal Connecting Principle.* Princeton, NJ: Princeton University Press.

————1964. *Flying Saucers: A Modern Myth of Things Seen in the Skies.*

————1973. Letter to Carl Selig, February 25, 1953. *C. G. Jung's Letters*, Vol. 2., Bollingen Series XCV. Princeton, NJ: Princeton University Press.

Koestler, A. 1971. *The Case of the Midwife Toad.* New York: Random House.

Mack, J. 1994. *Abductions.*

————1999. *Passport to the Universe.*

Macy, M. H. 2001. *Miracles in the Storm: Talking to the Other Side with the New Technology of Spiritual Contact.* New American Library.

————2005. "The miraculous side of instrumental transcommunication." A lecture at the Seventh International Conference on Science and Consciousness in La Fonda Hotel, Santa Fe, NM.

Mansfield, V. N. 1995. *Synchronicity, Science, and Soul-Making: Understanding Jungian Synchronicity through Physics, Buddhism, and Philosophy.* Chicago: Open Court Publishing.

Moody, R. A. 1975. *Life After Life: The Investigation of a Phenomenon—Survival of Bodily Death.* Atlanta: Mockingbird Books.

———1993. *Reunions: Visionary Encounters with Departed Loved Ones.* New York: Villard Books.

Perry, J. W. 1974. *The Far Side of Madness.* Englewood Cliffs, NJ: Prentice Hall.

———1976. *Roots of Renewal in Myth and Madness.* San Francisco: Jossey-Bass Publications.

Rawlins, D. October, 1981. "Starbaby." *Fate* 34.

Ring, K. 1982. *Life at Death: A Scientific Investigation of the Near-Death Experience.* New York: Quill.

Ring, K., and S. Cooper. 1999. *Mindsight: Near-Death and Out-of-Body Experiences in the Blind.* Palo Alto, CA: William James Center for Consciousness Studies.

Rogo, D. S., and R. Bayless. 1979. *Phone Calls from the Dead.* Englewood Cliffs, NJ: Prentice-Hall.

Sabom, M. 1982. *Recollections of Death: A Medical Investigation.* New York: Harper & Row.

Sagan, C. 1979a. "Amniotic Universe: Reflections on Birth, Death, and God." *Atlantic Monthly*: 39-45.

———1979b. *Broca's Brain.* New York: Random House.

———1983. *Cosmos.* New York: Random House.

———1997. *The Demon-Haunted World: Science as a Candle in the Dark.* New York: Ballantine Books.

Senkowski, E. "Instrumental Transcommunication (ITC)." An Institute for Noetic Sciences lecture at the Corte Madera Inn, Corte Madera, CA, July, 1994.

Schwartz, L. 1981. *World of the Newborn.*

Strieber, W. 1987. *Communion.*

Additional Resources

For information on Holotropic Breathwork workshops and facilitator training, please contact:

Grof Transpersonal Training
38 Miller Ave, PMB 516
Mill Valley, CA 94941
Web site: www.holotropic.com
E-mail address: gtt@holotropic.com
Phone: 415-383-8779
Fax: 415-383-0965

ABOUT THE AUTHOR

Stanislav Grof, M.D., Ph.D., is a psychiatrist with over fifty years experience of research into non-ordinary states of consciousness and one of the founders and chief theoreticians of transpersonal psychology. He was born in Prague, Czechoslovakia, where he also received his scientific training—an M.D. degree from the Charles University School of Medicine and a Ph.D. from the Czechoslovakian Academy of Sciences.

Dr. Grof's early research in the clinical uses of psychedelic substances was conducted at the Psychiatric Research Institute in Prague, where he was principal investigator of a program systematically exploring the heuristic and therapeutic potential of LSD and other psychedelic substances. In 1967, he was invited as Clinical and Research Fellow to the Johns Hopkins University, Baltimore, Doctor of Medicine.

After completion of this two-year fellowship, he stayed in the United States and continued his research as chief of psychiatric research at the Maryland Psychiatric Research Center and as assistant professor of psychiatry at the Henry Phipps Clinic of Johns Hopkins University, Baltimore, Doctor of Medicine. In 1973, Dr. Grof was invited to the Esalen Institute in Big Sur, California, where he lived until 1987 as Scholar-in-Residence writing, giving seminars, lecturing, and developing Holotropic Breathwork with his wife, Christina Grof. He also served on the board of trustees of the Esalen Institute.

He is the founder of the International Transpersonal Association (ITA) and is its past and current president. In this role, he, along with Christina, has organized large international conferences in the United States, the former Czechoslovakia, India, Australia, and Brazil. At present, he lives in Mill Valley, California, conducts training seminars for professionals in Holotropic Breathwork, transpersonal psychology, and writing books. He is also professor of psychology at the California Institute of Integral Studies (CIIS) in San Francisco and at the Pacifica Graduate School in Santa Barbara and gives lectures and seminars worldwide.

In 1993, he received an Honorary Award from the Association for Transpersonal Psychology (ATP) for major contributions to and development of the field of transpersonal psychology given at the occasion of the 25th Anniversary Convocation held at Asilomar, California.

He has published over 140 articles in professional journals, as well as numerous books, which have been translated into sixteen languages.

ABOUT SOUNDS TRUE

S ounds True was founded in 1985 with a clear vision: to disseminate spiritual wisdom. Located in Boulder, Colorado, Sounds True publishes teaching programs that are designed to educate, uplift, and inspire. With more than six hundred titles available, we work with many of the leading spiritual teachers, thinkers, healers, and visionary artists of our time.

To receive a free catalog of wisdom teachings for the inner life, please visit www.soundstrue.com, call toll-free 800-333-9185, or write: The Sounds True Catalog, P.O. Box 8010, Boulder, CO 80306.

SOUNDS TRUE
wisdom for the inner life